Routledge Revivals

Teacher Attitudes

Teachers' attitudes have been a subject of study and interest for many years. Originally published in 1986, this bibliography attempts to review the large field of research between the years 1965 and 1984. To identify all the sources of information, and to list documents that discuss research on teachers' attitudes. It does not include an assessment of the quality of the research reported in the listed documents, however, the value is in its comprehensiveness. Users of the bibliography can locate the listed studies and then evaluate the studies using criteria relevant to their individual purposes.

Teacher Attitudes

An Annotated Bibliography and Guide to Research

Marjorie Powell and Joseph W. Beard

Routledge
Taylor & Francis Group

THE GARLAND BIBLIOGRAPHIES IN CONTEMPORARY EDUCATION
(General Editor: Joseph M. McCarthy)

1. Issues in Adult Basic Education and Other Adult Education: *An Annotated Bibliography and Guide to Research*
by Darlene F. Russ-Eft, David P. Rubin, and Rachel E. Holmen

2. Contemporary Approaches to Moral Education: *An Annotated Bibliography and Guide to Research*
by James S. Leming

3. Teacher Effectiveness: *An Annotated Bibliography and Guide to Research*
by Marjorie Powell and Joseph W. Beard

4. Teacher Attitudes: *An Annotated Bibliography and Guide to Research*
by Marjorie Powell and Joseph W. Beard

TEACHER ATTITUDES
An Annotated Bibliography and Guide to Research

Marjorie Powell
Joseph W. Beard

GARLAND PUBLISHING, INC. · NEW YORK & LONDON
1986

Library of Congress Cataloging-in-Publication Data

Powell, Marjorie, 1942–
Teacher attitudes.

(The Garland bibliographies in contemporary education ; vol. 4) (Garland reference library of social science ; vol. 199)
Includes indexes.
1. Teachers—United States—Attitudes—Bibliography. 2. Teachers—United States—Attitudes—Research—Bibliography. I. Beard, Joseph W., 1942– II. Title. III. Series: Garland bibliographies in contemporary education ; v. 4. IV. Series: Garland reference library of social science ; v. 199.
Z5815.U5P68 1986 [LB2832.2] 371.1'00973 83-48213
ISBN 0-8240-9053-5 (alk. paper)

CONTENTS

INTRODUCTION:
TEACHERS' ATTITUDES

Teachers' attitudes have been a subject of study and interest for many years. The current number and variety of studies reflect a continuing interest. Some studies are purely descriptive, providing information about the attitudes that teachers hold. Other studies focus on describing the effects of teachers' attitudes on their teaching, their students, or their commitment to their profession. Still other studies investigate those factors that affect teachers' attitudes and the ways that such attitudes can be changed. Among all the varied efforts to describe existing attitudes, their effects, and ways that they can be modified, a considerable body of knowledge exists about teachers. This bibliography attempts to review that large field for the years 1965 through June, 1984, to identify all the sources of information, and to list documents that discuss research on teachers' attitudes. The bibliography does not include an assessment of the quality of the research reported in the listed documents; there are variations in the research methods and the veracity of the resulting information. However, the value of the bibliography is in its comprehensiveness. Users of the bibliography can locate the listed studies and then evaluate the studies using criteria relevant to their individual purposes.

1. STRUCTURE OF BIBLIOGRAPHY

Topics Covered

The bibliography includes studies of the attitudes of elementary and secondary school teachers. Within these two broad groups, some studies investigate the attitudes of groups of teachers, *e.g.*, teacher groups defined by subject area taught, such as mathematics, science or music; or by teacher characteristics, such as age and sex. Other studies that focus on teachers' attitudes toward educational issues are also included in the bibliography, for example, studies of teachers' attitudes toward students, toward instructional methods, toward subject areas. The bibliography includes studies of teachers' attitudes toward political issues but not toward political groups or parties. In addition to many descriptive studies, the bibliography includes studies of factors that influence teachers' attitudes and studies of the effects of those attitudes on teachers' behaviors and on students.

Studies with varied methodologies are included in the bibliography. Many of the studies are based on teachers' descriptions of their attitudes or selections of statements that represent their attitudes toward one or more subjects. Some studies focus solely on attitudes of teachers while others compare the attitudes of teachers with the attitudes of other groups, such as students, administrators, or parents. Some studies present a picture of teachers' attitudes at a specific point in time, a snapshot of attitudes. Other studies describe teachers' attitudes and changes in attitudes over a period of time. Some of these latter studies describe factors which influence those attitudes, describing reasons for changes. Still other studies describe teachers' attitudes and their effects on teachers' instructional behaviors or the attitudes of students resulting from those teachers' attitudes.

Entries in the bibliography have been divided into seven general categories. Each category is described in Section 3 of this introduction, with illustrations of entries. In addition, each entry has been assigned from one to four subject terms that are listed in the subject index. The author index and title index also list each entry in the bibliography.

Topics not Covered

Several topics are not covered in the bibliography. With the focus on elementary and secondary education, the bibliography does not include studies of attitudes of college teachers. Teaching at the post-secondary level is sufficiently different from teaching at the elementary and secondary levels that studies of attitudes of post-secondary instructors can be viewed as constituting an independent body of research, related to but separate from research on attitudes of teachers in elementary and secondary schools. On the other hand, studies of attitudes of pre-school teachers have been included because of the similarity of teaching at the pre-school and the early elementary years and because the numbers of such studies are small in comparison to the numbers of studies of attitudes of post-secondary education instructors.

Documents that exhort teachers to modify their attitudes, without including any research-based descriptive information about those attitudes, have been excluded from the bibliography. Likewise, documents that describe programs designed to change teachers' attitudes, without presenting any research-based information about teachers' attitudes, are excluded.

Studies which focus exclusively on teacher education, such as changes in attitudes of applicants for teacher education programs and changes in those attitudes resulting from the teacher training, are excluded. Teacher education is an important activity and numerous studies of all aspects of the process of training teachers have been conducted. However, people studying to become teachers differ from practicing teachers in many important characteristics, such as classroom experience. Studies of the attitudes of prospective teachers might reasonably be included in a bibliography of teacher education but are excluded from this bibliography.

A more general category of documents are excluded from the bibliography: conference papers that are not available through some normal distribution source, such as ERIC or a university publications department. A listing of documents only available by locating the author and requesting a copy has limited usefulness.

Sources of Reference

Four major index systems were reviewed to locate documents to be included in the bibliography: *Education Index*, *Dissertation Abstracts*, and both *Resources in Education* (*RIE*) and *Current Index to Journals in Education* (*CIJE*) of the Educational Resources Information Center (ERIC) system. The ERIC system, federally funded, makes documents available that would not otherwise obtain broad distribution. The system solicits documents from a variety of sources, including presenters at national and regional conferences and researchers in a variety of institutions. Documents are screened for appropriateness, copied onto microfiche, and announced in *Resources in Education* (*RIE*) or, if they have been published, *Current Index to Journals of Education* (*CIJE*). Both *RIE* and *CIJE* are monthly publications distributed to subscribers, usually organizations that also subscribe to the microfiche collection. The microfiche are distributed to libraries around the country and other institutions subscribing to the ERIC microfiche collection, such as state departments of education, county or regional education agencies (*e.g.*, BOCES and intermediate school districts) and large local school districts. Many documents that would be available only in limited numbers or for a limited period of time, such as evaluation reports of specific educational programs, become accessible through the ERIC system.

Different research terms were used in the four systems, because the classification systems and the labels for classes of documents differ among the systems. The search began with the 1965 volume of each index and continued through the June 1984 issues, with the objective of locating citations to documents through the middle of 1984. A few, but not many, early 1984 documents may be listed in later monthly collections of some indexes and thus not included in this bibliography. This is more apt to occur with *Dissertation Abstracts*, where the time lag results from delays in submitting dissertations to the system.

Additional steps were taken to cross-check the comprehensiveness of the bibliography. Publication lists from major education research organizations were reviewed to locate any documents not identified through the indexes. Reference lists from the major reviews of studies of teachers´ attitudes were checked to locate any citations which were not already included in the bibliography.

Types of Documents Included

The majority of the documents in the bibliography are research reports. These include technical reports describing results and methodologies as well as executive summaries of the research findings. The level of technical detail varies among these reports; some were written as final technical reports while others were written to communicate results to educators and other persons interested in teaching.

Some of the documents listed in the bibliography are reviews of research. Reviews may list and describe several studies or they may compile the information from several studies selected because of their focus on a single aspect of teachers´ attitudes. They are often a helpful source of initial information about a specific area of study, but may not include all documents related to that specific area of study.

Frequently two or more documents will describe the same study. Sometimes these documents have the same or a similar title. Where the two citations are clearly to the same document, they have been listed as multiple publications of the document. However, in other instances the documents differ and are listed separately.

2. HISTORY OF RESEARCH ON TEACHERS' ATTITUDES

Topics Studied

Many early studies of teaching assessed teachers' personality characteristics, including attitudes (as reviewed in Powell and Beard, 1984). Often these studies measured attitudes toward educational topics, such as the value of education or the characteristics of good teaching. Studies of teachers' attitudes toward general educational topics have continued throughout the history of the study of teachers' attitudes.

In addition to studies of teachers' attitudes toward general topics, studies of specific topics have been conducted as long as researchers have investigated teachers' attitudes. The specific topics have changed somewhat over the years, reflecting changes in important topics within education. For example, studies of teachers' attitudes toward team teaching (Borg, 1966) and toward science education, specific methods of instruction in science, and conditions for science teaching (*e.g.*, Blankenship, 1965; Wilson and Begle, 1972) were popular during the period when educational reform focused on team teaching and science education. Studies of teachers' attitudes toward science instruction have continued, though with a slightly lower frequency of occurrence (*e.g.*, Moon, 1977). During the heyday of accountability, researchers studied teachers' attitudes toward accountability (Good and others, 1975), while more recently researchers have focused on teachers' attitudes toward teacher evaluation reflecting a current concern of educators (Phelan, 1983; Paulin, 1981). Open education has been a topic of interest for a number of years; many researchers have investigated teachers' attitudes toward the open classroom and differences in attitudes among teachers who favor and oppose open education (*e.g.*, Coletta, 1974).

Sometimes major changes in the legal requirements relating to education influence the topics of interest to educators and the focus of research efforts. The most striking example of this phenomenon is the passage of Public Law 94-142, the Education for All Handicapped Children Act of 1975. The law requires that handicapped students receive educational services in the least restrictive environment, resulting in the mainstreaming of many handicapped students for all or a portion of the school day. The Act has changed the nature of educational services for handicapped students but also the nature of the instructional tasks and work environment for many teachers. One result of the Act has been an extensive effort to train teachers to teach handicapped students in classrooms with non-handicapped students. These efforts have included frequent measures of teachers' attitudes toward handicapped students (*e.g.*, Cruse, 1981), toward mainstreaming (*e.g.*, Hudson, 1979) and toward inservice and other programs to support teachers as they mainstream handicapped students (*e.g.*, Beverly Hudson, 1975).

Technological developments have prompted studies of teachers' attitudes. The advent of calculators in the classroom resulted in studies of teachers' attitudes toward calculators (Campbell and Virgin, 1976), while the advent of computers in the classroom led to studies of teachers' attitudes toward computers (Clement, 1981). Other technological developments, such as instructional television, have also spawned studies of teachers' use of and attitudes toward the specific technologies.

With increases in the number and frequency of educational innovations, usually associated with specialized funding from the state or the federal government, have come increases in studies of teachers' attitudes toward specific innovations. At the same time, some researchers have studied teachers' attitudes toward innovations in general and the process of change in education. Examples of such studies include Hall's studies of teachers' concerns about innovation (*e.g.*, Hall, 1976) and Loucks and Melle's study of levels of use of an innovation (Loucks and Melle, 1980).

Changes in major aspects of teachers' work environments have also led to studies of teachers' attitudes. Thus, the spread of collective bargaining between teachers' unions and school districts has prompted many studies of teachers' attitudes toward unions, collective bargaining and strikes. For example, Smith and Fox describe teachers' attitudes toward possible negotiation topics (Smith and Fox, 1971).

Some studies investigate teachers' attitudes toward educational research. While some of these studies assess teachers' generalized attitudes toward research, others focus on specific aspects of the research system. For example, Eaker and Huffman assessed teachers' attitudes toward dissemination of information resulting from research on teaching and sources that teachers find most useful for obtaining information about research results (Eaker and Huffman, 1981).

Sources of Research

Many studies of teachers' attitudes are completed as the research for a dissertation. These studies typically deal with teachers' attitudes toward a subject of interest to the doctoral candidate or the faculty at the institution where the dissertation is being completed. For example, during the period of extensive study of science education, many studies of teachers' attitudes toward science education were conducted, as dissertations, by graduate students in universities where faculty members were involved in development of modern science curricula and teacher training methods.

A number of studies of teachers' attitudes grow out of evaluations of educational programs. Many of these evaluations are conducted by school districts; they include assessments of the operation and effects of special programs funded by the district, the state or the federal government and assessments of educational needs as an initial step in developing special programs to secure funding from state or federal sources. For example, Kirkorian describes teachers' attitudes toward a particular instructional medium, closed-circuit television, as used within one school district (Kirkorian, 1971). Another school district conducted a study of teachers' satisfaction with their jobs and working conditions (Pontiac City School District, 1976). With the recent emphasis on inservice education for public school teachers, studies of teachers' attitudes toward inservice education abound (*e.g.*, McElhone, 1979; Lewandowski, 1980).

Other evaluations are conducted by state departments of education. For example, Enell assessed the impact of teachers' attitudes toward students with specific handicaps (Enell, 1982). In North Carolina, a state assessment of student learning included an assessment of attitudes of teachers and principals (North Carolina State Department of Public Instruction, 1975).

Both large and small federally funded programs have generated multiple evaluations, including studies of teachers' attitudes. The Alum Rock Voucher program is an example of a relatively small federally funded program that has been the focus of considerable evaluation attention; the Vanecko study of teachers' attitudes provides one example of studies of teachers' attitudes based on the voucher program (Vanecko, 1974). A very large federally funded program that has generated a large number of evaluation efforts, including studies of teachers' attitudes, is the Head Start program for disadvantaged children. The study by Meissner and others illustrates Head Start evaluations that include information about teachers' attitudes (Meissner and others, 1973).

Many studies are conducted by university faculty members on topics of continuing interest to them or topics of current interest because of their involvement in some specialized program. Researchers may also be located at research institutes; such institutes may have a specific topic focus or may conduct research on a variety of topics, both within and outside of education. Often, researchers at universities and research institutes conduct studies of teachers' attitudes as part of a larger evaluation of an education program.

RESEARCH METHODS

Researchers have used a variety of methods to study teachers' attitudes. One approach has been to conduct polls of large samples of teachers, often measuring attitudes toward a variety of topics. Such polls have been conducted periodically throughout the time period covered by the bibliography. National organizations sometimes conduct polls of a national sample of teachers (*e.g.*, the National Education Association polls, NEA, 1979). Sometimes state departments of education will poll a sample of teachers within the state on a topic of current interest within the state or the effects of new state legislation. More often, doctoral candidates conduct such polls as their dissertation research. Two examples of such dissertation studies are Ramsay's assessment of teachers' attitudes toward teacher evaluation system in Tennessee (Ramsay, 1980) and Roberts' assessment of teachers' attitudes toward New Jersey's statute establishing a standard for provision of education (Roberts, 1979). School districts and regional educational organizations also conduct such polls on topics of current interest.

Many studies of teachers' attitudes ask teachers to respond to specific statements. The statements are selected and organized to reflect teachers' attitudes toward the topic of interest within the study. Sometimes researchers expand the statements into descriptions of problems or situations and then ask teachers to respond to those descriptions by choosing the most serious problem descriptions, by describing their likely reactions, or by selecting the reaction that they believe is most appropriate. For example, teachers, students and mental health professionals were asked to respond to descriptions of student problem behaviors in one study (Vidoni and others, 1983). Some relatively sophisticated systems for eliciting teachers' attitudes allow teachers to analyze their own attitudes. For example, a system by Dobson & Dobson enables teachers to compare their attitudes toward different aspects of education by selecting alternative statements. The system graphically displays the information generated by the teachers' selection of alternative responses (Dobson and Dobson, 1983).

Other studies use interviews of individual teachers as the basic method of data collection. While development of descriptive statements requires considerable time, the actual collection and analysis of data from a relatively large sample of teachers can be conducted more quickly than can the collection and analysis of interview data for the same number of teachers. For this reason, studies using interview data typically include a smaller sample of teachers than do studies based on teachers' selections of alternative statements descriptive of their attitudes. For example, Peterson interview a relatively small sample of retired teachers to compile information about their career patterns and perceptions of influences on their careers (Peterson, 1979). A variation of the interview method involves analysis of documents produced by teachers. Data can be collected relatively quickly from groups of teachers but the analysis consumes considerable amounts of time. An example of such a study is Parkay's analysis of teachers' attitudes toward their work environment and the students they teach based on short stories that the teachers wrote for the researcher (Parkay, 1981).

Another approach has been to conduct case studies of teachers' attitudes. Usually case studies focus on one or a few teachers with information compiled over an extended period of time, *e.g.*, weeks, months or even a full school year. A case study may investigate one topic, such as a teacher's attitude toward open education (Holmes, 1980) or may cover several related topics (Carew and Lightfoot, 1977). Case studies often involve extended classroom observations, interviews, and analysis of documents.

Another research method used to study topic-specific attitudes is the assessment of attitudes before and after participation in an inservice education program. Because many of these studies focus on topics for which teachers are receiving inservice training, the specific topics studied parallel the topics of current interest within education. For example, with the recent efforts to implement mainstreaming and assist regular classroom teachers in working with handicapped students, many studies assess teachers' attitudes toward handicapped students or toward mainstreaming before and after participation in inservice training (*e.g.*, Salend and Johns, 1983).

3. OVERVIEW OF BIBLIOGRAPHIC TOPICS

The bibliography entries are divided into seven sections: A) descriptions of teachers' attitudes, B) variations in attitudes between groups of teachers, C) teachers' attitudes toward students, D) teachers' attitudes toward their own teaching, E) influences on teachers' attitudes, F) effects of teachers' attitudes and G) reviews of research on teachers' attitudes. Each section is discussed in turn. In addition, the bibliographic entries are listed in the author, title, and subject indexes.

I. Description of Teachers' Attitudes

Descriptive studies of teachers' attitudes toward specific topics span the years of the bibliography and cover a wide variety of topics. Many of the studies describe teachers' attitudes toward aspects of teaching, such as the curriculum (Gearhart, 1975), their role within their school setting (Borg, 1965), specific characteristics of the teaching environment (Lambert, 1980), and support services available to teachers (Hanes and Mulhern, 1981). The specific aspects of teaching on which descriptive studies focus change as the major issues of interest in education change. For example, descriptive studies have considered open education and mainstreaming, two of the several topics that have been of major concern to educators over the twenty years covered by the bibliography. Illustrative descriptive studies in these two areas include Amarel's description of teachers' attitudes toward open education, and changes in those attitudes (Amarel and others, 1973), description of teachers' attitudes toward mainstreaming (Williams and Algozzine, 1979) and descriptions of teachers' attitudes toward handicapped students mainstreamed into their classrooms (Enell, 1982). Teachers' attitudes toward teaching as a profession have been a continuing focus of descriptive studies, (*e.g.*, Coughlin, 1969) while the stresses teachers experience within the work environment constitute a relatively recent area of focus of descriptive studies, (*e.g.*, Pratt, 1978).

II. Variations in Attitudes between Groups of Teachers

Studies that compare attitudes of groups of teachers occur relatively frequently. Teacher groups have been defined by teacher characteristics. For example, Lipka and Goulet (1979) compare attitudes of teachers of different ages and years of teaching experience while Bruno (1981) describes differences in factors that cause stress among black, white and Hispanic teachers. Teachers are often grouped into those who have and have not received a specified type of training. Killian (1984), for example, compares attitudes of teachers who did and did not participate in a computer literacy training program. Relatively infrequently, studies compare attitudes of teachers in different countries. One study describes the perceptions of their degree of classroom autonomy of teachers in four countries, Brazil, Jordan, United States of America and Venezuela (Leon and others, 1982).

A large number of studies compare teachers with other groups, both within and outside of education. Comparisons of the attitudes of teachers and students occur frequently. Marsh's study of teachers' and students' perceptions of high schools illustrates this type of study (Marsh, 1979). Attitudes of teachers and principals are also often compared, *e.g.*, Farnsworth's study of teachers' and principals' attitudes toward effective methods of inservice education (Farnsworth 1981). A number of studies compare parents' attitudes with teachers' attitudes. Goulet, for example, compares attitudes of parents and teachers toward important instructional goals for kindergarten students (Goulet, 1975).

III. Teachers' Attitudes toward Students

Studies of teachers' attitudes toward students can be grouped into several types of studies. Some focus on teachers' attitudes toward specific groups of students. Racial characteristics define the student groups in many of these studies. Such studies have occurred throughout the time period covered by the bibliography. For example, Smith, in 1970, described teachers' attitudes toward Indian students (W. Smith, 1970) while Catalogna and others, in 1981, described teachers' attitudes toward students of different racial groups (Catalogna and others, 1981). Other studies compare differences in teachers' attitudes based on a student's sex, *e.g.*, a study of teachers' perceptions of male and female students (Miller and Asher, 1983). Other common groupings of students by characteristics are gifted students (*e.g.*, Rubenzer and Twaite, 1979) and handicapped students (*e.g.*, Ysseldyke and others, 1983). Some studies consider combinations of student characteristics, *e.g.*, a study of sex bias in teachers' referrals for speech therapy (Silverman and Van Opens, 1980).

Sometimes student characteristics relate specifically to educational concerns. Studies of these types of student characteristics are illustrated by studies of teachers' attitudes toward students with learning problems, *e.g.*, a study of teachers' and mothers' expectations for learning disabled students (Boersma and Chapman, 1982). Studies of teachers' attitudes toward handicapped and gifted students sometimes focus on student characteristics, such as comparisons of teacher and student attitudes toward handicapped or gifted students, and sometimes on educational concerns, such as studies of teachers' attitudes toward the teaching of handicapped or gifted students.

Some studies assess teachers' attitudes toward student behaviors, often their behaviors in the role of student, such as behavior in completing assigned tasks. Sometimes the studies measure teachers' attitudes toward student social behavior in the classroom. For example, Dobson and Brewer (1971) describe teachers' and principals' perceptions of the seriousness of student misbehavior problems. Occasionally these studies describe teachers' preferences for teacher responses to student problems. For example, Algozzine and others (1983) describe teachers' preferred responses to specific types of student misbehavior.

There are variations in the contexts in which studies of teachers' attitudes are conducted; some studies focus on the effects of these variations. Thus, studies have compared teachers' attitudes toward black and white students in segregated and desegregated schools, *e.g.*, Grant's study of teachers' attitudes toward male and female black and white students in desegregated classrooms (Grant, 1982). Other studies compare teachers' attitudes toward students by ability group by geographic location of the school (*e.g.*, Baldwyn Separate School District, 1982).

IV. Teachers' Attitudes toward Their Own Teaching

A few studies consider the school as a workplace and the effects of characteristics of the school on teachers' attitudes toward teaching as a profession and their own teaching. For example, Little reviews studies of the school as a workplace and relates school characteristics to behaviors and attitudes of teachers (Little, 1981).

Teachers' attitudes toward curriculum, theories of learning and of instruction, and of specific subject areas have been studied. One illustration of this class of studies is the work of Duffy and Anderson describing teachers' conceptions of reading and the relationship of those conceptions to planning and instructional behavior (Duffy and Anderson, 1982). Some studies focus on teachers' attitudes toward subject areas as those attitudes influence allocation of instructional time (Buchmann and Schmidt, 1981), while other studies consider teachers' attitudes toward instructional methods and materials, such as computers, as they relate to curriculum decisions (Wright and Stone, 1983). Teachers' attitudes toward sources of information about students, and the uses of that information in instructional planning, have been studied. For example, Salmon-Cox studied teachers' attitudes toward information obtained from standardized tests and their own observations of students (Salmon-Cox, 1981).

Several of these separate lines of research have been joined in studies of teachers' instructional decision making, *e.g.*, Leithwood and others (1982).

Another group of studies considers teachers' views about specific tasks associated with the profession. For example, teachers' attitudes toward parents and various ways of working with parents have been studied (*e.g.*, S. Williams, 1983). Some studies have considered teachers' attitudes toward all of their skills as professionals and the impact of those skills, or teachers' sense of efficacy. Studies of teachers' sense of efficacy investigate the extent to which teachers perceive that their work has a positive effect on students. For an illustration of such studies, see Ashton and others (1982).

V. Influences on Teachers' Attitudes

Studies have investigated a wide variety of factors that influence teachers' attitudes. The effects of participation in teaching as a profession have received attention over the years, typically in studies of changes in teachers' attitudes associated with teacher training and the first year of teaching. Other studies investigate changes in attitudes related to years of teaching experience. Occasionally, researchers combine these two types of studies. For example, Fuller reports changes in attitudes associated with teacher training, with early years of teaching and with several years of teaching experience (Fuller, 1969). Other studies consider the influence of specific aspects of teaching, such as use of a particular curriculum or instructional approach (*e.g.*, Tolman and Barufaldi, 1979) or use of a particular instructional medium (*e.g.*, Tobias, 1968). The composition of students in a classroom has been studied for its effects on teachers' attitudes. Many of these studies investigate the effects of teaching handicapped students on teachers' attitudes toward mainstreaming of handicapped students (*e.g.*, Mandell and Strain, 1978).

At a more comprehensive level, some studies investigate the effects of the school setting, or specific characteristics of the school or district, on teachers' attitudes. For example, Moeller and Charters describe the effects of the bureaucratic nature of the school on teachers' sense of power (Moeller and Charters, 1969). Laurento describes the effects of aspects of the employment contract on teachers' satisfaction with teaching (Laurento, 1980).

Interactions among teachers' attitudes exist and have been studied. For example, teachers' views of the value of education and of different patterns of instructional organization influence their attitudes toward their school and their students (Gies and Leonard, 1971). Teachers' attitudes toward teaching are related to their attitudes toward control of pupils within the school, or pupil control ideology (Willower and Landis, 1970).

One group of studies has investigated the effects on teachers' attitudes of participation in various types of programs. Bethel and Hord investigated the effects on teachers' attitudes toward teaching science of participation in an inservice training program that focused on both science content and instructional methods (Bethel and Hord, 1981). McFaul and Cooper describe the effects of participation in a program of peer clinical supervision on teachers' attitudes toward supervision (McFaul and Cooper, 1983).

VI. Effects of Teachers' Attitudes

Some studies have assessed the effects of teachers' attitudes on teachers' behavior. For example, teachers' behaviors in interactions with students have been related to teachers' sex role attitudes (Weber and others, 1978) and to teachers' attitudes toward individual students in their classrooms (*e.g.*, Good and Brophy, 1972). Teachers' attitudes influence teachers' external behaviors concerning individual students, such as referrals of students for special services (*e.g.*, Foley and Brooks, 1978).

The influence of teachers' attitudes on students have been the focus of several groups of studies. Some investigate the influence of teachers' attitudes on students' attitudes, as illustrated by a study of the effects of teachers' attitudes on students' perceptions of their school (Childress and Dobson, 1973). Other studies investigate the influence of teachers' attitudes on student learning, *e.g.*, a study of the effects of teachers' and students' attitudes on student achievement (Dillingham and Johnson, 1973).

Other studies assess the effects of teachers' attitudes in conjunction with aspects of the context in which they are teaching. An example is the study by Fielding and Gall investigating the relationship between teachers' attitudes and aspects of the work environment and teachers' perceptions of levels of stress in the work environment (Fielding and Gall, 1982). Some of these studies focus on major changes in the school environment, such as desegregation, *e.g.*, Peretti's study of the effects of teachers' attitudes on teachers' perceptions of the existence of discipline problems during desegregation (Peretti, 1976).

VII. REVIEWS OF RESEARCH ON TEACHERS' ATTITUDES

Reviews provide an overview of research on the topic of the review, describing consistent research results or indicating the absence of consistency of findings across the studies reviewed. Charts summarizing characteristics of studies in the field and research findings of the studies are commonly included in reviews. Individuals seeking to acquire a general understanding of a field of research can find initial help in reviews of the research.

Some reviews are organized to provide a history of a field of research, for example, the review of teachers' attitudes toward language by Daniels and others (1975). These reviews provide a perspective that may be missing from a review focusing exclusively on recent research.

Some reviews are comprehensive, including all studies that were located of the type reviewed for the time period covered by the review. Other reviews include only studies which meet specified selection criteria. An example of the latter is Flaxman's selected bibliography on teachers' attitudes and their effects on teachers' interactions with students (Flaxman, 1969). Some reviews contain annotated listing of the studies included in the review (*e.g.*, Jayatilleki, 1972). Some reviews critique the studies reviewed (Pedhazur, 1973) while other reviews conclude by describing types of additional research necessary to provide a more complete understanding of the topic of the review (Keavney and Sinclair, 1978).

Many reviews focus on specific topics related to teachers' attitudes. Some of these cover a specific curriculum area such as reading (Stern and Shavelson, 1983) or mathematics (Willoughby, 1969). Others are broader reviews of topics of general interest within the field of education. Brophy's review of research on teachers' expectations of students (Brophy, 1982), Cohen's review of factors affecting teachers' professional status (Cohen, 1967) and Yinger and Clark's review of teachers' decision making (Yinger and Clark, 1983) illustrate reviews on topics of current interest at the time they were completed. Sometimes that current interest is generated by specific external events, such as the interest in teachers' attitudes toward black English prompted by a court decision about the use of black English in the schools (Freeman, 1982).

4. FUTURE DIRECTIONS OF RESEARCH

Research on teachers' attitudes will probably move in two divergent directions between 1985 and 1990; some more complex studies of teachers' attitudes and many studies narrowly focused on specific topics will be conducted. The relatively complex studies will assess a variety of attitudes and multiple factors that may influence attitudes. These studies will focus on attitudes in a few areas, such as teachers' decision making about instruction and teachers' attitudes toward their work environment. Studies of teachers' decision making will grow out of the interests of researchers studying teacher behavior and researchers studying curriculum; both groups of researchers have moved toward studies of teachers' decision making in planning for and conducting instruction (see Powell and Beard, 1984). Much of this research draws upon more broadly based studies of decision making, applying concepts derived from studies of thinking to studies of teachers' thinking. As these studies include more aspects of teachers' thinking, they will include assessments of teachers' attitudes toward curriculum areas, instructional methods, students, and work environments.

Other studies will focus on narrow topics and teachers' attitudes toward those topics. These studies will largely grow out of district and state efforts to evaluate specific educational programs and innovations. The current limitations on funding for education and research in education will force educators to become increasingly concerned with program effectiveness. The resulting increase in program evaluations will be accompanied by an increase in measures of teachers' attitudes, as one means of understanding differential patterns of program effectiveness. Recent emphasis on teacher inservice training will also result in more studies of teachers' attitudes. Some of these studies will focus on specific innovations, such as the use of computers in the classroom. Others will focus on the effectiveness of methods of inservice education, such as coursework, workshops and classroom consultation.

Polls of both national and state samples of teachers will continue in future years. National organizations have a variety of reasons to conduct national polls of teachers' attitudes, as well as the general public's attitudes toward aspects of education. The reasons, such as documenting public and teacher support for specific types of educational programs, will continue to exist, resulting in continued national polls of attitudes toward education, including teachers' attitudes. State departments of education make a variety of uses of information derived from state polls, whether conducted by the department or by graduate students as dissertation research. The varied uses result in multiple pressures on state departments to conduct state-wide polls. For example, departments of education may use information from polls of teachers' attitudes to assist decision makers in selecting among alternative state-sponsored programs. Because they will continue to choose between potential programs, state departments of education will continue to conduct polls.

Studies of teachers' attitudes will continue to focus on topics of current educational interest. District administrators and state department of education personnel use information about teachers' attitudes as they plan programs to meet new educational needs or resolve problems identified within the educational system. This need for information about teachers' attitudes provides the impetus for some studies of teachers' attitudes. University faculty members' interests in current controversies, innovations and changes in emphasis within educational programs lead them to encourage doctoral candidates to conduct studies that focus on topics of current interest within education. This general force toward current topics pushes students of teachers' attitudes to conduct studies of attitudes toward the currently important educational topics. Thus, as computers become more prevalent in schools, more studies will measure teachers' attitudes toward computers and various instructional uses of computers. The broader interest in science and technology education will result in an upsurge in studies of teachers' attitudes toward science, technology, and science education. Studies of teachers' attitudes will continue to track areas of general educational interest.

It is hoped that this bibliography will form one base for future research on teachers' attitudes.

REFERENCES

Algozzine, Bob and others. "A Factor Analysis of Teachers' Intervention Choices for Dealing with Students' Behavior and Learning Problems," *Elementary School Journal, 84* (1983): 189-197.

Amarel, Marianne and others. Teacher Perspective on Change to an Open Approach. 1973. *ERIC ED* 076 568.

Ashton, Patricia T. and others. A Study of Teachers' Sense of Efficacy. 1982. *ERIC ED* 231 834.

Baldwyn Separate School District. A Gifted Model Designed for Gifted Students in a Small, Rural High School. 1982. *ERIC ED* 233 847.

Bethel, Lowell J. and Hord, Shirley M. A Case Study of Change: Inservice Teachers in a National Science Foundation Environmental Science Education Program. 1981. *ERIC ED* 200 589.

Blankenship, Jacob W. "Biology Teachers and Their Attitudes Concerning BSCS," *Journal of Research in Science Teaching, 3* (1965): 54-60.

Boersma, Frederic J. and Chapman, James W. "Teachers' and Mothers' Academic Achievement Expectations for Learning Disabled Children," *Journal of School Psychology, 20, No. 3* (1982): 216-221.

Borg, Walter R. Perceptions of the Teacher's Role in the Small Rural School. 1965. *ERIC ED* 010 968.

Borg, Walter R. Study of Human Interaction Variables in Successful and Unsuccessful Teacher Teams. 1966. *ERIC ED* 010 001.

Brophy, Jere E. Research on the Self-Fulfilling Prophecy and Teacher Expectations. 1982. *ERIC ED* 221 530.

Bruno, James E. "Morale-Affecting Stressors: An Analysis of Black, White, or Hispanic Elementary Schools," *Urban Education, 16* (1981).

Buchmann, Margret and Schmidt, William H. The School Day and Content Commitments. 1981. *ERIC ED* 204 282.

Campbell, Patricia and Virgin, Albert. A Survey of Elementary School Teachers and Principals' Attitudes to Mathematics and Utilizing Mini-calculators. 1976. *ERIC ED* 137 121.

Carew, Jean V. and Lightfoot, Sarah L. First Grade: A Multi-faceted View of Teachers and Children. 1977. *ERIC ED* 148 495.

Catalogna, Lenore and others. "Exploratory Examination of Teachers' Perceptions of Pupils' Race," *Journal of Negro Education, 50* (1981): 370-380.

Childress, Bill and Dobson, Russell. "Elementary Teachers' Philosophies of Human Nature and Students' Perceptions of the Elementary School," *Journal of the Student Personnel Association for Teacher Education 11, No. 4* (1973): 152-161.

Clement, Frank J. "Affective Considerations in Computer-Based Education," *Educational Technology, 21, No. 4* (1981): 28-32.

Cohen, Elizabeth G. "Status of Teachers," *Review of Educational Research 37* (1967): 280-295.

Coletta, Anthony J. "Do Open and Traditional Teachers Differ in their Beliefs about Learning?" *Phi Delta Kappan 55* (1974): 636-637.

Coughlin, R.L. "The Factorial Structure of Teacher Work Values," *American Educational Research Journal 6, No. 2* (1969): 169-189.

Cruse, Jeannette Elaine. Attitude of regular elementary school classroom teachers toward handicapped learners. Ph.D. dissertation. Pennsylvania State University. 1981.

Daniels, Harvey A. and others. What Teachers Believe: An Historical Investigation of Language Attitudes and the Implications for Bidialectalism in the Schools. 1975. *ERIC ED* 125 288.

Dillingham, McKinley and Johnson, T. Bradford. "The Effect of Teacher Attitudes and Self-concept on Academic Success," *Education of the Disadvantaged Child 1, No. 4* (1973): 15-21.

Dobson, Russell and Brewer, Leon. The Perception and Treatment by Teachers and Principals of the Behavioral Problems of Elementary School Children. 1971. *ERIC ED* 057 533.

Dobson, Russell L. and Dobson, Judith E. The Congruency of Teachers' Beliefs and Practices. 1983. *ERIC ED* 242 678.

Duffy, Gerald and Anderson, Linda. Conceptions of Reading Project. 1982. *ERIC ED* 218 583.

Eaker, Robert E. and Huffman, James O. Teacher Perceptions of Dissemination of Research on Teaching Findings. 1981. *ERIC ED* 205 501.

Enell, Nancy C. The effects of Regular Classroom Integration for Special Education Students with Visual, Auditory, Physical and Mental Impairments. 1982. *ERIC ED* 220 963.

Farnsworth, Briant J. "Professional Development: Preferred Methods of Principals and Teachers," *Education 10, No. 4* (1981): 332-334.

Fielding, Marianne A. and Gall, Meredith D. Personality and Situational Correlates of Teacher Stress and Burnout. 1982. *ERIC ED* 219 353.

Flaxman, E. A Selected Bibliography on Teacher Attitude. ERIC-IRCD Urban Disadvantaged. 1969. *ERIC ED* 027 357.

Foley, Walter J. and Brooks, Robert. "Pupil Control Ideology in Predicting Teacher Discipline Referrals," *Educational Administration Quarterly 14, No. 3* (1978): 104-112.

Freeman, Evelyn B. "The Ann Arbor Decision: The Importance of Teachers' Attitudes toward Language," *Elementary School Journal 83* (1982): 41-47.

Fuller, Frances F. "Concerns of Teachers: A Developmental Conceptualization," *American Educational Research Journal 6* (1969): 207-226.

Gearhart, George. "What Do Mathematics Teachers Think about the High School Geometry Controversy?" *Mathematics Teacher 68, No. 6* (1975): 486-493.

Gies, Frederick John and Leonard, B. Charles. "The Relationship between Teacher Perceptions of Organizational Climate and Values Concerning Disadvantaged Pupils," *The Negro Education Review 22* (1971): 152-159.

Good, Thomas L. and Brophy, Jere E. "Behavioral Expression of Teacher Attitudes," *Journal of Educational Psychology 63, No. 6* (1972): 617-624.

Good, Thomas L., Coop, R., Dembo, M., Denton, J. and Limbacher, P. "Teachers' View of Accountability: An Empirical Survey," *Phi Delta Kappan 56* (1975): 367-368.

Goulet, John E. "Curriculum Priorities of Teachers and Parents in Kindergarten Classrooms," *Reading Improvement 12, No. 3* (1975): 163-167.

Grant, Linda. Black Females' "Place" in Desegregated Classrooms. 1982. *ERIC ED* 224 844.

Hall, Gene E. "The Study of Individual Teacher and Professor Concerns about Innovations," *Journal of Teacher Education 27, No. 1* (1976): 22-23.

Hanes, Madlyn Levine and Mulhern, John D. The University Reading Clinic: A Needed and Viable Means of Servicing Community and Schools. 1981. *ERIC ED* 200 891.

Holmes, Margaret McCann. Teachers´ Perspectives on Open Education: A Case Study. Ph.D. dissertation. University of Wisconsin-Madison. 1980.

Hudson, Beverly S. An Assessment of the Attitudes of Secondary Level Teachers toward Incorporating Reading Skills with Content. 1975. *ERIC ED* 105 446.

Hudson, Floyd and others. "Mainstreaming: An Examination of the Attitudes and Needs of Regular Classroom Teachers," *Learning Disability Quarterly 2, No. 3* (1979): 58-62.

Jayatilleke, Raja. Human Relations in the Classroom. An Annotated Bibliography. ERIC ED Urban Disadvantaged. 1972. *ERIC ED* 064 417.

Keavney, Glenese and Sinclair, Kenneth E. "Teacher Concerns and Teacher Anxiety: A Neglected Topic of Classroom Research," *Review of Educational Research 48* (1978): 273-290.

Killian, Joyce E. Teachers Who Seek Computer Education: Their Attitudes, Needs, and Motivation. 1984. *ERIC ED* 242 715.

Kirkorian, Donald G. An Investigation of Teacher Attitudes toward Closed Circuit Television in the Fremont Union High School District, Sunnyvale, California. 1971. *ERIC ED* 087 378.

Lambert, Robert F. "Teacher Attitudes on Testing: A Multiple Perspective," *The College Board Review 118* (1980): 13-14, 29-30.

Laurento, Louis Michael. A Study Designed to Investigate the Relationship Between the Strength of the Professional Employee´s Contract and the Degree of Teacher Job Satisfaction. Ed.D. dissertation. Temple University. 1980.

Leithwood, Kenneth A. and others. Describing Teacher Decision Making. 1982. *ERIC ED* 220 464.

Leon, Anibal and others. A Cross-Cultural Study of Teacher Autonomy. 1982. *ERIC ED* 218 768.

Lewandowski, Jean Adele Dayton. Nebraska Social Studies Teachers' Perceptions about In-service Education Experiences and Self-initiated Professional Development Activities. Ed. D. dissertation. University of Nebraska-Lincoln. 1980.

Little, Judith Warren. The Power of Organizational Settings: School Norms and Staff Development. 1981. *ERIC ED* 221 918.

Lipka, Richard P. and Goulet, L.R. "Aging- and Experience-related Changes in Teacher Attitudes toward the Profession," *Educational Research Quarterly 4* (1979): 19-28.

Loucks, Susan and Melle, Marge. Implementing a District-wide Science Curriculum: The Effects of a Three-year Effort. 1980. *ERIC ED* 204 181.

McElhone, James Walter. A Study to Determine the Attitudes of Wyoming Teachers toward Inservice Education. Ph.D. dissertation. University of Wyoming. 1979.

McFaul, Shirley A. and Cooper, James M. "Peer Clinical Supervision in an Urban Elementary School," *Journal of Teacher Education, 34 No. 5* (1983): 34-38.

Mandell, Colleen J. and Strain, Phillip S. "An Analysis of Factors Related to the Attitudes of Regular Classroom Teachers toward Mainstreaming Mildly Handicapped Children," *Contemporary Educational Psychology 3, No. 2* (1978): 154-160.

Marsh, Colin J. "Teachers and Students Don't Agree about What Should Go On in High Schools," *High School Journal 63, No. 2* (1979): 67-71.

Meissner, Judith A. and others. Disadvantaged Children and Their First School Experiences. ETS Head Start Longitudinal Study: Preschool Teachers of Disadvantaged Children: Characteristics and Attitudes. 1973. *ERIC ED* 109 136.

Miller, Arden and Asher, William. "Gender Differences as a Factor in Teachers' Perceptions of Students: A Comment," *Perceptual and Motor Skills, 56* (1983): 856-58.

Moeller, Gerald H. and Charters, W.W. "Relation of Bureaucratization to Sense of Power among Teachers," in *Organization and Human Behavior: Focus on Schools*. Edited by Fred D. Carver and Thomas J. Sergiovanni. pp. 235-248. New York: McGraw-Hill Book Company. 1969.

Moon, Thomas C. "Selected Teacher Reactions to SAPA and SCIS Implementations," *School Science and Mathematics 77, No. 3* (1977): 227-232.

National Education Association. Nationwide Teacher Opinion Poll. 1979. *ERIC ED* 178 533.

Natriello, Gary and Cohn, Marilyn. Beyond Sanctions: The Evolution of a Merit Pay System. 1983. *ERIC ED* 238 140.

North Carolina State Department of Public Instruction. A Survey of Teachers and Principals: Grade 3. State Assessment of Educational Progress in North Carolina, 1973-74. 1975. *ERIC ED* 106 294.

O'Rourke, Bill. "'Lion Tamers and Baby Sitters': First-Year English Teachers' Perceptions of Their Undergraduate Teacher Preparation," *English Education 15* (1983): 17-24.

Parkay, Forrest W. Inner-City High School Teachers: Their Perceptions of Classroom Life as Revealed Through a Content Analysis of Projective Stories. 1981. *ERIC ED* 206 772.

Paulin, Pauline. The Politics of Evaluation at the Local Level: A View Through Teachers' Perspectives. 1981. *ERIC ED* 207 244.

Pedhazur, Elazar J. "Do Teacher Attitudes Make a Difference?" *New York University Education Quarterly 4, No. 3* (1973): 14-21.

Peretti, Peter O. "Effects of Teachers' Attitudes on Discipline Problems in Schools Recently Desegregated," *Education 97, No. 2* (1976): 136-140.

Peterson, Anne Allyn Rosher. Career Patterns of Secondary School Teachers: An Exploratory Interview Study of Retired Teachers. Ph.D. dissertation. Ohio State University. 1979.

Phelan, William T. "Governing Staff Reductions: The Use and Abuse of Teacher Evaluations," *Education and Urban Society, 15* (1983): 189-98.

Pontiac City School District. School Staff Attitudes and Job Satisfaction. 1976. *ERIC ED* 120 326.

Powell, Marjorie and Beard, Joseph W. *Teacher Effectiveness: An Annotated Bibliography and Guide to Research*. New York: Garland Publishing, Inc. 1984.

Pratt, John. "Perceived Stress among Teachers: The Effects of Age and Background of Children," *Educational Review 30, No. 1* (1978): 3-14.

Ramsay, Russell. Teachers' Perceptions of the Design and Implementation of Teacher Evaluation Systems in Tennessee Public Schools. Ed.D. dissertation. University of Tennessee. 1980.

Roberts, Albert George. New Jersey's Thorough and Efficient Mandate: Teacher Attitudes and Perceptions. Ed.D. dissertation. Columbia University Teachers College. 1979.

Rubenzer, Ronald L. and Twaite, James A. "Attitudes of 1,200 Educators toward the Education of the Gifted and Talented: Implications for Teacher Preparation," *Journal for the Education of the Gifted 2, No. 4* (1979): 202-213.

Salend, Spencer J. and Johns, Janet. "A Tale of Two Teachers: Changing Teacher Commitment to Mainstreaming," *Teaching Exceptional Children 15, No. 2* (1983): 82-85.

Salmon-Cox, Leslie. "Teachers and Standardized Achievement Tests: What's Really Happening?" *Phi Delta Kappan 62* (1981): 631-34.

Silverman, Ellen-Marie and Van Opens, Kathrine. "An Investigation of Sex-Bias in Classroom Teachers' Speech and Language Referrals," *Language, Speech and Hearing Services in the Schools 11* (1980): 169-174.

Smith, R.A. and Fox, F.H. Expressed Attitudes of Teachers toward Negotiations: A Factor Analytic Study. 1971. *ERIC ED* 048 628.

Smith, Waldron P. The Attitudes and Beliefs of Teachers Concerning the Education of American Indian Children in the Southwest. 1970. *ERIC ED* 051 957.

Stern, Paula and Shavelson, Richard J. "Reading Teachers' Judgments, Plans and Decision Making," *Reading Teacher 37* (1983): 280-86.

Tobias, S. "Dimensions of Teachers' Attitudes toward Instructional Media," *American Educational Research Journal 5* (1968): 91-98.

Tolman, Richard R. and Barufaldi, James P. "The Effects of Teaching the Biological Sciences Curriculum Study Elementary School Science Program on Attitudes toward Science among Elementary School Teachers," *Journal of Research in Science Teaching 16, No. 5* (1979): 401-406.

Vanecko, James J. Teachers' Reactions to the First Year of the Alum Rock Voucher Demonstration. 1974. *ERIC ED* 105 586.

Vidoni, Dennis O. and others. "Behavioral Problems of Children as Perceived by Teachers, Mental Health Professionals, and Children," *Psychology in the Schools, 20* (1983): 93-98.

Weber, Margaret B. and others. The Relationship between Teachers' Sex Role Attitudes and Stereotypic Reinforcement of Student Behaviors. 1978. *ERIC ED* 151 333.

Williams, Robert J. and Algozzini, Bob. "Teachers' Attitudes toward Mainstreaming," *Elementary School Journal 80, No. 2* (1979): 63-67.

Williams, Sheri S. "Colorado PTSA Studies the Home-School Partnership," *PTA Today 8, No.* 7 (1983): 31-32.

Willoughby, Stephen S. "Mathematics" in *Encyclopedia of Educational Research*. Edited by Robert L. Ebel. pp. 766-777. Toronto, Canada: The Macmillan Company. 1969.

Willower, Donald J. and Landis, Charles A., III. "Pupil Control Ideology and Professional Orientation of School Faculty, " *Journal of Secondary Education 45, No. 3* (1970): 118-123.

Wilson, James W. and Begle, Edward G. (Eds.). Correlates of Mathematics Achievement: Teacher Background and Opinion Variables. 1972. *ERIC ED* 084 125.

Wright, Benjamin D. and Stone, Mark H. Measurement as an Instrument of Learning. 1983. *ERIC ED* 238 411.

Yinger, Robert J. and Clark, Christopher M. Self-Reports of Teacher Judgment. 1983. *ERIC ED* 241 495.

Ysseldyke, James E. and others. Classroom Teachers' Attributions for Students Exhibiting Different Behaviors. 1983. *ERIC ED* 236 848.

Teacher Attitudes

I. DESCRIPTIONS OF TEACHERS' ATTITUDES

1. Ade, William. A study of relationships between teacher characteristics and congruity, incongruity, and inconsistency with policy positions of teachers organizations. ERIC ED 215 977.

   Reports that teachers' characteristics, e.g., age, were related to teachers' attitudes toward the policies of professional associations.

2. Adwere-Boamah, Joseph & others. Fundamental points of view of teachers on education: an investigation of the Kerlinger and Kaya Attitudinal Scale. Educational Research Quarterly 7 No. 2 (1982): 17-20.

   Describes teachers' views of education as progressive or traditional and assesses the characteristics of the measurement instruments.

3. Ahlum, Claude Leon, Jr. The support for and opposition to compulsory binding arbitration and the strike as collective negotiations impasse resolution procedures by public school teachers of Pennsylvania. Ed.D. dissertation. Temple University. 1980.

   Describes teachers as supportive of strikes and binding arbitration and reports that attitudes are not related to age, sex or whether the teacher's salary is the main support of a family.

4. Alden, Elaine F. & others. Austerity vs. aesthetics in the elementary school program. 1980. ERIC ED 205 283.

   Describes teachers' positive attitudes toward arts education; reports that they allocate limited instructional time to arts education; relates attitudes to teachers' characteristics.

5. Alexander, Donald K. & others. Measures of teacher attitude toward the open classroom. 1975. ERIC ED 108 888.

Describes teachers' attitudes toward the open classroom and the problems and benefits of teaching in an open environment.

6. Alexander, Livingston. A factor analytic study of teaching events stress inventory. ERIC ED 237 544.

Describes five factors which together account for teacher stress: (1) personal/professional threat, (2) interpersonal relationships, (3) racial issues, (4) non-contact teaching tasks, and (5) change in normal routine.

7. Alexander, Mary Sheron. A survey of high school social studies teachers' attitudes toward museum education programs. 1980. ERIC ED 190 469.

Describes the attitudes of secondary school teachers toward museums as educational institutions; they do not want to work with museum staff and do not view museum staff as educators.

8. Aloia, Gregory F. & Aloia, Stephen D. "Teacher expectation questionnaire: a scale to help determine the most appropriate placement for the mainstreamed handicapped student," Journal for Special Educators 19 No. 2 (1983): 11-20.

Describes initial expectations of teachers toward mainstreamed students and describes the data collection instrument.

9. Angello, Nancy Bryan. An analysis of Washington teachers' interest in selected priority areas of in-service training. Ph.D. dissertation. Washington State University. 1980.

Describes teachers' attitudes toward inservice training in specific areas, reporting a strong interest in training in instructional methods for specific subject areas and about mainstreaming.

10. Anglin, Leo W. & Dugan, Therese. Teachers' perceptions of existing and ideal school curriculum: an analysis of metaphors. ERIC ED 216 037.

Describes teachers' perceptions of an ideal and the actual curriculum and their perceptions of the views of parents and administrators.

11. Aotaki-Phenice, L. & Kostelnik, Marjorie. "Attitudes of early childhood educators on multicultural/multiethnic education," Journal of Multilingual and Multicultural Development 4: 41-46.

Describes teachers' attitudes toward multicultural education, the curriculum of early childhood education programs and factors associated with school success.

12. Arize, Augustine C. An econometric study of Arkansas secondary school teachers' attitudes toward and understanding of economic education. Ph.D. dissertation. North Texas State University. 1982.

Describes a relationship between college courses and inservice programs and teachers' attitudes toward and knowledge of economics and its role in social studies education.

13. Ashley, Susan & others. "Looking at the critical issues: the rural Pennsylvania teacher's perspective," Social Studies Journal 12 (1983): 27-35.

Reports that teachers in rural schools perceive that their schools face all the key educational problems and that conditions are not likely to improve.

14. Auton, Sylvia & others. "Staff development for secondary school teachers," NASSP Bulletin 66 No. 455 (1982): 116-20.

Describes attitudes of teachers toward aspects of inservice education programs and the teachers' participation in those programs.

15. Autotte, Norman Luke. Inquiry into the inclusion of social issues in Maine secondary social studies classrooms. Ed.D. dissertation. University of Maine. 1978.

Describes teachers' reports of behavior and attitudes when social issues are discussed.

16. Barman, Charles R. & others. "Attitudes of science and social studies teachers toward inter-disciplinary instruction," American Biology Teacher 44 (1982): 421-26.

Describes the attitudes of science and social science teachers toward inter-disciplinary instruction, including topics and methods.

17. Becker, Henry Jay & Epstein, Joyce L. "Parent involvement: a survey of teacher practices," Elementary School Journal 83 No. 2 (1982): 85-102.

Describes teachers' attitudes toward parent involvement in education of their children through home learning.

18. Becker, Henry Jay & Epstein, Joyce L. Parent involvement: teacher practices and judgements. ERIC ED 206 601.

Describes teachers' and administrators' attitudes toward parents teaching their children in specially-designed home learning activities.

19. Ben-Peretz, Miriam & Temir, Pinchas. What teachers want to know about curriculum materials. AERA presentaton. 1980. ERIC ED 190 484.

Describes things teachers consider important in selecting instructional materials, e.g., relevance of subject matter, textbook layout and readability, adaptability of instructional materials to student needs, instructional efficiency, practical usability.

20. Berben, E.A. A survey of attitudes of elementary educators concerning elementary counseling. 1968. ERIC ED 026 654.

Describes positive attitudes of teachers toward elementary school counseling programs.

21. Berkheimer, Glenn D. & Lott, Gerald W. "Science educators' and graduate students' perceptions of science education objectives for the 1980s," Science Education 68 No. 2 (1984): 105-116.

Describes attitudes of teachers toward science education and changes in science education objectives from kindergarten through grade 12.

22. Berryman, Joan D. & Berryman, Charles R. Use of the "Attitudes toward Mainstreaming Scale" with rural Georgia teachers. ERIC ED 201 420.

Describes attitudes of teachers toward mainstreaming; teachers were supportive of mainstreaming for students whose disabilities did not effect their learning but were resistant to mainstreaming disruptive students.

23. Berryman, Joan D. & Neal, W.R., Jr. "The cross validation of the Attitudes toward Mainstreaming

Scale," Educational and Psychological Measurement 40 (1980): 469-474.

Reports that teachers' attitudes toward handicapped students and mainstreaming consist of three major factors; student learning capability, traditional limiting disabilities and mainstreaming as an educational approach.

24. Bingham, Jane Sones. Teacher acceptance of global education in the social studies curriculum. Ph.D. dissertation. University of Michigan. 1979.

Describes teachers' attitudes toward the inclusion of global education goals in social studies.

25. Bintner, Stuart John. A study of the teaching methods, materials, class organizations, and opinions of American history teachers in selected Iowa high schools. Ed.D. dissertation. Drake University. 1978.

Describes attitudes of teachers toward teaching methods and materials.

26. Blair, Timothy R. Development of inservice models to implement teacher effectiveness research findings. ERIC ED 226 324.

Describes attitudes of teachers toward varied models of inservice education and the effects of varied programs on changes in teachers' behavior.

27. Blake, Robert W. Assessing English and language arts teachers' attitudes toward writers and writing. 1975. ERIC ED 113 718.

Describes teachers' attitudes toward writing and writing instruction.

28. Bliss, Samuel Stephen. An analysis of attitudes toward selected characteristics of minimum competency programs in mathematics as perceived by public school educators in Kansas, Nebraska, Iowa, Colorado, and Missouri. Ph.D. dissertation. Kansas State University. 1980.

Describes differences in specific components of attitudes but not overall attitude toward minimum competency testing between elementary and secondary teachers.

29. Bonds, Charles W. & Lindsey, John R. The principal in special education: the teacher's perspective. 1980. ERIC ED 213 209.

Describes the role that teachers perceive that the principal should play in implementing mainstreaming, including participation in staff training related to mainstreaming.

30. Bostrom, K. An evaluative study of the effects and effectiveness of microcomputer based teaching in schools. ERIC ED 224 461.

Describes teachers' use of computer assisted instruction and limited teacher interest in such instruction.

31. Brooks, Victor D., Jr. "Adversary to ally--the relationship of American television to history teaching strategies," Georgia Social Science Journal 15 No. 2 (1984): 11-15.

Describes positive teacher attitudes toward television as an educational tool, a change over a period of years.

32. Buckner, Edward M. Professional and political socialization: high school science teacher attitudes on curriculum decisions, in the context of a "scientific" creationism campaign. Ph.D. dissertation. Georgia State University, 1983.

Describes science teachers as divided in their responses to the "scientific" creationism campaign but generally the more strongly socialized teachers had less positive attitudes toward involvement of community members in curriculum decisions.

33. Bullough, Robert V., Jr. & others. "Rational curriculum: teachers and alienation," Journal of Curriculum Theorizing 4 No. 2 (1982): 132-43.

Describes teachers' perceptions of their work and as alienated from a new curriculum management system.

34. Burnes, Bruce. "Teaching about Native Americans in Minnesota public elementary schools," Journal of American Indian Education 22 No. 1 (1982): 1-6.

Reports that teachers feel inadequate to teach about native Americans; they note lack of content knowledge and human relations skills.

35. Calvano, Frank Anthony. Attitudes of elementary school teachers toward student nonpromotion. Ed.D.

dissertation. University of Southern California. 1981.

Describes support among teachers for nonpromotion, with no differences associated with teacher characteristics, e.g., age.

36. Campbell, W. "The teacher's view of teaching behavior," International Review of Education 18 No. 4 (1972): 540-546.

Presents views of teachers from several countries about their teaching and ideal teaching.

37. Carrick, Tessa. "Some biology teachers' goals for advanced level teaching," Journal of Biological Education 17 (1983): 205-14.

Describes attitudes of biology teachers toward the goals and methods of science education, reporting a concern for lower-level rather than higher-level cognitive skills.

38. Carson, Robert B. & others. Teacher participation in the community, role expectations and behavior. University of Oregon, Eugene. 1967. ERIC ED 014 798.

Reports teachers' views of their role in educational and community decisions; role seen as limited, with little involvement in decision making.

39. Caylor, Mary Jane. The attitudes of teachers toward the concept of collective bargaining in Alabama. Ed.D. dissertation. University of Alabama. 1981.

Reports teachers' attitudes toward collective bargaining; approximately half of the teachers believed that they would support a strike but teachers did not believe that collective bargaining would influence working conditions.

40. Childers, John H., Jr. & Podemski, Richard S. "Confronting idealistic teacher expectations: strategies for training programs and school districts," Teacher Educator 18 No. 3 (1982): 2-10.

Reports that beginning teachers have idealistic expectations toward several aspects of teaching, e.g., classroom activities, professional status.

41. Christenson, Sandra. "Institutional constraints and external pressures influencing referral decisions," Psychology in the Schools 19 No. 3 (1982): 341-45.

Describes aspects of the support system that teachers perceive as influencing their decisions to refer students for help.

42. Clay, Thomas. Music in Ohio schools. final report. ERIC ED 229 301.

Reports teachers' perceptions of the role of music in the school curriculum and the nature of school music programs.

43. Cohen, Martin & Fliess, Robert F. Minicalculators and instructional impact: a teacher survey. Pittsburg University, Pennsylvania. 1979. ERIC ED 178 360.

Teachers generally favor calculators, but not as a substitute for learning calculation skills, and allow the use of calculators in their classrooms.

44. Cortright, Richard W. "Teachers speak out about Public Law 94-142," Education Unlimited 2 No. 1 (1980): 20-21.

Reports that teachers believe that they need more training to work with mainstreamed students, that class sizes should be reduced when handicapped students are enrolled in regular classes and that paperwork associated with mainstreaming should be lessened.

45. Corwin, John K. & Sandiford, Janice R. "Results of the AVA National Teacher Concerns Survey," Voccational Education 549 (1984): 38-40.

Describes teachers' perceptions of the goals of vocational education and aspects of teaching.

46. Coughlan, Robert J. "An assessment of teacher work values," Educational Administration Quarterly 5 (1969): 53-73.

Describes five types of teachers in terms of work values: supervisory oriented, systems oriented, subject oriented, staff oriented or socially oriented.

47. Coughlan, R. J. "The factorial structure of teacher work values," American Educational Research Journal 6 No. 2 (1969): 169-189.

Describes five major dimensions of teacher work values: administrative focus, work emphasis, source of authority, educational concern and source of support.

48. Cowan, Elizabeth. How English teachers see the profession: an informal survey. ERIC ED 240 575.

Describes attitudes of English teachers toward the curriculum, teaching as a career and their teaching situation.

49. Cozine, Dean. Teacher perceptions of the acceptability of teacher training products. Research and Development Memorandum No. 141. Stanford University Center for Research and Development in Teaching. 1975. ERIC ED 118 566.

Describes teachers' attitudes toward different types of training products in terms of the products' perceived usefulness.

50. Cramer, Jerome. "Yes-Merit Pay can be a horror, but a few school systems have done it right," American School Board Journal 170 No. 9 (1983): 28, 33-34.

Describes the operation of and teachers' attitudes toward merit pay and the evaluation systems necessary to support merit pay.

51. Davies, Eirlys E. Error evaluation: the importance of viewpoint. ELT Journal 37 No. 4 (1983): 304-11.

Describes attitudes of teachers toward standard English and speech patterns of non-native speakers and their effects on teaching decisions.

52. Davis, William E. "The resource teacher's role as tutor and responsibilities for pupil grading," Journal for Special Educators 19 No. 1 (1982): 55-58.

Describes mainstreaming resource teachers' role and responsibilities for student achievement and relationships with classroom teachers.

53. DeGuire, Michael R. The role of the elementary principal in influencing reading achievement. ERIC ED 227 469.

Describes teachers' perceptions of and attitudes toward the principal's role as instructional leader in relation to the reading program.

54. Delemos, Valeria A. & Youngblood, Chester E. The St. Croix, United States Virgin Island, public school primary teacher: a profile. ERIC ED 228 169.

Describes attitudes and characteristics of teachers in the United States Virgin Islands.

55. Demetropoulos, Efstathios. G. The attitudes of secondary vocational teachers toward the establishment of decentralized teacher-centered career guidance in secondary schools. Ph.D. dissertation. Indiana University. 1979.

Reports concern for and willingness to assume roles related to career guidance among secondary school vocational teachers in Indiana.

56. Detroit Public Schools. Elementary school staff attitudes toward desegregation, 1979 survey. 1980. ERIC ED 208 116.

Reports that a majority of teachers believed that student academic achievement was increasing and that student discipline problems had not increased after school desegregation and that relations among teachers were good.

57. Detroit Public Schools. High school staff attitudes toward desegregation, 1979 survey. 1980. ERIC ED 208 818.

Describes the attitudes of teachers toward several aspects of their teaching situation, such as staff morale, student achievement, student discipline and staff relations that were associated with changes in school programs resulting from an integration program.

58. Detroit Public Schools. Middle school staff attitudes toward desegregation, 1979 survey. 1980. ERIC ED 208 117.

Describes attitudes of middle school teachers toward aspects of school programs that have changed, or may have been perceived to have changed, as a result of desegregation of the schools, such as discipline, relations with students and other staff.

60. DiSipio, Zina, Nake, Janet & Perney, Jan. "How classroom teachers view the resource room - part 1," The Journal for Special Educators of the Mentally Handicapped 14 (1978): 164-172.

Teachers surveyed felt resource rooms met the needs of special education students and the regular classroom teachers of those students.

59. Diem, Richard A. & Lawrence, Richard. "Violence, delinquency, and schools: a study of educators' attitudes," Texas Tech Journal of Education 10 #3 (198 175-80.

Describes teachers' attitudes toward student behavior problems, juvenile crime and the juvenile justice system.

61. Dreyfus, Amos. "An approach to the assessment of teachers' concerns in the context of curriculum evaluation," Studies in Educational Evaluation 8 No. 1 (1982).

Describes attitudes of experienced teachers toward aspects of a biology instructional program.

62. Drum, Randell L. & Wells, Tim J. A survey of teachers' opinions and practices regarding the teaching of problem solving skills. ERIC ED 240 075.

Describes teachers as having a positive attitude toward the teaching of problem solving skills and describes the personal descriptions associated with teaching of problem solving.

63. Duke, Daniel L. & others. "Teachers and shared decision making: the costs and benefits of involvement," Educational Administration Quarterly 16 (1980): 93-106.

Reports that teachers perceive that the costs to the teachers, in terms of time and effort, are greater than the benefits resulting from participation in school decision making.

64. Duvall, Charles R. A study of teachers and principals views of sponsored educational materials that may be provided schools by consumers power company. ERIC ED 232 940.

Reports a positive attitude among teachers toward social studies materials supplied by outside groups, provided the materials were unbiased.

65. Duvall, Charles R. A study of teachers' and principals' views of sponsored educational materials that may be provided schools by consumers power company. Part I: lower elementary (K-3) school teachers. ERIC ED 242 413.

Describes teachers' attitudes toward characteristics of instructional materials provided by a public utility company.

66. Eaker, Robert E. & Huffman, James D. Teacher perceptions of dissemination of research on teaching findings. ERIC ED 205 501.

Describes teachers views of the methods of dissemination of results of research on teaching.

67. Earl, Robert D. "Attitudes of elementary teachers toward science and science teaching," Science Education 61 (1977): 41-45.

Describes teachers' attitudes toward science and science teaching.

68. Eberts, Randall W. & Stone, Joe A. Unions and public schools: the effect of collective bargaining on American education. ERIC ED 242 084.

Describes teachers' attitudes toward unions and collective bargaining while describing the history and effects of collective bargaining for teachers.

69. Egertson, Harriet Ann. A description of the preparation, experience and educational orientation of teachers in prekindergarten programs in Nebraska. Ph.D. dissertation. University of Nebraska, Lincoln. 1980.

Describes preparation, experience and educational orientation of preschool and day care teachers in Nebraska.

70. Elbaz, Freema. Teacher thinking: a study of practical knowledge. ERIC ED 224 797.

Describes attitudes of teachers toward teaching and learning, toward English and reading instruction and toward teaching as a career.

71. Elsner, Priscilla Jo. "Criterion referenced assessment and its classroom uses as viewed by teachers," School Science and Mathematics 73 (1973): 730-734.

Describes teachers' attitudes toward criterion referenced testing systems and the additional training teachers received in use of test results.

72. Emond, Susie. English/language arts teachers take an introspective look: implications of a survey of elementary teachers. ERIC ED 233 395.

Describes teachers' attitudes toward elementary language arts instruction; classroom management and discipline were seen as the major problems.

73. Engler, Richard E., Jr. & others. Voices from the classroom: teacher concerns with new legislation for serving handicapped children. A report on a

study of reactions to Public Law 94-142. 1978. ERIC ED 176 437.

Describes teachers' knowledge of and attitude toward P.L. 94-142, the Education for All Handicapped Children Act.

74. Epstein, Joyce L. Single parents and the schools: the effect of marital status on parent and teaching evaluations. Johns Hopkins University. Baltimore, Maryland. Center for the Study of Social Organization of School. 1984.

Describes teachers' views of single parents and the problems that children of single parents may have in school.

75. Eubanks, Eugene E. "A study of teachers' perceptions of essential teacher attributes in defacto segregated high schools," Education 93 (1973): 373-380.

Describes teachers' perceptions of the important competencies needed in a segregated high school.

76. Evans, Mary Natalie. Propositional and functional patterns of selected kindergarten teachers as developed and interpreted by interaction analysis. Ed.D. dissertation. University of Cincinnati. 1969.

Describes Head Start kindergarten teachers as teacher-centered, content oriented, not encouraging student independent behavior, concerned with control of classroom, warm climate and encouraging student initiative.

77. Evans, Sylvia Arlene. Attitudes of teachers of the gifted and talented toward the concept of career education in the District of Columbia public schools. Ed.D. dissertation. Pennsylvania State University. 1982.

Reports positive attitudes toward career education for gifted students, with more positive attitudes associated with age and teaching experience, but perceptions that programs could be developed which were more effective if more money were allocated.

78. Fido, H.S.A. & Gayford, C.G. "Field work and the biology teacher: a survey in secondary schools in England and Wales," Journal of Biological Education 16 No. 1 (1982): 27-34.

Describes attitudes of secondary biology teachers toward field work and the problems encountered in doing field work.

79. Fischer, Thomas Ray. A study of educators' attitudes toward homosexuality. Ed.D. dissertation. University of Virginia. 1982.

Describes differences in attitudes toward homosexuality by educators' characteristics, e.g., age and job classification, with attitudes generally more negative than positive.

80. Fitzgerald, Sheila M. A career development study of elementary school teachers. 1972. ERIC ED 087 754.

Describes career attitudes of elementary teachers as not being happy ones.

81. Fitzgerald, Sheila Mary. Career needs and satisfactions of teachers: a replication study. 1978. ERIC ED 167 497.

Describes teachers' job satisfaction and career needs in 1977 compared to those identified in 1972; changes were related to teachers as individuals, not aspects of their instructional settings.

82. Fletcher, Ben C. & Payne, Roy L. "Levels of reported stressors and strains amongst schoolteachers: some UK data," Educational Review 34 No. 2 (1982): 267-78.

Describes characteristics of teacher stress and aspects of jobs which contribute to teacher stress.

83. Friesen, Charles D. The results of surveys, questionnaires and polls regarding homework. 1975. ERIC ED 109 174.

Describes teachers' attitudes toward student homework efforts as related to the amount of homework assigned.

84. Fris, Joe. "Perspectives on teachers' attitudes toward collective bargaining tactics," Canadian Administrator 19 No. 8 (1980): 1-6.

Describes the topics that teachers perceive to be appropriate for collective bargaining and the tactics that they think are acceptable within a negotiations setting.

85. Fuller, Mary Lou. "Teachers' perceptions of parents from intact and single parent families," Educational Horizons 62 No. 3 (1984): 94-95.

Describes attitudes of elementary teachers toward members of one- and two-parent families.

86. Gaug, Mary Ann. "Reading acceleration and enrichment in the elementary grades," Reading Teacher 437 No. 4 (1984): 372-76.

Describes teachers' perceptions of gifted students and the extent to which the teachers provide additional experiences for those students.

87. Gaus, Paula J. & Smith, Anne L. Evaluation of teacher's attitudes toward reading specialists. ERIC ED 211 950.

Describes teachers' attitudes toward reading specialists and their role in working with teachers; teachers' attitudes did not vary with the number of reading courses they had taken.

88. Gere, Anne Ruggles & others. Measuring teacher attitudes toward instruction in writing. 1980. ERIC ED 199 717.

Describes teachers' attitudes toward specific aspects of writing instruction, such as the relative role of student self-expression, i.e, the use of standard English and the role of linguistic maturity in effective writing instruction.

89. Gilson, Thomas Q. & Ramos, Elias T. "Public school teacher attitudes toward unionization," Journal of Collective Negotiations in the Public Sector 11 No. 2 (1982): 145-54.

Describes teachers' attitudes toward working conditions, unions and relations between teachers and administrators.

90. Goddard, William P. & Pereira-Mendoza, Lionel. "Three perspectives for computer applications in education," AEDS Journal 17 No. 3 (1984): 14-23.

Describes teachers' attitudes toward the use of computers for educational purposes as not associated with personal characteristics, e.g., sex, subject taught, grade taught.

91. Good, T.L., Coop, R., Denton, J. & Lunbacher, P. "Teachers' view of accountability: an empirical survey," Phi Delta Kappan 56 (1975): 367-368.

Reports the results of a survey of teachers' attitudes toward the concept and the process of accountability.

92. Gooding, C. Thomas. Faculty development and current problems in accountability in Great Britain. 1980. ERIC ED 202 900.

Reports that teachers were generally satisfied with the information about student achievement available from the national testing program, would prefer criterion- rather than norm-referenced tests, and did not have sufficient program information.

93. Gould, Jewell & Ward, James. Teachers and tests: the teacher union response. 1980. ERIC ED 193 259.

Reports that teachers view tests as useful in providing diagnostic information about students but as not useful for program evaluation or modification of curriculum content.

94. Graham, Steve & Deaton, William. "A factor analysis of the Rucker-Gable Educational Programming Scale," Educational and Psychological Measurement 43 No. 3 (1983) 927-33.

Describes teachers' attitudes toward mainstreaming and characteristics of the measurement instrument.

95. Green, Robert W. "Analysis of questions teachers ask about teaching modern mathematics in the elementary school," Arithmetic Teacher 23 No. 2 (1976): 98.

Describes teachers' concerns with various aspects of modern mathematics curricula.

96. Green, Virginia P. & Schaefer, Lyn. "Preschool teachers play materials preferences," Early Child Development and Care 14 No. 1-2 (1984): 85-92.

Describes the preferences of early childhood teachers for some materials available for preschool children.

97. Greenlaw, M. Jean & Kurth, Ruth Justine. Current research and analysis of definitions of comprehension. 1980. ERIC ED 194 878.

Describes teachers' perceptions of reading comprehension; most teachers had distinct conceptions of reading comprehension, selecting models similar to definitions of thinking.

98. Greer, Charles R. & Brown, M. Patricia. "Teachers' attitudes toward unions, working conditions, and

strikes following an illegal strike in the southwest," Journal of Collective Negotiations in the Public Sector 11 No. 3 (1982): 243-57.

Describes teachers' attitudes toward their teaching situations, with perceptions of low wages and unfair treatment associated with support for teacher strikes.

99. Griswold, Philip A. "Computer awareness and attitudes of prospective rural teachers," Rural Educator 5 No. 3 (1984): 11-15.

Reports attitudes of rural teachers toward the use of computers in education, noting general resistence to learning about computers.

100. Guenther, John. The importance of specific skills to high school social studies teachers. AERA presentation. 1973. ERIC ED 077 822.

Describes teachers' beliefs about what skills are important for students in social studies.

101. Gullickson, Arlen R. "Teacher perspectives of their instructional use of tests," Journal of Educational Research 77 No. 4 (1084): 244-48.

Describes attitudes of teachers toward testing their perceptions of the value of and uses for information provided by tests.

102. Gutkin, Terry B. & others. "Teacher reactions to school-based consultation services: a multivariate analysis," Journal of School Psychology 18 (1980): 126-134.

Reports that teachers who work with consultants in the classroom to learn to work with students with various behavioral and academic problems prefer that method rather than referral of students for assistance and occasional conversations with resource persons.

103. Handel, Charles Harold. Teacher attitudes and perceptions toward computer technology in education and the prototype computer-based Cincinnati instructional management system. Ed.D. dissertation. University of Cincinnati. 1982.

Describes attitudes of teachers toward computer technology and an instructional management system based on computer technology.

104. Hanes, Madlyn Levin & others. "Teachers' attitudes about psycholinguistic issues in reading:

implications and strategies for inservice training," Reading Improvement 20 (1982): 303-9.

Describes teachers' attitudes toward a theory of reading instruction and methods of inservice education in reading instruction.

105. Hanes, Madlyn Levine & Mulhern, John D. The university reading clinic: a needed and viable means of servicing community and schools. ERIC ED 200 891.

Reports that teachers are concerned about reading instruction and in support services available from university reading instruction programs.

106. Hanna, Charles Clifford. Teaching as a "central life interest" of metropolitan secondary teachers. 1972. ERIC ED 088 838.

Describes teachers' attitudes toward teaching as a career and its role within their lives.

107. Hargrove, Martha L. "Teachers' perceptions of ESEA Title I programs," Education 103 No. 2 (1982): 196-99.

Reports the attitudes of teachers participating in programs for disadvantaged students toward those programs.

108. Harste, Jerome C. & others. The teacher of reading. International Reading Association. 1976. ERIC ED 123 552.

Describes reading teachers' personal characteristics and beliefs.

109. Haughey, Margaret L. & Murphy, Peter J. "Quality of work life: rural teachers' perceptions," Canadian Administrator 23 No. 2 (1983): 1-6.

Describes attitudes of rural Canadian teachers toward aspects of their work and working conditions.

110. Helsel, A. Ray. "Value orientaton and pupil control ideology of public school education," Educational Administration Quarterly 7 No. 1 (1971): 24-33.

Pupil control is seen by educators as central to school operation.

111. Henning, Joel F. & others. "Teachers and authority," American Educator 4 No. 2 (1980): 20-25.

Reports that teachers are reluctant to take actions that question, or appear to question, the authority of school administrators and that they communicate this reluctance to question authority to students.

112. Hermanowicz, Henry J. "The pluralistic world of the beginning teacher," Kentucky School Journal 44 (1965): 18-19.

Reports a series of studies in which beginning teachers were interviewed about their perceptions of teacher education, fellow teachers, professional organizations and other aspects of teaching.

113. Hill, Ada D. & Reed, Daisy F. Overview of mainstreaming. ERIC ED 218 246.

Describes teachers' attitudes toward mainstreaming and support services available to teachers with mainstreamed handicapped students.

114. Hill, Charles H. "Oral reading as a content area teaching method," Clearing House 57 No. 2 (1982): 56-58.

Describes teachers' perceptions that oral reading is not an effective instructional method for social students and science instruction but reports that teachers use oral reading as an instructional method.

115. Hill, Charles H. "Round robin reading as a teaching method," Reading Improvement 20 (1983): 263.

Describes teachers' use of and attitudes toward student oral reading as an instructional method for science and social studies.

116. Holdaway, Edward A. "Facet and overall satisfaction of teachers," Educational Administration Quarterly 14 (1978): 30-47.

A survey of teachers in Alberta, Canada, found attitudes toward intrinsic facets of the profession were related to overall satisfaction with teaching.

117. Holyoak, Arlene. Secondary teachers' knowledge of legislation concerning the education of handicapped learners related to their attitudes toward handicapped individuals. Ph.D. dissertation. Pennsylvania State University. 1981.

Describes differences in knowledge about Public Law 94-142 but not in attitude toward handicapped students by teacher subject area.

118. Hoot, James L. & Lumsden, D. Barry. Aging education in the public schools--coming of age? ERIC ED 199 233.

Reports that teachers don't teach about aging but are generally willing to include instruction about aging if they have appropriate instructional materials.

119. Horak, Willis. "Behavioral priorities of science teachers: an analysis of perceptions about science teaching," School Science and Mathematics 80 (1980): 457-462.

Study found general agreement about the ranking of importance of teaching behaviors but many differences in beliefs about which types of teaching behaviors are valuable in teaching science.

120. Howard, Irvin. The attitudes and practices of early adolescent educators towards multiethnic education. Ed.D. dissertation. Illinois State University. 1980.

Describes differences between white and black teachers toward implementing multiethnic education programs, with teachers generally positive about inclusion of concepts but not teaching approaches.

121. Howard, Rose A. "Middle school discipline: what do teachers prefer?" Clearing House 54 (1980): 155-157.

Describes preferences of teachers identified as effective for teachers' responses to discipline problems; the highest agreement among teachers occurred in preferred responses to the most serious problems.

122. Hudson, Floyd & others. "Mainstreaming: an examination of the attitudes and needs of regular classroom teachers," Learning Disability Quarterly 2 No. 3 (1979): 58-62.

Describes teachers' negative attitudes; they have neither time nor support services to work with handicapped children in the classroom.

123. Hutson, Harry & Silvernail, David L. "Inservice education: a perception check," Education Unlimited 2 No. 1 (1980): 8-9.

Reports that teachers have perferences for topics and organizational methods for inservice education; participants should plan inservice programs and programs should be held during the school day.

124. Infantino, Robert Louis. Testing and accountability: a survey of the knowledge and attitudes of New York state secondary school English teachers. Ed.D. dissertation. State University of New York at Buffalo. 1976.

Describes attitudes and knowledge of a random sample of teachers toward testing and accountability.

125. Ingersoll, Gary M. & others. "Microcomputers in American public schools: a national survey," Educational Computer 3 No. 6 (1983): 28, 30-31.

Describes positive attitudes among teachers toward the use of computers as an instructional tool.

126. Instructor. "The American elementary teacher today: results of Instructor's first national teacher poll," Instructor 89 No. 6 (1980): 24, 26.

Reports the results of a poll of the teachers who read the magazine, covering a variety of educational topics, such as school violence, teacher unions, instructional methods and materials, and national political involvement of teachers.

127. Jacko, Carol M. Classroom teachers and sex-role stereotyping: awarenesses, attitudes, and behaviors. ERIC ED 199 256.

Describes teachers' attitudes toward sex-role stereotyping and their perceptions that sex-role stereotyping occurs both in society and in the classroom.

128. Jackson, James E. & Sui-Runyan, Yvonne Steinruck. The ten most important teaching skills in teaching reading. 1980. ERIC ED 189 584.

Reports teachers' identification of the teaching skills most important in teaching reading, including diagnosis of student skills through observation, motivation, classroom climate, and developing language skills.

129. Jackson, Phillip W. & Belford, Elizabeth. "Educational objectives and the joys of teaching," School Review 73 (1965): 267-291.

Describes the positive attitudes toward teaching and teaching experiences of a sample of teachers nominated by principals as exceptional teachers.

130. James, Arlos Ferrel. Educator attitudes concerning copyright. Ed.D. dissertation. University of Arkansas. 1981.

Reports that teachers have limited knowledge of the principles which underly copyright law and the application of those principles to specific copying activities of teachers.

131. Jenkins, Joseph R. & Bausell, R. Baher. "How teachers view the effective teacher: student learning is not the top criterion," Phi Delta Kappan 55 (1974): 572-573.

Presents the results of a survey of Delaware teachers toward the goals of schooling and criteria by which teachers are judged to be effective.

132. Johns, Kenneth W. "Wanted: money and time for science," School Science and Mathematics 84 No. 4 (1984): 271-276.

Describes attitudes of Nevada teachers toward science education and their perceptions of obstacles to teaching science, e.g., lack of time and equipment.

133. Johnson, Charles E. & others. Identifying and verifying generic teacher competencies. Georgia University. College of Education. 1978. ERIC ED 160 560.

Describes a process for developing a list of teacher competencies and teachers' ratings of the importance of those competencies.

134. Johnson, Lary. Staff members' preferences for characteristics of educational programs in Minneapolis west area schools. Minneapolis Public Schools. Department of Research and Evaluation. 1975. ERIC ED 114 429.

Reports teachers' attitudes toward curriculum, instructional methods, student groupings and parents.

135. Johnson, Warren Dale. Teachers' perceptions and circumstances that influence willingness to teach

environmental studies. Ph.D. dissertation. University of Illinois at Urbana-Champaign. 1980.

Describes teachers' perceptions of and attitude toward environmental studies.

136. Jones, Howard L. & others. "How teachers perceive similarities and differences among various teaching models," *Journal of Research on Science Teaching 17* (1980): 321-326.

Reports that teachers perceive certain aspects of various models of teaching as important and ignore other aspects; important aspects include affective orientation, emphasis on application and aspects of the structure of the environment.

137. Jones, Paul & Garner, Arthur E. "A comparison of middle school teachers' pupil control ideology," *Clearing House 51* (1978): 292-294.

Describes teacher pupil control ideology of a group of middle school teachers.

138. Joyce, Bruce & Birdsall, Les. Inservice teacher education in California: views of teachers. Occasional paper. California State Department of Education. Sacramento. 1977. *ERIC ED* 160 570.

Describes teachers as having generally negative views toward inservice education and its relationship to teacher concerns.

139. Jung, Steven M. & others. Experimental assessment of an incentive program to enhance school learning: a pilot study, final report. American Institutes for Researh in the Behavioral Sciences. Palo Alto, California. 1971. *ERIC ED* 055 115.

Describes an incentive program designed to change student achievement and teachers' attitudes toward the program.

140. Jung, Steven M. & others. Instructional practices questionnaire: mathematics. American Institutes for research in the Behavioral Sciences. Palo Alto, California. 1971. *ERIC ED* 055 117.

Presents the questionnaire used in study and results specific to mathematics.

141. Jung, Steven M. & others. Instructional practices questionnaire: reading. American Instututes for Research in the Behavioral Sciences. Palo Alto, California. 1971. *ERIC ED* 055 116.

Presents the questionnaire used in study and results specific to reading.

142. Kansky, Bob. Instructional computing in Wyoming: status and recommendations. _ERIC ED_ 202 675.

Describes the attitudes of Wyoming teachers toward computers and instructional uses of computers in the classrooms.

143. Kaplan, Robert M. "Teacher atitudes toward implementing career education in the classroom," _Journal of Educational Research 69 No. 3_ (1975): 106-108.

Describes attitudes teachers have toward implementing career education.

144. Kavale, Kenneth & Rossi, Constance. "Regular class teachers' attitudes and perceptions of the resource specialist program for educable mentally retarded pupils," _Education and Training of the Mentally Retarded 15_ (1980): 195-198.

Reports differences in attitudes toward resource room teachers and their roles in working with mentally retarded pupils among teachers by level of teaching assignment, with middle school teachers expressing more concerns than elementary or secondary teachers.

145. Kerlinger, Fred N. & Pedhazur, Elazar J. Attitudes and perceptions of desirable traits and behaviors of teachers: final report. 1967. _ERIC ED_ 019 742.

Presents results of questionnaires developed around educational attitude factors (progressivism, traditionalism), educational trait perceptions (person-oriented, task-oriented): progressive attitudes correlate positively with person-oriented perceptions.

146. Kerr, Alan. "Research report: are you afraid of research," _Australian Journal of Reading 6 No. 4_ (1983): 229-31.

Describes negative attitudes of teachers toward research and the reasons for those attitudes.

147. Khan, Nishat Ali & Hoge, Robert D. "A teacher-judgment measure of social competence: validity data," _Journal of Consulting and Clinical Psychology 51 No. 6_ (1983): 809-14.

Describes teachers' perceptions of the social competence of male and female kindergarten children.

148. Killian, Joyce E. "Preparing English teachers: the cooperating teachers' view," Education 15 No. 3 (1983): 136-42.

Describes attitudes of cooperating teachers toward student teachers and their preparation.

149. Kinghorn, Jan Bye. Inventory of teacher recommendations. Charles F. Kettering Foundation. Dayton, Ohio. ERIC ED 173 246.

Describes teachers' atitudes toward global education and the understanding of multiple cultures.

150. Kinzer, Charles K. & Stone, Ruth J. "A comparative study of educators' perceptions and use of mandated reading assessments," Reading Horizons 24 (1983): 64-68. ERIC ED 228 628.

Describes attitudes of teachers and principals toward the use of tests to assess student learning and teachers' uses of information from minimum competency testing.

151. Kirkorian, Donald G. An investigation of teacher attitudes toward closed circuit television in the Fremont Union High School District, Sunnyvale, California. Fremont Union High School District. Sunnyvale, California. 1971. ERIC ED 087 378.

Describes teachers' attitude toward closed circuit television.

152. Kiteley, James Walter. Secondary teachers' perceptions of content reading practices. Ph.D. dissertation. Arizona State University. 1980.

Although the majority of teachers had not had a reading course, they were supportive of reading practices and rated general teaching techniques as more important than specific techniques.

153. Knape, Carl. & Rosewell, Paul T. "The philosophically discerning classroom teacher," Educational Studies 11 (1980): 37-47.

Reports differences among teachers in their knowledge of and commitment to an educational philosophy and a relationship between degree of commitment to an educational philosophy and ability to justify teaching behaviors.

154. Knox, Gary Allen. An exploration of teacher perceptions concerning recommendations in social studies education. Ph.D. dissertation. Stanford University. 1980.

Describes teachers' acceptance of but lack of necessary knowledge about or commitment to implement a recommended new social studies curriculum.

155. Lampert, Magdalene. "Teaching about thinking and thinking about teaching," Journal of Curriculum studies 16 No. 1 (1984): 1-18.

Describes differences in teachers' intuitive and school-based knowledge and effects of that knowledge on teachers' attitudes.

156. Larrivee, Barbara. "Factors underlying regular classroom teachers' attitude toward mainstreaming," Psychology in the Schools 19 No. 3 (1982): 374-79.

Reports that four dimensions describe differences in teachers' attitudes toward mainstreaming; including teachers' views of the support for mainstreaming and the abilities and needs of mainstreamed students.

157. Lawrenz, Frances. "Factor validation of Kuhn's energy opinionaire," Journal of Environmental Education 15 No. 2 (1984): 42-44.

Describes the attitudes of teachers and students toward energy education and describes the data collection instrument.

158. Lentz, Kathleen Ann. Ego development and teaching-related attitudes in preschool teachers. Ph.D. dissertation. Arizona State University. 1980.

Describes few differences in the attitudes of preschool teachers by their perceptions of whether their classroom is open or directed and limited concerns about professional growth.

159. LeSourd, Sandra J. "An exploratory comparison of two methods of assessing teacher attitude toward instructional strategies," Theory and Research in Social Education 12 No. 1 (1984): 31-41.

Describes attitudes of teachers toward teaching approaches and greater detail in information obtained by interviews in comparison with a questionnaire.

160. Levin, Patricia G. "Teachers' perceptions, attitudes, and reporting of child abuse/neglect," Child Welfare 62 No. 1 (1983): 14-20.

Describes teachers' attitudes toward child abuse and factors which affect teachers' willingness to recognize and report instances of abuse.

161. Leyser, Yona & Abrams, Peter D. "Changing attitudes of classroom teachers toward mainstreaming through in-service training," Clearing House 57 No. 6 (1984): 250-55.

Describes changes in teachers' attitudes toward mainstreaming of handicapped students resulting from teachers' participation in an inservice training program.

162. Lingham, Marcella Erma. Variations in teachers' perceptions of parent involvement activities in working-class elementary schools. Ed.D. dissertation. Rutgers University. 1980.

Describes teachers' positive perceptions of parent involvement; the only difference by teacher perceptions of the teaching role occurred in one area of parent involvement.

163. Loble, Naomi Kaufman. The impact of P.L.94-142 on elementary teacher attitudes and needs for personnel, resources and staff preparation in an atypical New Jersey school district. Ph.D. dissertation. Rutgers University. 1980.

Elementary teachers were less receptive in the spring than in the fall to mainstreaming mildly handicapped students.

164. Logan, Jane Ramsey. The nutrition knowledge and sources of nutrition information used by elementary classroom teachers and elementary education majors. Ph.D. dissertation. Ohio State University. 1980.

Most teachers rate nutrition education as very or moderately important but report teaching it 0-3 hours per grading period; little relationship found between knowledge and courses taken.

165. Longstreth, Larry Eldon. Values and teaching: a study of teacher beliefs. 1970. ERIC ED 042 687.

Describes teachers' attitudes toward values, values education and values clarification.

166. Low, Harvey L. "Teacher's reactions to ungraded teaching," NASSP Bulletin 59 No. 394 (1975): 82-89.

Describes teachers' reactions to nongraded secondary schools.

167. McCaw, Steven C. "Teacher attitudes toward environmental education," Journal of Environmental Education 11 No. 2 (1979-80): 18-23.

Describes teachers' attitudes toward environmental education and their behaviors in using the environment to teach.

168. Machart, Norm. "The goal of social studies as perceived by some sixth grade teachers," Journal of Teaching and Learning 3 No. 3 (1978): 16-22.

Describes teachers' ratings of various goals of elementary social studies.

169. MacPherson, Ian George. Definitional orientations of young secondary social studies teachers in Pennsylvania: some implications for social studies teacher education. Ph.D. dissertation. Pennsylvania State University. 1979.

Describes the definitional orientation of social studies teachers.

170. Mahan, James M. "Major concerns of Anglo student teachers serving in Native American communities," Journal of American Indian Education 23 No. 3 (1984): 19-24.

Describes attitudes of Anglo teachers teaching in reservation schools, reporting concerns about teaching strategies, cultural sensitivity and adaptations to the reservation culture.

171. Mahan, James M. "The teacher's view of the principal's role in innovation," Elementary School Journal 70 (1970): 359-365.

Describes perception of teacher perception that principals and subject matter specialists are the major forces behind innovations.

172. Mark, Frank D. The attitudes of elementary teachers toward the mainstreaming of educable mentally retarded students in northwestern Ohio school districts: a summary of the study. 1980. ERIC ED 196 188.

Describes attitudes of teachers toward mainstreaming; attitudes varied between teachers who had and had not had experience with main-streamed students.

173. Martin, David Michael. A classification of Alabama public school kindergarten teachers according to their perceptions of selected developmental theories. Ed.D. dissertation. Auburn University. 1980.

Describes no differences in theoretical and philosophical viewpoints but differences between those and teachers' reports of behavior.

174. Meissner, Judith S. & others. Disadvantaged children and their first school experiences. Educational Testing Service. Head Start Longitudinal Study. Princeton, New Jersey. 1973. _ERIC ED_ 109 136.

A collection of background and language data based on a teacher questionnaire developed by Educational Testing Service.

175. Melancon, Jan G. & Thompson, Bruce. Perceptions of teacher brinkmanship behaviors. _ERIC ED_ 204 327.

Describes instances of teachers' brinkmanship behavior in relating to principals and reports no relationship between perceptions of such behavior and the perceiver's personality.

176. Mertz, Maia Pank & Zidonis, Frank. "Perceived preparation of Ohio English teachers," _Research in the Teaching of English 16 No. 3_ (1982): 279-84.

Describes attitudes of English teachers toward the secondary school English curriculum and their own preparation for teaching.

177. Michael, Charlene Belton & Riley, Marcia G. Workshop participants' perception rankings of second generation school desegregation issues. _ERIC ED_ 208 085.

Describes the attitudes of teachers and administrators toward problems encountered by schools after desegregation.

178. Mika, Walter J., Jr. "An NEA-VEA Response," _New Directions for Testing and Measurement No. 16_ (1982): 59-62.

Reports that teachers perceive that test scores have become a goal of education rather than a measure of the success of schools in achieving underlying goals.

179. Miller, David R., Splittgerber, Fred L. & Allen, Harvey. "We're in this thing together: teachers'

perceptions of middle school guidance," Elementary School Guidance and Counseling 15 (1980): 77-80.

Describes middle school teachers as optimistic about and supportive of guidance program based on a nationwide sample of state departments of education and principals and teachers in exemplary middle schools.

180. Miller, Maurice & others. "Student nonpromotion and teacher attitudes," Contemporary Education 51 (1980): 155-157.

Reports that teachers favor retention of students in grade and do retain students.

181. Miller, Texton R. & Strickland, Cecil L. Teacher attitudes and teacher adoption of concepts and practices in programs for the disadvantaged. North Carolina State University, Raliegh, School of Education. ERIC ED 067 459.

Describes differences in teacher and principal attitudes toward school programs for disadvantaged.

182. Milstein, Mike M. & others. "Organizationally based stress: what bothers teachers," Journal of Educational Research 77 No. 5; 293-97.

Reports that teachers perceive themselves as moderately stressed and view classroom factors as more important than organizational factors in determining their stress levels.

183. Mississippi State University. Public school teachers' perceptions of test validity and methods of interpreting test score data. ERIC ED 228 205.

Describes teachers' attitudes toward student testing and the uses of information from student testing.

184. Mitchell, Donald Leland. A study of attitudes, interests, and current practices related to career orientation activities in the elementary schools in Oklahoma. Oklahoma State Department of Vocational and Technical Education. Stillwater, Oklahoma. 1972. ERIC ED 057 248.

Describes teachers' perceptions of elementary school career orientation programs.

185. Moon, Thomas C. "Selected teacher reactions to SAPA and SCIS implementations," School Science and Mathematics 77 No. 3 (1977): 227-232.

Describes the range of teachers' attitudes toward the new science curricula.

186. Moracco, John C. & others. "Comparison of perceived occupational stress between teachers who are contented and discontented in their career choices," Vocational Guidance Quarterly 32 (1983): 44-51.

Describes the majority of surveyed teachers as not willing to select a teaching career if they were starting over in their working lives.

187. Morris, Jeanne Brown. The multiethnic education attitudes and practices of early childhood teachers. Ed.D. dissertation. University of Illinois at Urbana-Champaign. 1979.

Early childhood teachers had traditional attitudes toward and little training in beliefs appropriate for multiethnic classrooms and multiethnic education.

188. Munby, Hugh. A qualitative study of teachers' beliefs and principles. ERIC ED 228 215.

Describes the attitudes of teachers toward teaching, curriculum, content, innovation, and describes the research method used.

189. Murphy, Barbara C.T. A rationale for multicultural and multiethnic curriculum in early childhood education: assessment of inservce and preservice teacher attitudes toward selected concepts of ethnicity. Ph.D. dissertation. University of Pittsburgh. 1980.

Describes attitudes of teachers and teacher education students toward the concept of cultural pluralism and the extent to which preschool children should be made aware of their racial characteristics.

190. Murphy, Joseph & others. Academic press: translating high expectations into school policies and classroom practices. ERIC ED 272 636.

Describes attitudes of teachers as one aspect of academic press that encourages student achievement.

191. Muth, Rodney. "Power, conflict, and consensus: implications for teacher evaluation and school climate," NJEA Review 54 (1980): 19-20.

Reports that teachers' perceptions of principals' methods for making decisions and enforcing those decisions are related to teachers' reactions to the substance of the decisions made by principals.

192. Narang, Harbans Lel. "Factors associated with teacher knowledge of reading at the secondary level," Reading Horizons 21 (1980): 55-68.

Describes secondary school teachers' knowledge of reading instruction and sources of that knowledge, such as inservice training.

193. National Education Association. Nationwide teacher opinion poll. NEA research memo. National Education Association. Washington, D.C. 1979.

Describes demographic characteristics of teachers and their attitudes toward a number of issues based on teachers' responses to a national questionnaire.

194. National Education Association. A teacher survey NEA report: computers in the classroom. ERIC ED 229 343.

Describes teachers' attitudes toward the use of computers for instruction and limited knowledge about computers.

195. Neal, Stephen LeRoy. A determination of attitudes toward NCATE approved teacher education programs by selected public school teachers in a large metropolitan school system. Ed.D. dissertation. Memphis State University. 1981.

Reports no differences in attitudes toward their teacher education program by type of college attended and present teaching assignment, but variations in attitudes toward clinical experiences.

196. Neuman, Elizabeth M. & Harris, A. Christine. Comparisons of attitudes toward mainstreaming preschool and kindergarten children with special needs. 1977. ERIC ED 148 092.

Describes attitudes of teachers, special educators and parents toward aspects of mainstreaming.

197. Newman, Claude Arthur, Jr. Status and attitudes toward instructional computing in Arizona secondary schools with recommendations for a teacher education program in instructional computing. Ed.D. dissertation. Northern Arizona University. 1982.

Describes positive attitudes of teachers in Arizona secondary schools toward the use of computers for instructional purposes.

198. Nichols, Jeffery Brian. The attitudes of classroom teachers in selected north Texas school districts relative to collective bargaining. Ph.D. dissertation. North Texas State University. 1981.

Describes a slightly favorable attitude of teachers toward collective bargaining and variations in support for collective bargaining concerning specific topics of bargaining, e.g., salaries.

199. Nilsson, Beth Ann W. Participating teachers' perceptions of and attitudes toward a national writing project workshop. Ed.D. dissertation. Georgia State University-College of Education. 1981.

Describes a workshop in writing and changes in attitudes of participants toward the use of specific instructional strategies for teaching writing.

200. Norris, Cathleen A. & Lumsden, Barry. "Evaluating do-it-yourself computer inservice training packages: methodology and some findings," _Computing Teacher_ _11_ _No._ _6_ (1984): 65-66.

Describes teachers' attitudes toward a specific training program in the use of computers in the classroom.

201. Norris, Cathleen & Lumsden, Barry. "Functional distance in the attitudes of educators towards computers," _Technological_ _Horizons_ _in_ _Education_ _11_ _No._ _4_ (1984): 129-32.

Describes attitudes of teachers toward instructional users of the computer in the classroom.

202. Null, Eldon J. & Spence, Betty A. Selected variables of teachers and their perceptions of male and of female principals. AERA presentation. 1973. _ERIC_ _ED_ 196 315.

Describes teachers' perceptions of principals and their roles within the school setting.

203. Nussel, Edward J. & Johnson, Mildred. "Who obstructs innovation? a study of teacher perceptions of possible obstacles to innovation,"

<u>Journal of Secondary Education 44 No. 1</u> (1969): 3-11.

Describes teachers' perceptions of and responses toward innovations and the factors which make innovation difficult.

204. Ogden, William R. "The views of teachers as to the objectives of education: implications for curriculum development," <u>Southern Journal of Educational Research 9 No. 2</u> (1975): 95-109.

Describes teachers' opinions about education and the goals of education as they relate to specific curriculum decisions.

205. Ogletree, Earl J. Race and residence influence opinions of city residency ruling. <u>ERIC ED</u> 209 758.

Describes teachers' reactions to a Chicago Board of Education requirement that teachers must live within the school district.

206. Ogletree, Earl J. & Atkinson, Lillian M. Mainstreaming teachers favor mainstreaming. <u>ERIC ED</u> 223 027.

Describes favorable attitudes toward mainstreaming accompanied by teachers' desires for more inservice and support programs.

207. Olson, Francis Allen. Professional educators agreement on criteria for measuring teacher effectiveness. Ed.D. dissertation. Montana State University. 1979.

Describes attitudes of teachers and administrators toward criteria used to judge teacher effectiveness.

208. Olson, Linda Ann. Attitudes of educators and community leaders toward career education concepts, methods of delivery and community involvement. 1980. <u>ERIC ED</u> 189 371.

Describes the attitudes of teachers and community members toward inclusion of career education concepts within the elementary school curriculum; attitudes were positive.

209. Ortmeyer, Linda Elizabeth. Ageism and sexism: elementary public school teachers' attitudes toward a 70-85 year-old female, male, and person, and how attitudes relate to knowledge. Ph.D. dissertation. University of Washington. 1981.

Reports a relationship between both knowledge and demographic characteristics and attitudes toward older persons, with limited differences in attitude by sex of older person.

210. Page, Jane & others. Teacher education curricula: perceptions of first-year teachers. ERIC ED 229 364.

Describes teachers' attitudes toward their teaching experience, their learning and the likelihood that they will continue to teach.

211. Pajak, Edward F. & Glickman, Carl D. Teachers discrimination between information and control in response to videotaped simulated supervisory conferences. ERIC ED 243 842.

Describes attitudes of teachers toward supervision and methods used by supervisors to communicate information.

212. Palmer, Princess & others. "Florida's minimum competency program: a survey of teachers' opinions," High School Journal 66 No. 2 (1983): 104-09.

Describes teachers' attitudes toward a program of minimum competency testing and awareness of unintended consequences of the program.

213. Pate, Henri Elizabeth. Relationship of nutrition knowledge and attitude toward teaching nutrition of early education classroom teachers in Memphis city schools. Ph.D. dissertation. University of Alabama. 1983.

Reports a relationship between teachers' attitudes toward and knowledge of nutrition education but no relationship between attitudes and actual teaching of nutrition education.

214. Paulk, Larry. "Employee exit interviews," Spectrum 2 No. 1 (1984): 7-13.

Describes attitudes of teachers leaving a school district toward aspects of teaching as a career and their own teaching situations.

215. Payne, Cynthia Brooks. A comparative study of high school teachers' attitudes toward error in written composition compared wth key principles of Mina Shaughnessy's theory of composing. Ph.D. dissertation. Ohio State University. 1982.

Describes teachers' attitudes toward concepts of writing instruction, reporting that they are more positive than the literature would indicate but that teachers are frustrated in their ability to implement some of those concepts.

216. Penner, Karen P. & Kolasa, Kathyrn M. "Secondary teachers' nutrition knowledge, attitudes and practices," Journal of Nutrition Education 15 No. 4 (1983): 141-45.

Reports more favorable attitudes toward and knowledge about nutrition education among teachers who have taught nutrition education.

217. Peterson, Elizabeth L. & Nett, Emily M. "Sexuality in the classrooms of teachers with various sex role orientations," Theory and Research in Social Education 10 No. 3 (1982): 29-40.

Describes varied attitudes of three teachers toward sex roles and sexuality.

218. Petkau, H.P. & Wheeler, A.E. Inviting teacher professional growth. ERIC ED 200 598.

Reports that teachers' stages of professional growth are related to teachers' behaviors and attitudes.

219. Phelan, William T. Staff reductions and performance evaluations: teacher views on the roles of administrators and colleagues. ERIC ED 231 083.

Describes teachers' attitudes toward aspects of work, e.g. principals' control of evaluations and effects of the possibility of lay-offs on teacher attitudes.

220. Porter, Richard D. Dimensions of teacher militancy: a factor analysis of teacher attitudes. 1975. ERIC ED 103 359.

Describes teachers' attitudes toward militancy and aspects of their work situations which encouraged militancy.

221. Post, Thomas R. & others. "Teachers', principals', and university faculties' views of mathematics learning and instruction as measured by a mathematics inventory," Journal of Research in Mathematics Education 8 No. 5 (1977): 332-334.

Describes different attititudes toward philosophy of mathematics and its teaching.

222. Pratt, John. "Perceived stress among teachers: the effects of age and background of children taught," Educational Review 30 No. 1 (1978): 3-14.

Describes five areas that cause stress to elementary teachers; inability to cope with teaching problems, agressive students, non-cooperative students, concern for student learning and staff relations.

223. Pritchard, D.L. & Moodie, A.G. A survey of teachers' opinions regarding open areas. Vancouver Board of School Trustees (British Columbia). 1971. ERIC ED 057 102.

Presents results of a survey of teachers' opinions about open area education.

224. Proctor, John Edward. The attitudes of elementary principals and teachers from schools with three different racial student populations toward student behavior problems and principal responses to student behavior problems. Ed.D. dissertation. Northern Illinois University. 1979.

Describes attitudes of principals and teachers toward student behavior, definitions of problems and principals' responses to problems.

225. Provis, Malcolm. "Collective action by teachers," Ebel, Robert L. Encyclopedia of Educational Research. The Macmillan Company. (1969): 154-160.

Describes studies of teachers' characteristics, attitudes toward union activities and participation in those activities.

226. Queer, Glenn E. Discipline study. Pittsburgh Public Schools. Office of Research. 1971. ERIC ED 063 660.

Describes results of a survey of teachers', principals' and parents attitudes toward corporal punishment and other discipline techniques.

227. Quintana, Susan & Ramirez, Albert. "Educators' attitudes, perceptions, and knowledge about bilingual-bicultural education," Atisbos Journal of Chicano Research (1976-1977): 97-106.

Describes teachers' and principals' attitudes toward bilingual education.

228. Raines, Bob Gene. Personal, situational, and behavioral predispositional factors related to the elementary teacher's attitude toward teaching

mathematics. Ed.D. dissertation. University of Virginia. 1970.

Relates teachers' mathematics attitudes to their attitude toward teaching, type of training and their attitudes toward elementary schools.

229. Rajpal, Puran L. "Teacher judgements of minority children," Integrated Education 10 No. 9 (1972): 33-36.

Describes teachers' ratings of behavioral problems exhibited by minority children.

230. Rajpal, Puran. "What behavior problems do teachers regard as serious?" Phi Delta Kappan 53 (1972): 591, reprinted in Discipline and Learning: an Inquiry into Student-Teacher Relationships (revised edition). National Education Association. Washington, D.C. 1977.

Presents ratings by teachers of a list of student behavior problems with a comparison to teachers' ratings in 1928.

231. Ramsey, Russell W. "How much can the school house control?," Adolescence 18 No. 72 (1983): 899-906.

Describes attitudes of teachers toward community support for the schools and reports that teachers perceive a lack of consequence about programs for disadvantaged students.

232. Rangel, Robert Edward. Perceptions of public school teachers in an ESEA Title I, nonpublic schools program. Ph.D. dissertation. University of Southern California. 1979.

Describes perceptions of teachers involved in a program toward aspects of the program.

233. Ray, James Earl. A study to examine belief patterns about teaching, learning, and classroom organization among teachers, administrators engaged in implementing national management models, and elementary principals. Ph.D. dissertation. Michigan State University. 1978.

Describes the attitudes of teachers and principals, and differences in attitudes toward teaching, classroom organization and learning.

234. Ream, Marsha A. Status of the American public school teacher, 1975-1976. National Education Association. Washington, D.C. 1977. ERIC ED 159 163.

Describes characteristics and attitudes of teachers toward teaching and their job situation, based on a survey.

235. Reddick, Thomas L. & Fields, Joseph C. A study of professional attitudes of teachers in five public school systems in Tennessee and Michigan. Mid-south Educational Research Association. 1978. ERIC ED 161 863.

Describes teachers' attitudes toward the profession and the negative effect of professional negotiations on teachers' attitudes.

236. Reddick, Thomas L. & others. A study of professional attitudes of teachers in the Cumberland County and Putnam County public school systems in Tennessee. 1980. ERIC ED 199 915.

Describes attitudes of teachers toward their teaching situation, the contracts under which they work, teaching as a career, and the unionization of the teaching profession.

237. Redwine, Judith A. & Dubick, Robert A. Teachers' perceptions of instructional leadership and teacher evaluation processes. 1978. ERIC ED 157 892.

Describes teachers' attitudes toward the principal as leader and toward the teacher evaluation process.

238. Reed, Carol Larkin. A comparison of kindergarten goals as perceived by public school superintendents, elementary principals, first grade teachers, kindergarten teachers, and parents in the state of Mississippi. Ed.D. dissertation. Mississippi State University. 1979.

Describes attitudes of several groups toward kindergarten goals.

239. Rees, Richard T. & Grogan, Jane. "The relationship of sexism and authoritarianism in teacher attitudes," Phi Delta kappan 59 (1978): 564.

Teachers high in authoritarianism attitude are also high in sexism.

240. Rescigno, Ronald C. A study of the relationship between parent and teacher satisfaction with their involvement in a school's decision-making process and student attitude toward school. Ed.D. dissertation. University of Northern Colorado. 1977.

Describes attitudes of parents and teachers: teachers had a more positive attitude when decisions were made at school, not district, level.

241. Reynolds, William M. & Greco, Victor T. "The reliability and factorial validity of a scale for measuring teachers' attitudes towards mainstreaming," Educational and Psychological Measurement 40 (1980): 463-468.

Reports that teachers' attitudes toward mainstreaming are composed of two main factors, educational and administrative factors.

242. Rice, Robert Jean. Role understanding and role acceptance in curriculum decision making and their affect upon curiculum change in school organizations. Ed.D. dissertation. Colorado State College. 1966.

Disagreements between teachers, administrators and school board members in reported perceptions of role of each group in making curriculum decisions.

243. Richardson, Ann Skerratt. Educators' attitudes toward goals and theories of art education. Ph.D. dissertation. University of Southern California. 1982.

Describes the attitudes of secondary school art teachers and administrators toward art programs as they exist within their districts and ideal art programs.

244. Richey, Linda S. & Ysseldyke, James E. "Teachers' expectations for the younger siblings of learning disabled students," Journal of Learning Disabilities 16 No. 10 (1983): 610-15.

Reports that teachers have lower expectations for the siblings of learning disabled than of other children.

245. Ringlaben, Ravic P. & Price, Jay R. "Regular classroom teachers' perceptions of mainstreaming effects," Exception Children 47 No. 4 (1981): 302-4.

Describes the perceptions of classroom teachers toward mainstreaming and its effects on the classroom and other students.

246. Rist, Marilee C. "But U.S. teachers oppose scarcity bonuses," American School Board Journal 170 No. 9 (1983): 25.

Describes teachers' attitudes toward bonus pay in areas of teacher shortage and effects on teachers' attitudes of teachers' characteristics such as years of teaching and union membership.

247. Rist, Marilee C. "Teacher comments: from growls to gratitude," American School Board Journal 170 No. 9 (1983): 27.

Describes teachers' attitudes toward merit pay systems and nine areas that teachers see as potential problems.

248. Roberts, Albert George. New Jersey's thorough and efficient mandate: teacher attitudes and perceptions. Ed.D. dissertation. Columbia University Teachers College. 1979.

Describes attitudes of teachers toward the New Jersey law mandating a "thorough and efficient" education for all students.

249. Roberts, Fannie M. "Attitudes toward mathematics of faculty and students in three high schools," School Science and Mathematics 70 No. 9 (1970): 785-793.

Describes students' and teachers' attitudes toward mathematics and mathematics instruction.

250. Roberts, Jane M.E. & Woolf, Beth. State-sponsored inservice: a pilot study of impact. ERIC ED 243 808.

Describes teachers' attitudes toward various types of inservice programs and the extent of behavioral change resulting from program participation.

251. Robertson, James R. & Haas, John D. "Teacher personality and the new social studies," Journal of Educational Research 64 No. 3 (1977): 133-138.

Presents data on teacher personality and attitudes of a group of social studies teachers.

252. Robinson, Richard D., Goodacre, Elizabeth J. & McKenna, Michael C. "Psycholinguistic beliefs: a cross-cultural study of teacher practice," Reading Improvement 15 (1978): 134-137.

Teachers in the United States and England reported little knowledge of psycholinguistics and beliefs about teaching which are contrary to basic tenets of psycholinguistics.

253. Rooks, Donald O. Attitudes of teachers, principals, superintendents, board members, and legislators toward collective bargaining for teachers. Ed.D. dissertation. University of Georgia. 1980.

Describes differences among different groups toward teacher collective bargaining by personal characteristics, e.g., age, group membership.

254. Roscoe, Bruce & Peterson, Karen L. "Teacher attitudes toward material availability for teaching visually impaired students," _Reading Improvement_ _20_ (1983): 239-44.

Reports that teachers view more training and materials as necessary for effective instruction of visually impaired mainstreamed students.

255. Rosenfeld, Lawrence B. An investigation of teachers' stereotyping behavior: the influence of mode of presentation, ethnicity and social class on teachers' evaluation of students. New Mexico University. Albuquerque. 1973. _ERIC_ _ED_ 090 172.

Describes impacts of stereotyping on teachers' evaluations of students, tendancy to respond to stimulus materials, e.g., social class, ethnicity, audio and visual modes.

256. Ross, Elbert Milton. The effect of structured verbal communication on principals' and teachers' perceptions of the adequacy of instructional materials and teaching conditions. Ph.D. dissertation. Ohio State University. 1978.

Presents a comparison of teachers' and principals' perceptions of school environment and teaching conditions.

257. Ruck, Jane E. Weber. Teachers' attitudes toward teacher evaluation in selected Connecticut school districts in relation to level of compliance of teacher evaluation programs with P.A. 74-278 (an act concerning teacher evaluation). Ph.D. dissertation. University of Connecticut. 1979.

Describes attitudes teachers have toward teacher evaluation - not related to type of evaluation or legal compliance.

258. Rush, Gary & Wood, Judy. "In-service education of teacher educators: a national survey," _Action in Teacher Education_ _4_ _No. 2_ 71-73.

Describes attitudes toward inservice education, topics covered, training methods and factors which encourage participation.

259. Sadoski, Mark C. A study of the theoretical bases of reading instruction and a comparison of programs. ERIC ED 236 543.

Describes teachers' attitudes toward reading, reading instruction and five programs of reading instruction.

260. Safran, Stephen P. "Resource consultant communication and teacher expectations of behaviorally disordered children," Behavioral Disorders 8 No. 1 (1982): 25-31.

Describes teachers' views of behaviorally disordered children as children with special problems but generally within the range of normal behavior.

261. Salemi, Anthony Joseph. A factor analysis of the perceived problems of parents, teachers and students of a local school district. Ph.D. dissertation. Southern Illinois University at Carbondale. 1978.

Describes perceptions of three groups toward a set of educational problems.

262. Sandefur, Walter S. III & Smith, Howard W., Jr. "A case of contrasting perceptions: profs vs. practitioners," Phi Delta Kappan 62 (1980): 59-60.

Reports agreement on large classes as a problem but disagreement in ranking of other problems by teachers and college professors of education.

263. Sanders, James R. & others. Elements of quality in elementary education. AERA presentation. 1978. ERIC ED 155 135.

Describes teachers' rankings of attributes of effective classroom teachers.

264. Sanders, John. Individualized instruction: teacher assessment, a research study. 1976. ERIC ED 127 284.

Describes teachers' interest in individualized instruction.

265. Sanders, Nicholas M. & Wallace, Joan. Teacher and parent opinion concerning moral/ethical education in the public schools: a report of an institute for

survey research study. Research for Better Schools. Philadelphia, Pennslyvania. 1975.

Describes attitudes of teachers and parents toward moral education in the public schools.

266. Sauders, Robert Ronald & Watkins, J. Foster. Teacher burnout/stress management: an exploratory look in an urban school system in Alabama. ERIC ED 236 109.

Describes attitudes of Alabama teachers toward aspects of their teaching situations and factors associated with teacher stress.

267. Scanland, Worth & Slattery, Diane. "The impact of computer-based instruction upon teachers: two perspectives," Educational Technology 23 No. 11 (1983): 7-12.

Describes teachers as generally resistant to the use of computers as instructional tools.

268. Scharffe, William G. "Attitudes toward pupil progress reporting," Phi Delta kappan 59 (1978): 555.

Describes teachers' attitudes toward reporting with teachers' feeling that narrative reporting is better than letter grades, parent conferences better, but not "much better" than letter grades.

269. Scheckman, Leslee J. The attitudes of secondary content area teachers toward the disabled reader, teaching reading, and inservice workshops. ERIC ED 200 918.

Describes positive attitudes among secondary school teachers toward the teaching of reading and participation in inservice education programs focused on reading instruction.

270. Schlageter, J. Noel. Student cognition, attitudes, and action orientation and teacher attitudes toward environmental education concepts at the seventh grade level. Ed.D. dissertation. University of Rochester. 1980.

Describes positive teachers' and students' attitudes toward environmental management concepts and the study of environmental issues.

271. Schonborn, Barbara Gail. An investigation of the attitudes of elementary school teachers toward sex-role behaviors of elementary school children. Ph.D.

dissertation. University of Illinois at Urbana-Champaign. 1975.

Teachers stereotype boys and girls when attributing motivation but report no differences in their responses to boys and girls.

272. Schulte, Sharon Louise. A survey of attitudes toward moral education. Ed.D. dissertation. University of Toledo. 1982.

Describes no differences in the attitudes of parents, teachers, administrators and school board members toward moral education, but differences in teacher attitudes by years of teaching experience.

273. Seeley, Kenneth R. "Competencies for teachers of gifted and talented children," Journal for the Education of the Gifted 3 (1979): 7-13.

Teachers and college faculty rated areas of teacher competence that are important in teaching gifted and talented students.

274. Selinger, Alphonse D. "Attitudes of Ontario secondary school teachers toward aspects of professional negotiations and sanctions," Canadian Journal of Education 5 No. 3 (1980): 34-54.

Reports that teachers favored collective bargaining but were less supportive of strikes unless they believed that their interests were seriously threatened; teacher characteristics were related to attitudes.

275. Shadiow, Linda. "A twist of the kaleidoscope: the voices of teachers," English Journal 73 No. 3 (1984): 38-42.

Describes attitudes of teachers toward teaching English from the late nineteenth and early twentieth centuries.

276. Sharan, Sholmo & others. "What teachers think about small-group teaching," British Journal of Teacher Education 5 No. 1 (1979): 49-62.

Describes teachers' attitudes toward small group versus recitation teaching.

277. Shirer, William Roe. The purposes of school evaluation as perceived by teachers, principals, superintendents, and school board presidents of schools holding membership in the Wisconsin North Central Association. Ph.D. dissertation. University of Wisconsin - Madison. 1979.

Describes nine factors teachers and administrators perceive to be the purpose of school evaluation and want to pursue and three factors which they might be forced to pursue.

278. Silva, Aurora Chavez. An analysis of teachers' attitudes toward state bilingual education programs of selected school districts in the Texas coastal bend area, K-6. Ed.D. dissertation. Texas A & I University. 1980.

Describes attitudes of teachers toward aspects of bilingual education programs; teachers believe that reading and mathematics instruction should be offered in the child's language, support for and training associated with bilingual programs is inadequate.

279. Silver, Paula F. & Davis, William J. Attitudes toward sex-role differentiation in secondary education. AERA presentation. 1978. ERIC ED 156 949.

A survey which found six dimensions that teachers and administrators identify in sex-role differentiation.

280. Silver, Paula F. & Davis, William J. "Educators' attitudes regarding sex equity," Planning and Changing 9 No. 4 (1978): 236-243.

Teachers' attitudes toward sex roles and affirmative action.

281. Silvernail, David L. "Survey results: how do administrators, teachers rank educational goals?" NASSP Bulletin 64 (1980): 101-108.

Describes similarities in teachers' and administrators' goals for students among Maine teachers and administrators; goals include development of skills and attitudes as well as knowledge.

282. Simms, Richard Leslie. "Attitudes of Oklahoma teachers toward House Bill 1706," Journal of Teacher Education 34 No. 2 (1983): 26-28.

Describes teachers' attitudes toward proposed changes in teacher education requirements and toward minimum competency testing.

283. Simpson, Ronald D. & Brown, Dean R. "Attitudes toward selected concepts among junior high science teachers," School Science and Mathematics 70 No. 3 (1970): 207-213.

Describes attitudes of junior high teachers toward science and the teaching of science.

284. Singer, James Donald. The role of the principal as perceived by UniServe representatives and teachers. Ph.D. dissertation. Kansas State University. 1978.

Describes attitudes teachers have toward the principal's role.

285. Sklarz, David P. "The apple orchard is bearing fruit in our school," _Clearing House_ _57_ _No. 6_ (1984): 284-85.

Describes the uses of computers in classrooms and teachers' and students' attitudes toward the use of computers in school.

286. Sloan, Charles A. & Triplett, DeWayne. Parents' and teachers' perceptions of handwriting. 1977. _ERIC ED_ 155 723.

Parents and teachers have similar preceptions of handwriting and instructional needs.

287. Smith, Allen G. "Causal ascriptions in the classroom: the varieties and uses of causal explanations for behaviors within the classroom," _Council on Anthropology and Education Quarterly_ _6_ _No. 2_ (1975): 13-16.

Describes the ways Montessori teachers attribute causation to teacher and student behavior.

288. Smith, Arthur E. "Attitudes of British and American teachers toward reading instruction," _Reading World_ _18_ _No. 1_ (1978): 13-21.

Describes attitudes of British and American teachers toward methods of reading instruction.

289. Smith, Bernice Dunbar. Fostering affective development in young children: an inquiry into the perceptions of parents and teachers. Ph.D. dissertation. Ohio State University. 1979.

Describes the objectives of parents, preschool and primary teachers for affective development and finds agreement among them.

290. Smith, Peggy B., Flaherty, Carol, Webb, Linda J. & Mumford, David M. "The long-term effects of human sexuality training programs for public school teachers," _Journal of School Health_ _54_ _No. 4_ (1984): 157-159.

Describes teachers' attitudes toward human sexuality and limited long-term changes in attitudes resulting from participation in an inservice program.

291. Smithman, Harold H. & Lucio, William H. "Supervision by objectives: pupil achievement as a measure of teacher performance," Educational Leadership 31 (1974): 338-344.

Finds no differences in teachers' and students' attitudes in groups where the supervision was based on objectives agreed upon by the teacher and supervisor but greater student achievement in math among students where the objectives were selected by the supervised teachers.

292. Snow, Albert J. "A teacher's view of Project Advance Chemistry," Journal of Chemical Education 61 No. 4 (1984): 379.

Describes positive attitudes of teachers toward a specific high school chemistry course.

293. Snyder, Fred A. "Teachers' perception of para-professionals," Contemporary Education 39 (1968): 145-147.

Describes attitudes of teachers toward para-professionals (65 percent rated them very helpful) and lists duties performed by para-professionals.

294. Sorenson, Garth & Gross, Cecily F. Teacher appraisal, a matching process. University of California, Los Angeles. 1967. ERIC ED 016 299.

Presents a three dimensional model of factors to include in an evaluation of teachers and the responses of professionals to those factors; kinds of objectives endorsed by teacher, kinds of instructional methods used and kinds of relations with pupils.

295. Speigel, Dixie Lee & Wright, Jill D. "Biology teachers' use of readability concepts when selecting texts for students," Journal of Reading 27 (1983): 28-34.

Describes teachers' attitudes toward characteristics of textbooks, e.g., readability level, subject matter content.

296. Spellman, Judith B. & others. Adapting to changing racial and ethnic composition: a survey of San Francisco teachers and principals. Research

Memorandum No. 5. Stanford Research Institute. Palo Alto, California. 1967. ERIC ED 164 738.

Describes characteristics of teachers and their attitudes toward the racial composition of schools and changes in the composition.

297. Spiegel, Dixie Lee & Wright, Jill D. "Biology teachers' preferences in textbook characteristics," Journal of Reading 27 No. 7 (1984): 624-628.

Describes perceptions of textbooks as instructional tools among high school biology teachers.

298. Spivey, James R. "Dogmatism and the secondary social studies teacher's perspective," Illinois School Research 11 No. 2 (1975): 26-31.

Presents secondary social science teachers' views of teachers' roles.

299. Sponseller, Doris Bergen & Fink, Joel S. "Early childhood education: a national profile of early childhood educators' views," Education and Urban Society 12 (1980): 163-173.

Reports that early childhood education teachers are generally supportive of the value and goals of early childhood education but that differences in attitude are associated with instructional setting, public or private.

300. Stainback, William C. & others. "Teachers' attitudes toward integration of severly handicapped students into regular schools," Teacher Educator 19 No. 3 (1984): 21-27.

Describes the attitudes of teachers as neutral or mildly accepting toward mainstreaming of handicapped students.

301. Stallard, Sandra Faye. Perceptions of selected teachers regarding knowledge and skill competencies needed for teaching black students. Ph.D. dissertation. University of Virginia. 1979.

Describes the several skills and knowledge that successful teachers of black students believe are necessary, e.g., knowledge of culture, history, language, learning problems and learning strengths of black students.

302. Stansfield, Charles. Teachers' attitudes toward publishers' tests. 1974. ERIC ED 117 991.

Describes foreign language teachers' attitudes toward publishers' tests.

303. Stapleton, James C. Teacher brinkmanship and job satisfaction. AERA presentation. 1979. ERIC ED 171 655.

Describes teachers' attitudes toward their jobs as related to acts of brinkmanship.

304. Stapleton, James C., Thompson, Bruce, Frankiewicz, Ronald G. & others. "Teachers' perceptions of teacher behavior," Education 100 (1980): 286-291.

Presents at least five attitude dimensions which can be used to describe the attitudes of teachers toward the brinkmanship behavior of other teachers (challenging authority while avoiding negative sanctions from authority).

305. Stapleton, James C. & others. "The relationship between teacher brinkmanship and teacher job satisfaction," Planning and Change 10 No. 3 (1979): 157-168.

Teachers' job satisfaction is related to teachers' acts of brinkmanship in working with the principal.

306. Stebbins, Robert A. "The meaning of disorderly behavior: teacher definitions of a classroom situation," Sociology of Education 44 No. 2 (1971): 217-236.

Describes teachers' definitions of disorderly student behavior.

307. Steere, Margarett L. An analysis of teacher interpersonal relationships, attitudes, and instructional behavior as perceived by pupils, parents, teachers, consultants, and administrators within a large metropolitan school district. Ed.D. dissertation. Memphis State University. 1978.

Describes teachers' and others' attitudes toward teachers' behaviors in interacting with others in the school setting.

308. Stern Mark Ezra. Teacher sense of power relative to curriculum in a suburban school district: a case study. Ph.D. dissertation. Michigan State University. 1978.

Describes teachers' perceptions that curriculum control rests with administration - the principal and superintendant.

309. Stetz, Frank P. & Beck, Michael D. Comments from the classroom: teachers' and students' opinions of achievement tests. 1979. ERIC ED 171 779.

Presents a generally positive attitude among students and teachers toward standardized achievement tests.

310. Stevens, Dorothy Jo. "Educators' perceptions of computers in education: 1979 and 1981," AEDS Journal 16 (1982): 1-15.

Reports more positive attitudes among teachers toward the use of computers for educational purposes in 1981 than in 1979 but a continuing feeling of inadequacy to teach computer literacy.

311. Stevens, Dorothy Jo. "How educators perceive computers in the classroom," AEDS Journal 13 (1980): 221-232.

Teachers favored courses to teach computer literacy in secondary school but did not feel qualified to teach such courses.

312. Stevens, Gwendolyn & Gardner, Sheldon. "A study of attitudes toward hyperkinesis using Q methodology," Behavioral Disorders 8 No. 1 (1982): 9-18.

Describes consistency in teachers' definitions of aspects of hyperkinesis among children but differences in the conception of the causes of the problem.

313. Stevenson, Chris. A phenomenological study of user and non user perceptions of a teacher center and inservice. ERIC ED 219 342.

Describes attitudes of teachers toward voluntary and mandatory inservice education programs and reports a relationship between those attitudes and teachers' perceptions of themselves as professionals.

314. Stewart, Ida Santos. Cultural differences in the attributions and intentions of Anglos and Chicanos in an elementary school. AERA presentation. 1974. ERIC ED 088 627.

Students', teachers', and parents' attributions and intentions differ but the study reports no clear pattern of relationships.

315. Stewart, Larry Relna. Attitudes of rural Nevada administrators, school board members, and teachers

concerning selected major problems. Ed.D. dissertation. University of Nevada. 1979.

Describes attitudes of three groups toward major education issues.

316. Stiggins, Richard J. & Bridgeford, Nancy J. The use of performance assessment in the classroom. Northwest Regional Educational Laboratory. Portland, Oregon. Center for Performance Assessment. 1984. ERIC ED 242 718.

Describes teachers' attitudes toward assessment of student performance and teachers' uses of information gathered from classroom measurement of student skills.

317. Stoker, W.M. Fred. Four hundred elementary school teachers look at the elementary school principal. 1975. ERIC ED 122 414.

Presents teachers' attitudes toward elementary school principals.

318. Stoops, Charles E. & Willower, Donald J. "Teacher militancy and pupil control ideology," *Texas Journal of Education 9 No. 2* (1982) 111-15.

Reports no relationship between teachers' militancy and preferences for strict control of students.

319. Stout, Candance. "Why cooperating teachers accept students," *Journal of Teacher Education 33 No. 6* 22-24.

Describes the attitudes of secondary cooperating teachers toward student teachers and the process of training new teachers.

320. Strein, William Olin. Expert opinion regarding the key skills, concepts, and attitudes for elementary and secondary teachers to facilitate the development of student emotional well-being and a survey of teachers' self-assessments in this regard. Ed.D. dissertation. Pennsylvania State University. 1979.

Describes attitudes teachers and a panel of experts hold as identified by their responses to a list of important teacher skills, concepts and attitudes.

321. Stronck, David R. A comparison between teachers aware of the population explosion and their students. 1972. ERIC ED 064 109.

Presents differences in students' and teachers' attitudes toward the population explosion.

322. Summers, Beulad Wilkinson. An assessment of teacher attitude toward a K-12 education for parenthood program. Ph.D. dissertation. Kansas State University. 1981.

Reports that teachers believe that all students need to learn about parenting, but that attitudes vary by teachers' characteristics, e.g., sex, years of teaching experience and subject taught.

323. Sunday, Christy. A study of elementary school teacher attitudes toward a new program in language in Baltimore County, Maryland. Ed.D. dissertation. George Washington University. 1978.

Describes elementary teachers' attitudes toward a new language program.

324. Tabatabaeian, Maryam. Construction and application of a test measuring teachers' attitudes towards creativity. Ph.D. dissertation. University of Oregon. 1981.

Describes development of an instrument to measure attitudes of teachers toward creativity, and responses of participants in teacher training programs.

325. Tait, Pearl E. & Wolfgang, Charles. "Mainstreaming a blind child - problems perceived in preschool day care programs," Early Child Development and Care 13 No. 2 (1984): 155-67.

Describes attitudes of teachers toward mainstreaming and problems encountered in actually mainstreaming a blind student.

326. Taylor, Jesse Leon. Teacher perception of educational television: its availability, use and value in San Diego County Schools, California. 1977-1978. Ed.D. dissertation. Brigham Young University. 1979.

Describes teachers' attitudes toward educational television and its uses in the classroom.

327. Taylor, Nancy E., Pichert, Sarah & Chase, Martha. "Views on language and reading: a comparison of the opinions of university faculty, teachers and parents," Educational Research Quarterly 5 No. 3 (1980): 74-84.

Describes differences in views of reading and language instruction between three groups with general agreement on importance of language for success in school.

328. Teague, P. Terrett, Jr. Selected attitudes and perceptions of beginning teachers as related to their teaching situations. AERA presentation. 1972. ERIC ED 065 461.

Beginning teachers' perceptions of their teaching situation, preparation and educational attitudes and feelings of acceptance by the community.

329. Thein, Marguerite Nyun. Motivation strategies: the perception of administrators and teachers as to the effectiveness of selected instructional strategies for motivation of students to read. Ed.D. dissertation. Brigham Young University. 1980.

Found no differences between teachers and principals in their perceptions of three strategies to motivate students.

330. Thomas, A. Ross & McTaggart, Elizabeth A. "Organizational climate in Catholic schools: the development of a concept," Australian Journal of Education 27 (1983): 78-93.

Describes attitudes of teachers in Catholic schools who had previously taught in public schools; teachers rated Catholic schools higher in seven of eight components, e.g., staff relations, parent interaction.

331. Tiou, Josiah & Bennett, Clifford. "Teacher perceptions of discipline problems in a central Virginia middle school," Journal of Social Studies Research 7 No. 2 (1983): 37-59.

Describes teachers' perceptions of the multiple and complex causes of student discipline problems, including lack of parent supervision.

332. Torbe, Mike. "Where have we come from? where do we go?" English Quarterly 13 (1980): 26-34.

Describes teachers' perceptions, and changes in perceptions, of student learning and the factors associated with student learning.

333. Trueblood, Cecil R. Measuring attitudes toward inservice education. ERIC ED 211 545.

Describes teachers' attitudes toward inservice education and the development of the data collection instrument.

334. Tucker, Jan L. "Teacher attitudes toward global education: a report from Dade County," Educational Research Quarterly 8 (1983): 65-77.

Describes teachers' attitudes toward global education and the inadequacies of available instructional materials.

335. Tudor, Kay Pasley. "An exploratory study of teacher attitude and behavior toward parent education involvement," Educational Research Quarterly 2 No. 3 (1977): 22-28.

Describes differences in teachers' attitudes toward parent involvement.

336. Vanecko, James J. Teachers' reactions to the first year of the Alum Rock voucher demonstration. AERA presentation. 1974. ERIC ED 105 586.

Describes teachers' attitudes toward and value conflicts with vouchers as a means of assigning pupils to schools and allowing parental involvement in school assignments.

337. Villeme, Melvin G. & Hall, Bruce W. "Higher ability education graduates: do they enter and stay in teaching?" Teacher Educator 19 No. 3 (1984): 11-15.

Describes teachers' attitudes as positive toward teaching as a career and their own teaching assignment.

338. Wah, William. A study of teacher perceptions of selected middle school programs in Michigan. Ph.D. dissertation. Michigan State University. 1980.

Describes teachers' attitudes toward teaching in a middle school and teachers' characteristics, e.g., years of experience.

339. Walker, Hill M. & Rankin, Richard. "Assessing the behavioral expectations and demands of less restrictive settings," School Psychology Review 12 (1983): 274-84.

Describes attitudes of teachers toward mainstreaming and behaviors of handicapped students in the classroom and describes the data collection method used to collect the attitude information.

340. Walker, Laurie. "English teachers' beliefs about teaching writing," English Quarterly 15 No. 4 (1982): 56-62.

Describes teachers' perceptions of writing and writing instruction as congruent with recent research findings.

341. Wallace, Michael Vincent. A survey of the attitudes of public high school teachers regarding moral education in public high schools. Ed.D. dissertation. Temple University. 1980.

Describes teachers as supporting integration of moral education throughout the high school curriculum.

342. Wang, Ray-John. Elementary and secondary teachers' understanding and attitudes toward career education. Ph.D. dissertation. Pennsylvania State University. 1982.

Reports relationships between teachers' attitudes toward career education and knowledge of career education, subject matter taught and sex.

343. Ward, James G. "The news of testing: the good, the bad, and the useful," American Educator 4 No. 3 (1980): 24-27.

Describes teachers' desires for test information to diagnose pupils' learning needs and problems, rather than to assess program effectiveness.

344. Ward, James Gordon. "An overview of the AFT's 'Teaching and Testing,'" New Directions for Testing and Measurement 16 (1982): 47-52.

Reports that teachers, while critical of tests, use test information for instructional purposes but see tests as only one source of information.

345. Ward, James G. Teachers and testing: a survey of knowledge and attitudes. 1980. ERIC ED 193 258.

Reports that teachers use test information for diagnosis of student learning needs, for planning instructional activities and for grouping students for instruction; they perceive many problems with the current minimum competency testing programs.

346. Warren, Richard L. "Context and isolation; the teaching experience in elementary school," Human Organization 34 No. 2 (1975): 139-148.

Describes origins of teachers' responses to aspects of the teaching profession, including working in isolation from other teachers in self-contained classrooms.

347. Washington, Valora. "Teachers in integrated classrooms: profiles of attitudes, perceptions, and behavior," Elementary School Journal 80 (1980): 192-201.

Describes the attitudes and behaviors of black and white teachers in integrated classrooms, focusing on attitudes toward students and their instructional setting.

348. Watkins, Marley W. & Brown, Robert D. "Competency and interpersonal ratings of teacher specialists: what teachers think of each other," Psychology in the Schools 17 No. 1 (1980): 102-105.

Describes teachers' ratings of the interpersonal skills of teachers by teaching assignment, with teachers of mentally retarded students rated higher than elementary and secondary teachers.

349. Weber, Margaret B. & others. Attitudes of public school teachers towards mainstreaming the mentally retarded. Preliminary draft. 1977. ERIC ED 150 817.

Describes attitudes of teachers toward mainstreaming; teachers have limited knowledge about EMR and TMR students and limited belief that such students would benefit from mainstreaming.

350. Weber, Wilford A. Teaching Perceptions regarding the importance of specified teaching competencies. ERIC ED 228 219.

Describes teachers' attitudes toward specific teaching opportunities; inservice and preservice teachers had similar views of the importance of specific competencies.

351. Wehling, L.F. & Charters, W.W., Jr. "Dimensions of teacher beliefs about the teaching process," American Educational Research Journal 6 (1969): 7-30.

Presents eight dimensions of teachers' beliefs; subject matter emphasis, personal adjustment ideology, student autonomy/teacher direction, emotional disengagement, student viewpoint, classroom order, student challenge, and integrative learning.

352. Wexler, Lillian K. Teacher excellence in Oregon 1955-1976: a study of selected excellent teachers. Ph.D. dissertation. University of Oregon. 1977.

Describes characteristics, attitudes and beliefs, and role behaviors of teachers nominated for "teacher of the year."

353. White, Arthur L. & others. A study of the research priorities as perceived by elementary and secondary school science personnel. 1980. ERIC ED 186 264.

Describes the areas of science education in which elementary and secondary teachers believe that more research is needed to improve science instruction.

354. White, John H. A field study on a bonus program to reduce teacher absenteeism. ERIC ED 229 869.

Describes attitudes of teachers in favor of a program to reward teachers with few absences; teachers believe that students would benefit from such a program.

355. Whitehead, Jesse, Jr. Assessment of teacher attitudes toward behavior modification: implications for behavioral consultation in the secondary school. Ph.D. dissertation. Rutgers University. 1983.

Describes teachers' attitudes toward use of behavior modification as associated with teaching level and teacher characteristics, e.g., years of teaching experience.

356. Whittaker, Muriel. "An investigation into teacher attitudes to objectives for primary science education," School Science Review 58 No. 203 (1976): 360-366.

Contrasts two groups of teachers, one that prefers student active exploration objectives and the other that prefers objectives focusing on orderly critical processing of information.

357. Whorton, James E. & others. "Single concept fliers: an alternative to in-service training," Reading Improvement 20 No. 4 (1983): 316-18.

Describes attitudes of teachers toward mainstreaming and approaches to training teachers to work with handicapped students.

358. Wiles, David K. "Racial attitudes of inner-city teachers," Urban Education 6 No. 2-3 (1971): 273-278.

Describes attitudes of teachers toward integration and toward different compositions of student groups within schools.

359. Wilkinson, W.J. "Science teachers' opinions of the pupil and measurement of pupil role," Educational Review 25 No. 1 (1972): 46-53.

Describes teachers' views of the ideal science student and of factors related to science learning.

360. Williams, Robert J. & Algozzine, Bob. "Teachers' attitudes toward mainstreaming," Elementary School Journal 80 No. 2 (1979): 63-67.

Describes attitudes of regular classroom teachers toward special education and mainstreaming, such as teachers' needs for training and assistance.

361. Wilson, James W. & Begle, Edward G. (eds.) Correlates of mathematics achievement: teacher background and opinion variables. N.L.S.M.A. Reports. No. 23. parts A, B, & C. 1972. ERIC ED 084 125.

Describes mathematics teachers' attitudes and backgrounds and relates background variables to teachers' attitudes toward mathematics and student learning.

362. Wright, E. & others. Survey of secondary school teachers' perceptions of school and education. North York Board of Education. Willowdale, Ontario. 1972. ERIC ED 084 290.

Presents results of a survery of teachers' attitudes toward schools and education.

363. Wyatt, Flora. "Responsibility for gifted learners--a plea for the encouragement of classroom teacher support," Gifted Child Quarterly 26 No. 3 (1982): 140-43.

Describes attitudes of teachers of gifted students toward characteristics of effective teachers of and programs for gifted students.

364. Yinger, Robert J. & Clark, Christopher M. Understanding teachers' judgments about instruction: the task, the method, and the meaning. ERIC ED 228 194.

Reports teachers' perceptions of the effectiveness of various language arts activities and the criteria teachers used in evaluating the activities.

365. Yuen, Chi-Yuen. An analysis of vocational teachers' understandings of and attitudes toward using microcomputers in vocational education. Final Report. Vocational-Technical Education Research Report. V. 22 No. 1.

Describes the attitudes of vocational education teachers as supportive of the use of microcomputers for instruction; teachers had limited knowledge of how they might be used.

366. Zahorik, John A. "Teacher experiential knowledge about teacher verbal behavior," Journal of Teacher Education 31 (1980): 44-49.

Describes teaching behaviors reported by teachers to be important or inappropriate and the reasons teachers give for their recommendations of important behaviors.

367. Zahorik, John A. "Teaching practices and beliefs in elementary specialty schools," Elementary School Journal 80 (1980): 144-157.

Describes the attitudes toward education of teachers in selected schools that focus on the type of instructional method used by the teacher.

368. Zeigler, H. The political world of the high school teacher. University of Oregon, Eugene. 1966. ERIC ED 014 789.

Describes conservative political attitudes and limited political participation of high school teachers in Oregon.

369. Zimmerman, Isa Kaftal. Bright meadows: a study of teachers' attitudes and feelings in an unorthodox school. final report. Newton Public Schools. West Newton, Massachusetts. 1971. ERIC ED 064 256.

Presents results of interviews with teachers about students in an alternative school.

II. VARIATIONS IN TEACHERS' ATTITUDES

370. Abbott, David W. Attitudes of selected groups of parents and educators toward Public Law 94-142. Ed.D. dissertation. Brigham Young University. 1981.

Reports similar attitudes among teachers and parents toward important aspects of mainstreaming and educational services to handicapped students.

371. Adams, Michael & others. Educational perspectives: a survey of 10,000 Ontario students, teachers and parents. Ontario Institute for Studies in Education. Toronto, Canada. 1976. ERIC ED 141 401.

Describes attitudes of teachers, students and parents toward the education system.

372. Adams, Ronald D. & others. A developmental study of teacher concerns across time. 1980. ERIC ED 189 181.

Describes differences and similarities in the concerns of student teachers, beginning teachers and experienced teachers toward aspects of teaching and their working environment; all teachers were concerned about academic impact on students.

373. Aftreth, John Jordan. Differences among elementary school teachers, administrators, and parents in the comparison of teacher competencies. Ed.D. dissertation. Northern Arizona University. 1978.

Describes attitudes of parents, teachers and administrators toward teacher competencies.

374. Allen, D.I., Hamelin, R. & Nixon, G. "Need for structure, program openness and job satisfaction among teachers in open area and self-contained classrooms," Alberta Journal of Educationl Research 22 No. 2 (1976): 149-153.

Teacher self-reports about their open programs conducted in open and self-contained areas indicate greater job satisfaction among teachers in self-contained areas and in open programs; results are related to the particular teachers' low need for structure.

375. Allen, Harvey A. & Splittgerber, Fred. Teachers' and principals' attitudes about the characteristics and functions of middle schools. 1980. ERIC ED 206 086.

Describes teachers' and principals' attitudes toward education, their school and the role of the principal as an instructional leader within the middle school setting.

376. Aloia, Gregory F. & Aloia, Stephen D. "Variations in expectations of the mainstreamed handicapped child by regular and special education teachers," Journal for Special Educators 19 No. 1 (1982): 13-19.

Reports that teachers had lower expectations for mainstreamed students than did special education resource teachers.

377. Anastasi, Anne & Geisinger, Kurt F. Use of tests with school children. 1980. ERIC ED 194 635.

Describes attitudes of parents and teachers toward the use of standardized achievement and ability tests in the schools; teachers' characteristics and knowledge of tests and testing concepts are also reported.

378. Anderson, Roedean S. An analysis of opinions from black scientists and the responses of elementary school teachers concerning science education for inner-city youth. Ph.D. dissertation. Walden University. 1979.

Describes beliefs black teachers and black scientists have toward teaching science in inner city schools and the role of the teacher.

379. Anonymous. "Doing a better job," USA Today 110 No. 2443 (1982): 10.

Describes attitudes of parents, students and teachers toward integrated and segregated schools.

380. Apostle, Alexander Paul. Citizen involvement in teacher negotiations. Ph.D. dissertation. University of Idaho. 1979.

Reports a belief among educators that schools boards represent citizens and therefore citizens should have a very limited role in negotiations, with stronger belief by citizen leaders that they should participate in such negotiations.

381. Arnold, Kenneth Harold. Attitudes towards public school teachers strikes. Ed.D. dissertation. University of the Pacific. 1981.

Describes support for teacher strikes among teachers but not among other groups, e.g., administrators and parents; strikes were viewed as disruptive to the school system and to the public image of teachers.

382. Ashton, Patricia & others. Middle school organization, teacher job satisfaction and school climate. ERIC ED 215 426.

Compares attitudes toward their school and job of teachers in junior high schools and middle schools; middle school teachers were more satisfied with their jobs.

383. Atkinson, Trudie L. "Race as a factor in teachers' responses to children's grief," Omega: Journal of Death and Dying 13 No. 3 (1982): 243-50.

Describes no differences in beliefs about life after death but differences in responses to students' grief among black and non-black teachers.

384. Ayabe, Carol & Peterson, Sarah. A descriptive study of the Mesa public schools learning disability - extended program. ERIC ED 233 032.

Describes a program for learning disabled students and the attitudes of students, parents, teachers and principals toward the program and toward learning disabled students.

385. Ayers, Jerry B. & Quallis, Glenda S. "Authoritarianism and teachers' classroom behavior," Reading Improvement 19 No. 3 (1982): 219-22.

Describes current teachers as having more authoritarian attitudes than did teachers twenty-five years ago.

386. Bacharach, Samuel B. & Mitchell, Stephen M. Labor relations in school systems: attitudes toward teachers unions across school district hierarchies. ERIC ED 243 180.

Describes the attitudes of teachers, administrators and school board members toward teachers' unions and their effects on the operation of the schools.

387. Bandy, Helen. The identification of skills and characteristics needed by country school teachers. 1980. ERIC ED 234 042.

Describes consistencies and differences in the attitudes of teachers and administrators toward the values and disadvantages of rural schools for students, teachers and the community.

388. Barner, Ann E. "Do teachers like to teach?" Pointer 27 No. 1 (1982): 5-7.

Describes regular and special education teachers' attitudes toward teaching as generally positive, with concerns for burnout and maintenance of discipline.

389. Barr-Johnson, Virginia & Hiett, Sharon Lee. A comparison of the concerns related to student discipline held by teachers who have studied classroom management techniques with the concerns of other classroom teachers. 1980. ERIC ED 222 461.

Describes teachers' perceptions of the causes of student classroom behavior problems (attributed to parent and family attitudes) and greater teacher concern for student motivation than student drug and sex problems.

390. Beck, Michael D. Student and teacher attitudes toward standardized tests: a summary of two surveys. 1980. ERIC ED 193 292.

Describes the attitudes of students and teachers toward standardized testing; both groups view it as one component of an effective system for evaluating student learning.

391. Beck, Michael D. & Stetz, Frank P. Standardized testing as viewed by test specialists and users. 1980. ERIC ED 191 876.

Describes teachers' attitudes toward and knowledge of concepts related to standardized tests as more favorable than predicted by a group of test specialists; students' attitudes are likewise more positive than predicted.

392. Belmont Elementary School District. Homework surveys for teachers, parents and students. ERIC ED 233 464.

Describes attitudes of teachers, parents and student toward homework, the amount of homework and whether teachers correct homework.

393. Blacher, Jan & Turnbull, Ann P. "Teacher and parent perspectives on selected social aspects of preschool mainstreaming," Exceptional Child 29 No. 3 (1982): 191-99.

Describes differences in parents' and teachers' views on the value of mainstreaming by personal characteristics, e.g., years of teaching experience and experience with mainstreamed students.

394. Blai, Boris, Jr. Faculty perceptions of "effective" teachers: a parallel-perceptions inquiry. ERIC ED 219 029.

Describes teachers', administrators, and college faculties' perception of factors associate with teacher effectiveness.

395. Blust, Ross S. & Kohr, Richard L. A survey of teacher perceptions on school conditions and school related conditions. ERIC ED 213 757.

Describes attitudes of various groups of Pennsylvania teachers toward instructional activities, classroom management, school management, and parent-teacher relations.

396. Borg, Walter R. Perceptions of the teacher's role in the small rural school. 1965. ERIC ED 010 968.

Reports the results of a survey of teachers, principals and teacher educators of the role of teachers in a rural school.

397. Borg, Walter R. Study of human interaction variables in successful and unsuccessful teacher teams. ERIC ED 010 001.

Surveys teachers and principals on their attitude toward team teaching; presents a description of teams and how they operate.

398. Bowen, Charles & Dalton, Tom. Divergent perceptions of school psychological services. ERIC ED 205 848.

Reports discrepencies in the perceptions of teachers and school psychologists about the role and responsibilities of school psychologists.

399. Brande, Richard Thomas. Supervisory behaviors which contribute to the improvement of instruction: an

analysis of teacher and supervisor perceptions. Ed.D. dissertation. Hofstra University. 1980.

Teachers and principals agree that some teacher behaviors are more effective, with behaviors related to content seen as making a greater contribution to teacher effectiveness than process variables.

400. Branscum, James D. & others. "Competencies of rural Oklahoma school principals," High School Journal 66 No. 2 (1983): 141-48.

Reports attitudes of teachers, administrators and school board members toward the responsibilities of principals.

401. Brophy, John Richard. An assessment of the attitudes and knowledge of teachers, counselors and administrators in the Commonwealth of Massachusetts toward norm-referenced standardized testing: implications for educational decision-making. Ed.D. dissertation. Northeastern University. 1982.

Describes attitudes of teachers and administrators to norm-referenced testing, with variations by educational position and some relationship among administrators between expenditure level of the district and attitude toward testing.

402. Brown, Lewis M. Relationships between progressivism, traditionalism, dogmatism, and philosophical consistency in science, English and elementary school teachers. 1974. ERIC ED 098 056.

Reports that teachers' life philosophy is related to teaching philosophy.

403. Buletya, R. Wayne. Knowledge and attitudes expressed toward the mainstreaming process by preservice and certified elementary teachers. E.D. dissertation. Western Michigan University. 1979.

Describes a relationship between level of knowledge and attitude toward mainstreaming.

404. Burch, Barbara G. & Danley, W. Elzie. "Teachers', supervisors, and superintendents' perceptions of the priority of supervisory responsibilities," Kappa Delta Pi Record 16 No. 3 (1980): 94-96.

Reports differences in the perceptions of administrators and teachers about the appropriate roles for persons who supervise teachers and the relative time to be spent within each of the several roles associated with supervision.

405. Burleson, Barbara & others. "Elementary teachers' and mothers' attitudes toward affective education," Elementary School Guidance and Counseling 15 (1980): 147-151.

Reports that teachers were more supportive than were mothers of affective educational goals in early childhood education programs; mothers thought that teachers did not value affective education.

406. Burton, Fredrick. A study of the letter grade system and its effect on the curriculum. ERIC ED 238 143.

Describes the attitudes of teachers, administrators, parents and students toward grading and the use of letter grades.

407. Buser, Robert L. & Banks, Freddie A., Jr. "The why, what, how and by whom of evaluating principals," NASSP bulletin 68 No. 468 (1984): 1-4.

Describes attitudes of teachers and administrators toward the evaluation of principals with agreement that the purpose of evaluation is professional growth.

408. Butterfield, Dennie. Professional concern of the eighties. ERIC ED 211 524.

Reports that teachers and school board members have different perceptions of the purposes and effects of teacher tenure.

409. Byhee, Rodger. "The ideal elementary science teacher perceptions of children, pre-service and in-service elementary science teachers," School Science and Mathematics 75 (1975): 229-235.

Describes teachers' and student teachers' perceptions of important traits of elementary science teachers.

410. Byrd, David Martin. A survey of teachers', administrators', and professors' perceptions of the need for teacher inservice education. Ph.D. dissertation. Syracuse University. 1980.

Describes areas in which members of three groups see a need for teacher inservice education and the similarity of perceived that need.

411. Caire, Warren Francis. A study of attitudes and perceptions of Catholic school parents and teachers in New Orleans parochial schools as compared to selected Catholic schools in Washington, D.C. and Denver, Colorado. Ed.D. dissertation. George Peabody College for Teachers. 1979.

Describes no differences in teachers' attitudes and their perceptions of parents' attitudes among the three cities, but differences in parents' attitudes.

412. Campbell Lloyd R. & Williamson, John A. "Administrators and teachers on reform in education," Clearing House 54 (1980): 133-134.

Teachers and administrators differ in their attitude toward community and student involvement in school governance, minimum competencies, student job placement services and corporal punishment.

413. Campbell, James Reed & Swanchak, John. Why do teachers choose to implement or reject drug abuse prevention programs? ERIC ED 201 620.

Describes a limited relationship between teacher characteristics and actual implementation of drug abuse prevention programs in their classrooms; teachers perceive as more effective programs that are oriented toward values, rather than the provision of information.

414. Campbell, Patricia & Virgin, Albert. A survey of elementary school teachers' and principals' attitudes to mathematics and utilizing mini-calculators. North York Board of Education. Willowdale, Ontario, California. 1976. ERIC ED 137 121.

Describes teachers' attitudes toward calculators and their use in schools after children develop proficiency in calculation.

415. Caria, Antonio. Attitudes of students, teachers, administrators and parents regarding modern language study in the Edmonton Separate School District. Ph.D. dissertation. University of Oregon. 1981.

Reports consistent support among the groups for modern language instruction, differences in perceptions of the quality of instruction and reasons for student discontinuance of modern language instruction.

416. Carter, Marion Austin. A study of attitudes of parents, students, and professional educators toward Dublin County schools in North Carolina. Ed.D. dissertation. University of Wyoming. 1979.

Reports that educators had more positive attitudes but that all three groups had positive attitudes toward the schools; insufficient information about the schools might account for some responses to the attitude measure.

417. Cavin, Janis Ivie. Attitudes toward programs for gifted children. 1980. ERIC ED 198 672.

Describes differences in attitudes of parents, teachers and administrators toward programs for, and the need for programs for, gifted students; parents were less aware of the need for and characteristics of programs.

418. Cawelti Gordon & Reavis, Charles. "How well are we providing instructional improvement services?" Educational Leadership 38 (1980): 236-240.

Reports that teachers have more concerns than do administrators about the level of services provided by school distircts to improve instruction; concerns focus on curriculum improvement, teacher supervision, staff development, and evaluation.

419. Center for Social Organization of Schools. Study of teachers practice of parent involvement: results from surveys of teachers and parents. ERIC ED 238 558.

Describes differences in attitudes toward parent involvement and toward specific activities to involve parents between urban and suburban teachers.

420. Chapman, David W. & Hutcheson, Sigrid M. "Attrition from teaching careers: a discriminant analysis," American Educational Research Journal 19 No. 1 (1982): 93-105.

Describes differences between teachers who remain in or leave teaching toward their own skills and the criteria for success in teaching.

421. Chavez, Annette & Widmer, Connie Carroll. "Math anxiety: elementary teachers speak for themselves," Educational Leadership 39 No. 5 (1982): 387-88.

Reports no differences between male and female teachers and no dislike of math among most elementary teachers.

422. Chesley, Gary Michael. Attitudes of secondary teachers, administrators, parents, and non-parent taxpayers toward reduction in force decisions. Ed.D. dissertation. Saint Louis University. 1980.

Reports differences among the three groups in factors considered important in making decisions about which teachers to release when reduction in force is necessary.

423. Christensen, Judith C. & Burke, Peter J. "Principals and teachers assess professional development in elementary schools," Phi Delta Kappan 63 No. 6 (1982): 417.

Describes teachers' and administrators' perceptions of aspects of effective inservice education, e.g., cooperative planning.

424. Ciaglia, Anthony F. Parents' social background and pupil control attitudes of students and teachers. Ph.D. dissertation. Fordham University. 1980.

Describes consistencies among and factors relating to the pupil control ideologies of students, teachers and parents.

425. Cockfield, Reamer Lorenzo. School and community attitudes and perceptions toward secondary education in Florence County School District Three. Ed.D. dissertation. University of South Carolina. 1980.

Describes attitudes of teachers, students and commmunity members toward aspects of the educational program.

426. Cohen, Elaine Linenberg. Administrative behavior of the principal as viewed by principals, teachers, and parents. Ed.D. dissertation. University of San Francisco. 1978.

Describes attitudes of three groups toward the behavior of the principal as a school manager.

427. Colangelo, Charles Wylie & Moraghan, Robert E. A factor analytical study of the attitues of principals, teachers, and parents towards grading and reporting practicies. Ed.D. dissertation. St. John's University. 1981.

Reports general agreement within but disagreement between groups of teachers and administrators in grading and reporting practices of the schools in one county.

428. Coletta, Anthony J. "Do open and traditional teachers differ in their beliefs about learning?" Phi Delta Kappan 55 (1974): 636-637.

Teachers in open and traditional classrooms report different beliefs toward learning, role of teacher, use of tests, intuition, learning styles.

429. Collins, H.W. "A comparative study of public school teacher opinion and state laboratory teacher opinion," Illinois School Research 7 No. 2 (1971): 38-42.

Laboratory teachers have a more favorable opinion than other teachers of the satisfactions of teaching, teachers' status, school facilities and services and community pressures.

430. Cooke, Robert A. & others. "Michigan teachers vs. a national sample of workers on quality of worklife," Phi Delta Kappan 63 No. 9 (1982): 636-37.

Describes teachers as less satisfied with aspects of their employment situations than a sample of workers.

431. Cookson, Peter W., Jr. Teacher evaluation in independent schools. an empirical investigation. Independent School 39 No. 4. 1980. 47-54.

Compares attitudes of teachers and principals in private schools toward the increasing formalization of systems of teacher evaluation in private schools.

432. Cooley, Denice & others. "Gifted females: a comparison of attitudes by male and female teachers," Roeper Review 6 No. 3 (1984): 164-167.

Describes male teachers as having more traditional attitudes than do female teachers toward gifted female students.

433. Crane, Robert Lee. A study of Michigan public middle school teacher and administrator attitudes toward the use of grades as compared with selected alternative forms of pupil progress reporting. Ph.D. dissertation. Michigan State Univerisity. 1979.

Describes similarities and differences in the attitudes of teachers and principals toward grades and other systems of reporting pupil progress.

434. Crase, Dixie R. & Crase, Darrell. "Parental attitudes toward death education for young children," Death Education 6 No. 1 (1982): 61-73.

Reports that teachers were more positive than parents toward education about death for young children.

435. Crismore, Avon. Students' and teachers' perceptions and use of sixth grade social studies textbooks in Champaign middle schools. ERIC ED 232 952.

Describes the attitudes of teachers, students, parents and administrators toward social studies instructional material.

436. Darom, Efraim, & Bar-Tal, Daniel. "Causal perception of pupils' success or failure by teachers and pupils: a comparison," Journal of Educational Research 74 No. 4 (1981): 233-39.

Reports that teachers and students were similar in the assignment of the causes of student success or failure on a test.

437. Davidson, Cleo. "Parents' and teachers' responses to mainstreaming," Education Unlimited 2 No. 2 (1980): 33-35.

Describes the attitudes of a small sample of parents of handicapped children and regular classroom teachers with mainstreamed students about mainstreaming and handicapped pupils.

438. Dawson, Gaye Carol. A comparison of attitudes of Virginia high school business education teachers and social science teachers toward competency-based education. Ph.D. dissertation. University of Maryland. 1979.

Reports more favorable attitudes toward competency-based education among business education than social science teachers.

439. Deaton, Edward Veal. A comparison of attitudes toward career education among public school administrators, academic teachers, vocational teachers, and counselors in high school. Ph.D. dissertation. Georgia State University. 1982.

Describes differences in the attitudes of members of the four groups toward different aspects of career education, with vocational teachers more positive than other groups.

440. DeGracie, James & Rule, Judy. How elementary schools are perceived by parents, teachers, and students: 1977 vs. 1981. ERIC ED 221 930.

Describes the perceptions of teachers, parents and students toward the strengths and problems of specific elementary schools.

441. DeMedia, Dwayne L. & Kish, John P., Jr. A study of attitudes of teachers and principals toward middle school certification. 1980. ERIC ED 195 560.

Describes teachers and administrators teaching at the middle school level as favoring but elementary and secondary teachers and administrators as not favoring certification for middle school teaching.

442. Dempsey, Arthur D. Anglo-American and Cuban-American teachers' perception of elementary school boys and girls. ERIC ED 213 684.

Describes differences in expectations for behaviors of boys and girls among Anglo-American and Cuban-American elementary school teachers.

443. Diem, Richard A. "The nature of conflict in a high school," Texas Tech Journal of Education 7 (1980): 139-149.

Reports that teachers, parents and students have different perceptions of and attitudes toward conflict situations within high schools, with limited communication occurring.

444. Dierenfield, Richard B. Classroom disruption in English comprehensive schools. ERIC ED 235 124.

Describes differences in attitudes toward and perceptions of pupil disruptive behavior in English and American high schools.

445. District of Columbia Public Schools. Assessment of services provided by paraprofessionals. ERIC ED 240 205.

Reports that teachers and principals valued the services provided by paraprofessionals in the classroom.

446. Dorhout, Albert. "Student and teacher perceptions of preferred teacher behaviors among the academically gifted," Gifted Child Quarterly 27 No. 3 (1983): 122.

Describes attitudes of gifted students toward teachers and teachers' perceptions of students' attitudes toward teachers with differing person-social and cognitive-intellectual characteristics.

447. Dow, Ian I. & Whitehead, Ruth Y. New perspectives on curriculum implementation: a survey of teacher, principal and consultant/co-ordinator concerns. ERIC ED 220 445.

Reports teachers' and administrators' perceptions of curriculum innovations and barriers to curriculum change.

448. Doyle, Larry Michael. An investigation of the attitudes of school board presidents, superintendents and association presidents in St. Louis County, St. Charles County, Franklin County, and Jefferson County, Missouri, concerning the nature and scope of collective negotiations. Ph.D. dissertation. Saint Louis University. 1979.

Reports variations among school districts in perceptions of what subjects should be included in negotiations and what procedures should be followed in conducting negotiations.

449. Dreibelbis, Robert M. The perceptions of special education teachers in Pennsylvania toward Public Law 94-142. Ed.D. dissertation. Indiana University of Pennsylvania. 1980.

Describes attitudes of special education teachers toward P.L. 94-142, e.g., not enough time to prepare IEPs; the bill has not ended inadequate education for handicapped students.

450. Duane, Edward A., Bridgeland, William M. & Stern Mark E. "Teacher power perceptions: curriculum politics in three suburban school districts," Educational Research Quarterly 5 (1980): 59-69.

Describes teachers' perceptions of their power to influence curriculum.

451. Duchi, Steve Andrew. An exploratory study of the middle school climate as perceived by students, teachers, and administrators and the relationship of these perceptions with selected behavioral characteristics. Ph.D. dissertation. University of Pittsburgh. 1978.

Describes attitudes teachers, students and administrators have toward school climate in the middle school.

452. Dyson, Lily L. & Kubo, H. Richard. Attitudes of preschool teachers toward the integration of handicapped children. International Convention of the Council for Exceptional Children. Philadelphia. 1980. ERIC ED 187 043.

Teachers and supervisors report supportive attitudes toward integration of handicapped children into regular classrooms and a need for more training and support services for that integration.

453. Ebbeck, Marjory. Education for the future: is it a reasonable and attainable goal? 1980. ERIC ED 190 241.

Describes consistencies in the attitudes of parents and teachers toward the goals and methods of preschool education in Australia, the social, emotional and self development of the children.

454. Eberwein, Howard Jacob. An analysis of staff and parent attitudes and understanding relative to mainstreaming in the Pittsfield, Massachusetts public school system. Ed.D. dissertation. University of Massachusetts. 1981.

Reports positive attitudes among teachers and parents toward mainstreaming; teachers believed that training for mainstreaming was not adequate and that time was not available to talk with special education teachers about main-streamed students.

455. Eiland, Belva Haynes. A study of attitudes of parents, teachers, and students toward the pilot programs for gifted and talented students in selected school districts in Michigan. Ph.D. dissertation. Michigan State University. 1982.

Reports similar positive attitudes toward programs for the gifted among teachers and parents.

456. El-Bouhy, Farouk Shawky S. Secondary school teachers' perceptions of preservice teacher education: a comparative study in the U.S.A. and Egypt. Ph.D. dissertation. University of Pittsburgh. 1980.

Describes attitudes of teachers in the United States and Egypt toward their secondary teacher education programs, based on teachers' responses to a survey; also describes teacher education programs in the two countries.

457. Elliott, Peggy G. & others. Trends and attitudes in the use of educational media and materials," Educational Technology 24 No. 4 (1984): 19-24.

Describes attitudes of teachers and administrators toward instructional media and changes in those attitudes, identifying characteristics of media associated with positive responses.

458. Enell, Nancy C. The effects of regular classroom integration for special education students with visual, auditory, physical and mental impairments. ERIC ED 229 963.

Describes attitudes of acceptance among teachers and students toward mainstreaming of handicapped students.

459. Engel, Larry Eldon. Attitudes of administrators, school board members, and teachers relating to labor peace. Ed.D. dissertation. Western Michigan University. 1981.

Reports differences in attitudes toward types of labor peace but not between respondent groups, e.g., school board members and teachers.

460. Engel, Ross A. & Else, David. "The impact of collective bargaining on schools in a rural setting: a retrospective assessment," Research in Rural Education 2 No. 1 (1983): 9-14.

Describes attitudes of teachers, administrators and school board members toward collective bargaining for teachers.

461. Engstrom, Gerald A. An examination of the viability of class climate as a useful construct in secondary schools. ERIC ED 214 891.

Describes teachers' and students' attitudes toward aspects of the classroom that constitute classroom climate.

462. Etheridge, George W. & others. Discipline: beliefs of student teachers and directing teachers. ERIC ED 215 958.

Describes preferred discipline philosophies of student teachers and their supervising teachers and changes in student teachers' attitudes to be more like their supervising teachers' attitudes.

463. Evans, Joyce & Stewart, Patricia. Toy preference and safety knowledge: a pilot study of teachers of young children. 1980. ERIC ED 191 593.

Describes teachers' and students' preferences for specific toys and teachers' knowledge of the factors that make toys safe and unsafe.

464. Faas, Larry A. Stress producing factors among regular educators and various types of special educators. ERIC ED 242 728.

Describes factors associated with stress, as reported by regular classroom and special education teachers, including paperwork, discipline and behavior problems and disinterested parents.

465. Faddis, Bonnie J. & Hutchison, Barbara. Sex equity in Lincoln County schools: a report of a needs assessment. 1980. ERIC ED 212 695.

Describes attitudes of teachers, administrators, and students toward aspects of sex equity, reporting agreement on the need for additional information, teaching methods and materials, and career counseling for students.

466. Fait, Linda. Attitudes of parents and teachers concerning retention of elementary students in the state of Utah. Ed.D. dissertation. Brigham Young University. 1982.

Reports that teachers view retention as more important than parents do; teachers have inadequate information about district policies regarding retention; no relationship found between teacher attitude and personal characteristics, e.g., age.

467. Falce, William Roger, Jr. The perceived role expectations of the middle school teacher. Ed.D. dissertation. University of Pittsburgh. 1979.

Describes perceptions of experts, school board members, administrators, teachers, parents and students toward the role of middle school teachers.

468. Fawcett, Claude W. The skills of teaching. University of California, Los Angeles. 1965. ERIC ED 016 605.

Describes different patterns of valued skills as perceived by teachers and administrators; describes teacher and principal conference-setting to identify leadership skills.

469. Feldman, David. "The effects of differential labeling on professional concepts and attitudes toward the emotionally disturbed/behaviorally disordered," Behavioral Disorders 8 No. 3 (1983): 191-98.

Reports that perceptions of regular classroom and special education teachers toward the likely success of mainstreaming of handicapped students is influenced by labels applied to students.

470. Finnegan, Harry. Discipline study. Spokane School District. Washington. 1976. ERIC ED 122 450.

Teachers, parents, students, citizens, and administrators rank student discipline concerns.

471. Fisher, Darrell L. & Fraser, Barry J. "A comparison of actual and preferred classroom environments as perceived by science teachers and students," Journal of Research in Science Teaching 20 No. 1 (1983): 55-61.

Reports that science teachers perceived their classroom environment as more favorable than did their students.

472. Florida State Depart of Education. Assessing assessment: a review of parents', teachers', and administrators' attitudes toward and utilization of statewide assessment results. Florida State Department of Education. Tallahassee, Florida. 1977. ERIC ED 144 948.

Reports attitudes of the three groups toward the results of one type of assessment program.

473. Fraser, Barry J. "Differences between student and teacher perceptions of actual and preferred classroom learning environment," Educational Evaluation and Policy Analysis 4 (1982): 511-19.

Describes attitudes of teachers and students toward actual and preferred classroom environments and the development of a questionnaire.

474. Frataccia, Enrico V. & Hennington, Iris. Satisfaction of hygiene and motivation needs of teachers who resigned from teaching. ERIC ED 212 612.

Describes differences in motivation and job satisfaction between teachers who leave the profession and teachers who remain.

475. Freiberg, H. Jerome. Parent-teacher responses to importance and use of affective teacher characteristics in the classroom. AERA presentation. 1977. ERIC ED 137 291.

Compares attitudes of parents and teachers toward affective teacher characteristics in teaching.

476. Futch, Angela Sumpter. A comparison of the opinions toward education held by citizens, school board members, and teachers in a predominantly black-populated town in southern Illinois, using selected items of the annual Gallup poll of the public's attitudes toward the public schools. Ph.D. dissertation. Southern Illinois University at Carbondale. 1983.

Describes the attitudes of members of the three groups toward the public schools, based on the procedures used by the Gallup poll.

477. Gagne, Francoys. "Perceptions of programs for gifted children: agreement on principles, but disagreement over modalities," British Columbia Journal of Special Education 7 No. 2 (1983): 113-27.

Describes attitudes of teachers and parents toward gifted children and the need for and methods for special instructional programs.

478. Gans, Karen Derk. Regular and special education teachers: life values and attitudes toward integrating handicapped students in to the regular education classroom. Ph.D. dissertation. Kent State University. 1983.

Reports differences between regular classroom and special education teachers in attitudes toward major life goals, a relationship between teachers' attitudes toward specific student handicaps and willingness to work with handicapped students.

479. Gardner, George Robert, Jr. A study of the relationships between attitudes of teachers and chief school administrators' perceptions of teachers' attitudes toward collective action. Ph.D. dissertation. George Peabody College for Teachers of Vanderbilt University. 1983.

Describes the attitudes of teachers and administrators toward collective bargaining and relates those attitudes to demographic characteristics, e.g., age and years of teaching experience.

480. Gargiulo, Richard M. & Yonker, Robert J. "Assessing teachers' attitude toward the handicapped: a methodological investigation." Psychology in the Schools 20 No. 2 (1983): 229-33.

Describes attitudes of preservice and inservice teachers toward handicapped students.

481. Gehrke, Nathalie J. Reading in content areas: a comparative study of attitudes, perceptions, and practices of preservice and inservice secondary teachers. ERIC ED 205 331.

Describes the attitudes toward reading instruction of secondary content teachers and teacher education students; more positive attitudes were associated with more learning about reading instruction.

482. Goodspeed, Madonna Theresa & Celotta, Beverly Kay. "Professors' and teachers' views of competencies necessary for mainstreaming," Psychology in the Schools 19 No. 3 (1982): 402-07.

Reports that teachers rated a set of competencies more necessary for successful mainstreaming than did college professors.

483. Gorman, William Joseph. Student evaluation and reporting: perceptions of administrators, teachers, parents and students. Ph.D. dissertation. George Peabody College for Teachers of Vanderbilt University. 1980.

Describes differences in perceptions among the four groups about the purpose of student evaluations.

484. Goulet, John E. "Curriculum priorities of teachers and parents in kindergarten classrooms," Reading Improvement 12 No. 3 (1975): 163-167.

Describes teachers' and parents' priorities for goals of kindergarten instruction.

485. Graeber, Anna O. & others. A survey of classroom practices in mathematics: reports of first, third, fifth, and seventh grade teachers in Delaware, New Jersey, and Pennsylvania. Research for Better Schools, Inc. Philadelphia, 1977. ERIC ED 180 820.

Reports teachers' attitudes toward hand held calculators, classroom practices in areas of opportunity, motivators, structure and instructional events.

486. Graham, Donna Regina. An investigation of teachers' and administrators' decision-making behaviors and attitudes concerning the promotion and retention of elementary students. Ed.D. dissertation. Catholic University of American. 1981. ERIC ED 215 433.

Describes teachers' attitudes toward promotion policies and the amount of teacher involvement in the development of those policies.

487. Graham, Steve & others. "Educational personnel's perception of mainstreaming and resource room effectiveness," Psychology in the Schools 17 (1980): 128-134.

Reports that regular classroom and resource room teachers have different attitudes toward and different expectations for the effectiveness of mainstreaming of handicapped students.

488. Grandgenett, Myrna Marie. A trilevel assessment of inservice needs among teachers: perceptions of teachers, principals and area education agency personnel. Ph.D. dissertaton. University of Iowa. 1978.

Describes perceptions of members of the three groups about teachers' inservice education needs.

489. Grant, LaRue Tucker. A comparative study of attitudes of students, parents, educators, and business leaders toward selected concepts of career education. Ed.D. dissertation. University of Houston. 1979.

Describes attitudes of four groups toward career education and its importance within the curriculum.

490. Grant, Stephen & Carvell, Robert. "A survey of elementary school principals and teachers: teacher evaluation criteria," Education 100 (1980): 223-226.

A survey of teachers and principals found a high degree of agreement on evaluation criteria for teachers and agreement on the importance of 19 of 21 behaviors identified as important.

491. Greenwood, J. Robert. An investigation of the current perceptions and ideal expectations of junior high/middle school principals and teachers regarding the principal's role in supervision of

instruction. Ed.D. dissertation. Boston College. 1979.

Describes perceptions teachers and principals have of actual and ideal behavior of principals in the evaluation of instruction.

492. Gring, Stephen Robert. The opinions of mathematics teachers and industrial employers regarding basic mathematics skills priorities: a comparative study within Lancaster County (Pa.). Ed.D. dissertation. University of Pennsylavania. 1979.

Describes areas of agreement on whether skills (computation and geometric) are more or less basic between teachers and members of industry.

493. Grossman, Gloria Pines. Teachers' political knowledge and attitudes: a comparison of education seniors, other university seniors, and teachers in the field. Ph.D. dissertation. Arizona State University. 1981.

Describes political knowledge and attitudes of teachers and teacher education students, reporting greater interest among teachers than students in civic participation.

494. Guskey, Thomas R. Differences in teachers' perceptions at the causes of positive versus negative student achievement outcomes. <u>ERIC ED</u> 200 624.

Describes some differences by teaching grade level in teachers' beliefs about the causes of student achievement; elementary teachers more often attributed lack of success to lack of effort.

495. Haas, Toni J. A convergence of two cultures in the implementation of P.L. 94-124. <u>ERIC ED</u> 238 193.

Describes attitudes and perceptions of regular classroom and special education teachers toward teaching and students.

496. Hall, Gene, (ed.) "Research briefs," <u>Journal of Teacher Education 33 No.6</u> (1982): 45-46.

Describes attitudes of teachers, preservice teachers and students toward teaching as a profession, aspects of teaching and toward mainstreaming.

497. Handler, Janet R. Views of educators, students, and parents regarding important discipline problems,

related influences and corrective actions. ERIC ED 203 506.

Describes parents', students' and teachers' attitudes toward discipline and specific discipline problems; apathy and inattention were viewed as the leading problems.

498. Harmon, David J. Intensive communication strategy: the gifted program. 1980. ERIC ED 209 270.

Describes attitudes of teachers and administrators toward a program for gifted students and an inservice training strategy that resulted in positive changes in attitudes.

499. Harris, J. John, III. Student discipline and instructionally effective schools. ERIC ED 235 257.

Reports differences in teachers' and principals' attitudes toward discipline, the school environment and characteristics of effective schools.

500. Hart, James C., Jr. "Role performance vs. role expectations of elementary school principals," *Capstone Journal of Education* 1 No. 1 (1980): 39-44.

Reports differences in perceptions of the principal's role between principals and teachers and between teachers teaching in different organizational settings.

501. Hartnett, Marjorie S. A comparison of concerns of elementary teachers, administrators, and special educators toward the concept of mainstreaming the mildly handicapped in selected Nebraska public schools. Ed.D. dissertation. University of Nebraska-Lincoln. 1979.

Describes attitudes of the three groups of educators toward mainstreaming mildly handicapped elementary students.

502. Haynes, Richard Morrill. Knowledge and attitudes of administrators, teachers and students about student rights. Ed.D. dissertation. Duke University. 1978.

Describes attitudes of three groups toward students' rights within the school setting.

503. Hegenbart, Gary Lee. How teachers and parents perceive parental involvement in elementary school. Ed.D. dissertation. University of Illinois at Urbana-Champaign. 1980.

Describes differences in views of parents and teachers about how much parent involvement does and should occur, with teachers seeing more involvement already occurring than parents see.

504. Henfield, Paul & Steiglitz, Maria. Comparisons of parent and teacher attitudes toward mainstreaming. ERIC ED 207 281.

Describes similarities and differences in teachers' and parents' perceptions of issues related to mainstreaming of handicapped students.

505. Herman, Joan L. & Yeh, Jennie P. Some effects of parent involvement in schools. 1980. ERIC ED 206 963.

Describes the attitudes of parents, teachers and administrators toward the school and the early childhood education program involving parents; more parental involvement was associated with greater satisfaction with the school program.

506. Hiebert, Bryan & others. "Affective influences on learning disabled adolescents," Learning Disability Quarterly 5 No. 4 (1982): 334-43.

Describes teachers, parents and learning disabled students as having lower expectations for learning disabled than for regular students.

507. Holdaway, Steven Lee & Jensen, Larry C. "Self-, teachers', and mothers' perceptions of the behaviorally disordered child," Psychology in the Schools 20 (1983): 388-94.

Reports that teachers view the behaviors of behaviorally disordered children in less positive ways than do parents and the children themselves.

508. Hood, Paul D. & Hayes, Tamara C. The communication program survey, spring 1967. A survey of public elementary and high school teachers and principals in twelve San Francisco bay area counties regarding their interest in and attitude toward educational innovation, research and development. Far West Laboratory for Educational Research and Development. San Francisco. 1967. ERIC ED 087 462.

Describes public school educators' interest in and support for innovation and research.

509. Horowitz, David. Relationships between the attitudes toward student rights and the pupil control ideology of New York State public school

teachers and administrators. Ed.D. dissertation. State University of New York at Albany. 1980.

Describes teachers as less knowledgeable about student rights, less favorable toward laws concerning student rights and with less humanistic beliefs about pupil control than administrators.

510. Hoy, James Michael. A survey of secondary student and teacher attitudes in selected schools in the Commonwealth of Pennsylvania differing in architectural design. Ed.D. dissertation. Pennsylvania State University. 1980.

Describes teachers' and students' attitudes but finds no differences associated with differences in architectural design of the schools.

511. Huber, Joseph D. "Comparison of disciplinary concerns in small and large schools," Small School Forum 4 No. 2 (1983): 7-9.

Describes attitudes of parents, principals and teachers toward school discipline, including attitudes toward use of drugs, alcohol, and tobacco.

512. Hughes, Dean Mark. Perceptions of parents, teachers, and administrators regarding procedures of the individualized education program in selected South Dakota schools. Ed.D. dissertation. University of South Dakota. 1980.

Describes consistency in school personnel's perceptions of implementation of individualized education programs across types of schools but differences between their perceptions and parents' perceptions.

513. Ignatovich, Frederic, Cusick, P.A. & Ray, J.E. Value/belief patterns of teachers and those administrators engaged in attempts to influence teaching. Research Series No. 43. Institute for Research on Teaching. Michigan State University. Lansing. 1979. ERIC ED 181 007.

Describes differences between teachers', principals' and administrators' attitudes toward the nature of management of children in educational contexts - they differ by degree of closeness to children.

514. Information Science, Inc. Goals of secondary education as perceived by education consumers. Volume IV. Quantitative results. New Mexico

University. Albuquerque. Institute for Social Research and Development. 1979. ERIC ED 159 170.

Describes attitudes of parents and teachers in two commuinities toward several aspects of secondary education.

515. Jacobs, Theodore Charles. A comparison of measures of attitudes of high school teachers and administrators toward student behavioral problems. Ph.D. dissertation. Boston College. 1982.

Reports that teachers viewed as more serious those student behavior problems which disrupt the classroom.

516. Jenkins, Jerry A. Elementary school science programs: pupil and teacher attitudes. ERIC ED 062 146.

Describes teachers' and students' moderate satisfaction with and low interest in elementary science programs.

517. Jensen, Bruce Frederick. An investigation of factors related to educators' attitudes toward the educational integration of exceptional children. Ph.D. dissertation. University of Iowa. 1979.

Reports more positive attitudes toward mainstreaming among regular than special class teachers.

518. Johnson, Charles E. & others. Verifying teacher competencies for their generic qualities. AERA presentation. 1978. ERIC ED 173 264.

A report of teachers' and teacher educators' ratings on the desirability of statements of teacher competence.

519. Jones, Norman Hooper. A survey of student, parent, and staff attitudes toward and perceptions of Nashville's ESL/bilingual program: an evaluation procedure. Ed.D. dissertation. George Peabody College for Teachers of Vanderbilt University. 1981.

Describes consistencies and differences in attitudes among members of the three groups, with teachers concerned about staff recruitment.

520. Joyce, Bruce R. & others. Interviews: perceptions of professionals and policy makers. 1977. ERIC ED 142 546.

Describes attitudes teachers and educational policy makers have toward inservice teacher education.

521. Joyce, William W. & others. "Teachers', supervisors', and teacher educators' perceptions of social studies," _Social Education_ _46_ _No. 5_ (1982): 357-60.

Describes attitudes of teachers, administrators and teacher educators toward the goals of social studies instruction and the groups responsible for defining these goals.

522. Katz, Sheldon F. Curriculum innovation: teacher commitment, training, and support. Ed.D. dissertation. Columbia University Teachers College. 1980. _ERIC_ _ED_ 200 546.

Describes the presence of teacher commitment during the implementation of an innovation and teacher recognition of the need for support and training.

523. Keen, Mark Francis. A study of the relationship between philosophic positions and attitudes toward education. Ed.D. dissertation. University of Missouri-Columbia. 1981.

Describes few differences in the philosophies and attitudes toward education of teachers and parents, with parental attitudes not well defined.

524. Keene, Mary Emma. Knowledge and beliefs of reading by high school students and elementary teachers. 1980. _ERIC_ _ED_ 192 250.

Reports that secondary students have well-defined conceptions of reading instruction and that those conceptions parallel the conceptions of reading instruction held by elementary teachers.

525. Kerlinger, Fred N. "Attitudes toward education and perceptions of teacher characteristics: a Q study," _American Educational Research Journal_ _3_ _No. 3_ (1966): 159-168.

Describes the attitudes of a small sample of teachers and teacher educators and reports that attitudes toward education and perceptions of teachers are related.

526. Kerns, Thomas Elliott. An analysis of the attitudes of South Carolina school board members and educators toward alternatives for alleviating the

teacher shortage in mathematics and science. Ed.D. dissertation. University of South Carolina. 1983.

Reports agreement among board members, personnel administrators, superintendents and teachers toward some methods of alleviating the teacher shortage but disagreement about other methods.

527. Kerwood, Mary Margaret. Acceptance attitudes of parents, teachers, and school administrators toward use of parental participation booklets in selected Arizona school districts. Ed.D. dissertation. Northern Arizona University. 1983.

Describes positive attitudes toward the booklets among all groups with differences among the groups in attitudes toward some aspects of the program, e.g., degree of training needed for parents to use the booklets effectively.

528. Khan, Sar B. & Traub, Ross E. "Teachers' attitudes in open and traditional schools," Canadian Journal of Education 5 No. 3 (1980): 5-14.

Reports that teachers in open-space schools had more positive attitudes than teachers in traditional schools toward education, their teaching and pupils, and toward educational innovation.

529. Kiley, Thomas Patrick. A study of the relationships between attitude toward consolidation of schools and certain characteristics and attitudes on the part of students, parents, teachers, administrators and supervisors in the public schools of Sullivan County, New York. Ed.D. dissertation. St. John's University. 1979.

Describes attitudes of four groups toward consolidation in relation to characteristics and other attitudes.

530. Killian, Joyce E. Teachers who seek computer education: their attitudes, needs and motivation. ERIC ED 242 715.

Describes differences in attitudes and motivations of teachers who did and did not participate in computer literacy training.

531. King, Barbara Lynn. Two modes of analyzing teacher and student attitudes toward writing: the Emig attitude scale and the King construction scale. Ed.D. dissertation. Rutgers University. 1979.

Describes teachers' and students' attitudes toward writing and a program to change those attitudes.

532. Kleine, Glen Albert W. Congruence and divergence of teacher-school board member attitudes in selected Kentucky school districts 1973 and 1982. Ed.D. dissertation. East Tennessee State University. 1982.

Describes more congruence among attitudes of teachers and board members in 1982 than in 1973, the result of changes in teachers' attitudes, and variations in the degree of congruence by characteristics of the school districts.

533. Kleparchuk, Harry. Supervisory services considered desirable by teachers and principals in "open space" elementary schools. Oregon School Study Council. Eugene, Oregon. 1970. ERIC ED 081 074.

Describes the type of supervision that teachers and principals want in open space classrooms.

534. Koppel, Irene E. "The perceived contribution of foreign language to high priority educational goals," Foreign Language Annals 15 No. 6 (1982): 435-39.

Describes teachers' and administrators' perceptions of the value of foreign language instruction in relation to other subjects, e.g., science.

535. Krahm, Barbara. Attitudes and opinions of principals and teachers involved in an experimental earth science program in New York state. 1972. ERIC ED 064 108.

Describes teachers' and principals' attitudes toward a new science program.

536. Kraus, D.L. A study of present practices and attitudes concerning the letter grading system of secondary school language arts teachers and administrators of Oahu, Hawaii. Ed.D. dissertation. University of South Dakota. 1969.

Most teachers felt that the letter grade system had more weaknesses than strengths and met parent needs moı than teacher and pupil needs.

537. Kremer, Kevin Philip. Parent and teacher attitudes toward parent-teacher conferences in Bismarck elementary schools. Ed.D. dissertation. University of North Colorado. 1981.

Describes attitudes of parents and teachers as positive toward parent-teacher conferences, but teachers would like them scheduled on half-days without students.

538. Kreutter, Karole J. Student and teacher attitudes toward disciplinary practices in a junior high school setting. Ph.D. dissertation. Temple University. 1983.

Describes differences in teachers' and students' attitudes toward stealing within the school; teachers selected stronger responses than did students to incidents of stealing.

539. Lambert, Robert F. "Teacher attitudes on testing: a multiple perspective," College Board Review 118 (1980): 13-14.

Describes differences in attitudes toward testing and the uses of information from testing among teachers, administrators, teachers' union representatives.

540. Landers, Maria Anne. An analytic survey of educator's attitudes toward competency testing. Ph.D. dissertation. North Texas State University. 1982.

Describes attitudes of teachers, counselors and administrators toward minimum competency testing programs for students in operation in their districts; teachers perceive that the programs identify students needing remediation but do not lower standards.

541. Langenbrunner, Mary R. & Thornburg, Kathy R. "Attitudes of preschool directors, teachers, and parents toward parent involvement in the schools," Reading Improvement 17 (1980): 286-291.

Describes differences between the three groups in their perceptions of the actual and the preferred levels of parent involvement.

542. Leam, Stanley M. & Gough, Pauline B. "Comparing lay and professional opinion on Gallup Poll questions," Phi Delta Kappan 62 (1980): 47-48.

Describes differences and similarities in the opinions of educators and community members toward major issues in education; educators reported more problems and cost questions than did community members.

543. Lehrer, Sande. A comparative analysis of selected aspects of a local school system as perceived by teachers and the parents of their students. Ph.D. dissertation. University of Southern Mississippi. 1978.

Describes teachers' and parents' attitudes toward the schools and particular school programs.

544. Leon, Anibal & others. A cross-cultural study of teacher autonomy. _ERIC ED_ 218 768.

Describes consistencies and differences in teachers' perceptions of the extent to which they have autonomy in decision making.

545. Levin, James. "Lay vs. teacher perceptions of school discipline," _Phi Delta Kappan 61_ (1980): 360.

Describes attitudes of teachers in two schools toward teachers, student discipline, and the role of parents in student behavior control.

546. Lipka, Richard P. & Goulet, L.R. "Age and intergroup differences in attitudes toward the teaching profession: how do teachers and students view themselves and each other?" _Contemporary Educational Psychology 6 No. 1_ (1981): 12-21.

Reports no differences in teachers' attitudes toward teaching associated with teachers' age, but differences between teachers and student teachers.

547. Lock, Corey & Lichtenstein, Joseph M. "Some research implications for the development of teacher inservice programs," _Kappa Delta Pi Record 17_ (1980): 11-13.

Reports no differences between beginning and experienced teachers in the needs that they perceive they have that could be met through inservice education programs.

548. Logan, Bayne. "Teacher self-perception and curricular innovation," _Phi Delta Kappan 63 No. 10_ (1982): 705-06.

Describes differences in attitudes among inner-directed and outer-directed teachers.

549. Lott, Dorthy Lee M. A survey of the opinions of administrators and supervisors and teachers concerning appropriate goals and the implementation of Public Law 94-142. Ed.D. dissertation. University of Southern Mississippi. 1980.

Describes perceptions of members of the three groups that the schools could do a better job in meeting the goals of P.L. 94-142.

550. Lowther, Malcolm A. & others. "Perceptions of work-related conditions among teachers and persons in other occupations," Journal of Educational Research 77 No. 5 (1984): 277-282.

Describes attitudes of teachers and persons trained as teachers but not teaching toward aspects of their jobs, e.g., advancement prospects.

551. Lucas, Ann. Educational goals and values of students and teachers: an exploratory study. 1979. ERIC ED 175 801.

Study identified few differences at grade 12 between students' and teachers' selections of important educational goals.

552. Lux, Yvonne Meyer. Teacher and principal perceptions of evaluation criteria. Ed.D. dissertation. University of Southern California. 1980.

Teachers consistently rated teaching tasks related to instruction as important but there were variations in ratings for tasks related to custodial care, community linkage, housekeeping and collaboration.

553. Lynch, James & Burns, Bob. "Non-attenders at INSET functions: some comparisons with attenders," Journal of Education for Teaching 10 No. 2 (1984): 164-177.

Reports different attitudes toward types of inservice education among teachers who did and did not attend a specific inservice program.

554. Lynch, P.P. & Ndyetabura, V.L. "Practical work in schools: an examination of teachers' stated aims and the influence of practical work according to students," Journal of Research in Science Teaching 20 No. 7 (1983): 663-71.

Describes attitudes of teachers and students toward instructional goals of student assignments in science.

555. McCoy, Arthur L. Attitudes of teachers and students toward race and ethnicity in the Department of Defense Dependents School System, European Region. Ed.D. dissertation. University of Southern California. 1979.

Teachers have more positive attitudes than students toward the several ethnic groups studied.

556. McCroskey, James C. & Richmond, Virginia P. Power in the classroom I: teacher and student perceptions. ERIC ED 215 389.

Reports that teachers and students hold some common and some divergent views about the way teachers use power in the classroom.

557. McKinley, Wayne Edwin. Attitudes and perceptions of attitudes toward the disciplinary behaviors of teachers and administrators within a selected school. Ph.D. dissertation. Northwestern University. 1974.

Indicates differences in attitudes toward teacher disciplinary behavior by differenct role groups in school, with generally accurate perceptions by one group of the attitudes of the other groups.

558. McTeer, J. Hugh & others. "Comparing views of students, parents, teachers and administrators on objectives for the secondary school," Education 98 No. 3 (1978): 259-263.

Describes and compares the views of parents, teachers, students and administrators about educational goals.

559. McVeigh, Ronald Joseph. A descriptive analysis of teachers' and students' beliefs relative to seven specific dimensions of the classroom teaching-learning process. Ed.D. dissertation. University of California, Los Angeles. 1970.

Identifies differing teacher and student beliefs with respect to the teaching-learning process.

560. Mahan, James M. "Toward more effective use of professor-consultants by public school districts," Planning and Change 11 (1980): 133-140.

Reports that administrators and teachers agree in having a limited view of the role that college professors of education might play in assisting schools to improve instruction or increase teachers' skills.

561. Mahmoud, Hussein Bashir. Secondary school science curricula practices: a ten-year longitudinal study of schools in ten states. ERIC ED 206 513.

Describes teachers' attitudes toward the science curriculum and to changes in the curriculum.

562. Mallette, David Leon. The acceptance of the goal of scientific literacy by science educators, supervisors and secondary school science teachers in North Carolina. Ph.D. dissertation. North Carolina State University at Raleigh. 1980.

Describes differences in attitudes of three groups toward goals of secondary school science instruction.

563. Maloy, Robert W. & Seldin, Clement A. Dimensions of school and classroom climate: a comparison of teacher, student and parent attitudes in one Massachusetts community. ERIC ED 243 205.

Describes the attitudes of teachers, students and parents toward the goals, climate and instructional programs in the secondary schools in one district.

564. Markley, Edgar Thomas. Professional expectations for the role of the substitute teacher as identified by selected administrators, classroom teachers, experienced and inexperienced substitute teachers in the Howard County, Maryland, public school system. Ed.D. dissertation. George Washington University. 1980.

Describes expectations, limits in expectations and lack of planning for substitutes by teachers, administrators and substitutes themselves.

565. Marr, Timothy & others. "Nutrition education for grades 7-12: the perspective of Pennsylvania teachers and administrators," Journal of Nutrition Education 12 (1980): 149-152.

Describes consistent positive support for nutrition education among secondary teachers and administrators; educators perceived a need for methods to incorporate nutrition education into ongoing instruction.

566. Marsh, Colin J. "Teachers and students don't agree about what should go on in high schools," High School Journal 63 No. 2 (1979): 67-71. ERIC ED 222 846.

Describes differences in teachers' and students' attitudes toward school goals, instructional objectives, lesson content, learning activities and assessment of student performance.

567. Marsh, Jean Crawford. Attitudes of preservice and inservice teachers toward disabled children. Ed.D. dissertation. Texas Tech University. 1983.

Reports no differences in attitude toward handicapped students between preservice and inservice teachers or by teacher demographic characteristics, but more positive attitudes among teachers with prior experience with handicapped people.

568. Martin, Wilfred B.W. & others. "Observations from teachers and students on school discipline," Clearing House 54 (1980): 80-82.

Reports that teachers are frustrated by the school organizational constraints on student discipline, describes teachers' perceptions of the causes of discipline problems, describes students' reactions to homework and suspension as punishment.

569. Mascitelli, Sally Ann. A comparison of management preferences among elementary, regular and special education teachers. Ed.D. dissertation. Pennsylvania State University. 1981.

Describes attitudes of teachers toward student management; regular teachers viewed some student behaviors more unfavorably than did special education teachers.

570. Massey, Barbara P. A comparative analysis of sex-role attitudes of administrators and teachers in the public schools of Mississippi. Ed.D. dissertation. University of Southern Mississippi. 1979.

Describes attitudes of principals and teachers toward women in school administration roles.

571. Mayfield, Margie I. "Orientation to school and transitions of children between primary grades," Alberta Journal of Educational Research 29 No. 4: 272-84.

Describes the attitudes of parents, teachers and administrators toward aspects of student adjustment to grade level changes.

572. Mehaffie, Shamus. Quality of education and effects of size in small west-Texas high schools: 1973 vs. 1983 surveys. ERIC ED 230 363.

Describes teachers and adminsitrators as having positive attitudes toward small high schools and the quality of the support service for teachers.

573. Mercer, B. Jill. Factors influencing reading achievement. 1980. ERIC ED 189 580.

Reports consistency in perceptions in parents' and teachers' perceptions of the factors that influence reading achievement; television is seen to have a limited relationship to achievement.

574. Messina, Antoinette J. Expanding career choices for students by reducing mathematics anxiety. 1980. ERIC ED 199 090.

Describes a program designed to change the attitudes of teachers and students toward mathematics as a field of study; both teachers and students had more positive attitudes after participation in the workshop.

575. Michener, Laura Ann. A survey of the attitudes of administrators, teachers, and community members toward the education of gifted children and youth. Ed.D. dissertation. University of Pennsylvania. 1980.

Describes positive attitudes toward education of gifted children, with more positive attitudes associated with personal characteristics, e.g., participation in a program for gifted students.

576. Miller, Eugenia Porretta. Qualifications needed by teachers of English: ratings by English curriculum coordinators and English educators. Ph.D. dissertation. University of New Mexico. 1979.

Describes consistency of attitudes between coordinators and teachers, importance of language arts and technology in preparation of teachers, low priority given to individual students' dialect, diverse cultures and work with diverse ethnic groups.

577. Miller, P.J. "Student and teacher attitudes towards education: an exploratory study," Alberta Journal of Educational Research 20 No. 3 (1974): 251-258.

Describes teachers' and students' attitude toward education and the instrument used to measure students' and teachers' attitudes.

578. Mills, Helene Audrey. Attitudes of a suburban middle school parent and teacher population toward the meaning of a basic education. Ed.D. dissertation. Wayne State University. 1983.

Reports that teachers and parents favor greater attention to basics but that they do not favor basics to the exclusion of other aspects of the curriculum.

579. Minor, James A. Elementary versus special education teachers' perceptions in handling learning behavior and neurological problems. Ed.D. dissertation. University of South Dakota. 1976. ERIC ED 131 624.

Describes teachers' feelings of adequacy working with students with various types of handicaps; indicates more requests for help as failure is experienced.

580. Moracco, John C. Stress in teaching: a comparison of perceived stress between special education and regular teachers. ERIC ED 202 828.

Reports no differences between regular and special class teachers' perceptions of stress; personality characteristics are related to perceptions of stress.

581. Morrill, Robert W. & others. Discriminating between parent and teacher perceptions of an alternative school. 1980. ERIC ED 207 159.

Reports that parents were more satisfied than teachers with the philosophy and operation of a private school and its effects on student learning; parents saw the school as less different from public schools than did teachers.

582. Morris, John E. & Garcia, Jesus. "Social studies in rural America," Social Education 46 No. 2 (1982): 115-20.

Reports than rural teachers and students perceive that rural life is misrepresented in curricular materials.

583. Mueller, Doris L. "Teacher attitudes toward reading," Journal of Reading 17 (1973): 202-205.

Reports differences in attitudes and behavior of student teachers and experienced teachers with respect to reading behavior and differences in ratings of the importance of reading in the elementary curriculum.

584. Murray, Frank B. "Credibility of information for educational innovation," Journal of Educational Research 64 (1970): 17-20.

Describes different types of information that teachers and professors of education found valuable regarding an innovation - teachers rated standardized test information as of limited importance and professors rated that information as most important.

585. Muse, Ivan D. & Stonehocker, Loya. A study of small rural high schools of less than 200 students: perceptions of teachers and administrators. AERA presentaton. 1979. ERIC ED 168 778.

Describes characteristics and attitudes toward education of teachers in small rural schools.

586. Muse, Ivan D. & others. A study of rural teachers and the rural schools as perceived by school administrators, teachers, parents and students. 1976. ERIC ED 119 921.

Describes teachers' attitudes toward rural areas and parents and students' attitudes toward teachers.

587. Mutimer, D.D. & Rosemier, R.A. "Behavior problems of children as viewed by teachers and the children themselves," Journal of Consulting Psychology 31 No. 6 (1967): 583-587.

Describes differences in the perceptions of teachers and students in grades 7-12 on the seriousness of student problem behavior.

588. Nagy, Philip & Drost, Dale. "A comparison of scaling and correlational analysis of perceptions of mathematics objectives," Alberta Journal of Educational Research 29 No. 3 (1983): 180-95.

Describes attitudes of teachers and college faculty toward goals of mathematics education; also discusses research methods used.

589. Nerren, George Nolen, Jr. Attitudes of high school teachers perceived as effective or ineffective managers of student/teacher conflicts. Ed.D. dissertation. University of Tennessee. 1980.

Reports differences between teachers considered by building managers to be effective or ineffective; more effective teachers have greater trust in students and more positive teacher self-confidence.

590. Ngandu, Kathleen M. "Why Do Kids Read?" Reading Horizons 21 No. 1 (1981): 128-33.

Reports that teachers and students both view gaining knowledge as the most important reason for reading.

591. Norton, G.R. "Acceptability of time out from reinforcement procedures for disruptive child behavior: a further analysis," Child and Family Behavior Therapy 5 No. 2 (1983): 31-42.

Describes teachers as rating more positively than did parents several methods for responding to student disruptive behavior.

592. Ntukidem, Peter James. A comparative analysis of elementary school teachers' attitudes toward visual art education: Nigeria -- United States of American. Ph.D. dissertation. George Peabody College for Teachers of Vanderbilt University. 1982.

Describes attitudes of teachers in the United States and Nigeria toward visual arts education and describes factors related to negative attitudes.

593. Oaster, T.R.F. Are differences guaranteed in "teachers versus the public"? ERIC ED 225 978.

Reports that teachers have more positive attitudes toward schools and educational programs than do parents.

594. Oaster, Thomas R.F. Reservation and off-reservation parent, teacher and student perceptions of student rights. ERIC ED 220 740.

Describes differences and similarities in attitudes of parents, teachers and students toward discipline and students' rights for Indian students.

595. Oglesby, Shirley Ann. A comparison and analysis of attitudes of parents and teachers of kindergarten children on selected issues related to kindergarten education. Ed.D. dissertation. Jackson State University. 1983.

Reports differences in attitudes between parents and teachers about some aspects of kindergarten programs: both groups agreed on the importance of emotional growth and psychological development as program goals and that teachers failed to foster creativity.

596. Olson, Arthur H. Attitude of high school content area teachers toward the teaching of reading. 1967. ERIC ED 015 851.

Describes principals' and teachers' responses to a checklist of the extent of teachers' reading skills and ability to adapt materials; teachers reported positive results (male less than female) with principals not always so positive.

597. O'Neal, E.C. Relationships of zones of indifference to directives and levels of authoritarianism of coaches and teachers in selected schools in Mississippi. ERIC ED 239 399.

Describes relationships between teachers' and coaches' attitudes toward authority and conformity with principals' directives.

598. Ornstein, Allan C. Selected teacher behaviors rated as desirable by ninth-grade disadvantaged students and ninth-grade teachers of the disadvantaged. Ed.D. dissertation. New York University. 1971.

Describes the differences between students' and teachers' ratings of desirable teacher behaviors.

599. Ortega, Joel Christian. A study of attitudes of general and special education teachers affected by a least restrictive alternative educational program. Ph.D. dissertation. Kent State University. 1981.

Describes differences in the attitudes of teachers toward mainstreaming associated with differences in personal characteristics, e.g., experience with mainstreamed students.

600. Ortiz, Flora Ida. Work-orientations and incentive systems and their effect in the delivery of education in a multi-cultural institution. ERIC ED 233 436.

Describes differences in work orientations and attitudes toward aspects of the work situation between teachers and principals.

601. Otunga, Moses Daniel. The relationship between teachers' attitudes toward participation in decisions about school issues and the perceptions of principals, superintendents, and board members concerning these attitudes. Ed.D. dissertation. Northern Illinois University. 1980.

Describes teachers as perceiving limited involvement in school decision making while principals perceived that they had more extensive involvement.

602. Overman, Bette C. Variety and intensity of school-related problems as perceived by teachers, parents and students. 1980. ERIC ED 214 887.

Describes differences and similarities in perceptions of the behaviors that constitute behavior problems in the classroom among teachers, parents and students.

603. Owen, James Ernest, Jr. An analysis of the perceptions held by public elementary school teachers and administrators of selected goals for kindergarten programs in Alabama. Ed.D. dissertation. Auburn University. 1978.

Describes attitudes teachers and administrators have toward kindergarten goals - no differences found.

604. Page, Fred M., Jr. & Page, Jane A. "Perceptions of teaching that may be influencing current shortage of teachers," College Student Journal 16 No. 4 (1982): 308-11.

Describes the attitudes of inservice and preservice teachers toward teaching as a career.

605. Page, Jane A. The teaching profession as a career opportunity: perceptions of high school seniors, pre-service teachers, and in-service teachers. ERIC ED 214 924.

Describes the attitudes of teachers, students and teacher education students toward teaching as a career and the factors that make teaching unattractive.

606. Page, Jane A. & Page, Fred M., Jr. Pre-service and in-service teachers' perceptions of teaching profession. ERIC ED 213 671.

Reports that the attitudes of preservice and inservice teachers toward teaching as a career varied by personal characteristics such as race and sex.

607. Parkay, Forrest W. & Conoley, Colleen. Discipline in the schools: the relationship of educators' attitudes about corporal punishment to selected variables. ERIC ED 199 208.

Reports that male teachers favor corporal punishment more than female teachers; dogmatism is also related to attitudes toward corporal punishment.

608. Parker, Sandra. In-service training programs for teachers in Teacher Corps and non-Teacher Corps

schools utilizing a questionnaire instrument. 1980. ERIC ED 196 842.

Reports differences in attitudes toward staff development and specific aspects of inservice education programs between teachers in schools with and without Teacher Corps programs.

609. Penner, Karen P. & Kolasa, Kathryn M. Secondary teachers' nutrition knowledge, attitudes, and practices. ERIC ED 212 564.

Describes differences in teachers' knowledge of nutrition and attitudes toward nutrition education and subject matter taught.

610. Phelan, William T. Governing staff reductions: the use and abuse of teacher evaluations. ERIC ED 278 929.

Reports that teachers and principals believe that teachers' evaluations should be considered in making decisions about teacher lay-offs.

611. Pickle, Judy. "Perspectives of educators across clinical and scholarly/scientific work settings," College Student Journal 17 (1983): 190-95.

Describes differences in teachers' and teacher educators' views of classroom events, based on videotapes of classrooms.

612. Pint, Robert F. Staff and student attitudes toward innovative programs at the middle school level. 1973. ERIC ED 102 109.

Describes middle school participants' attitudes toward innovative instructional programs.

613. Pisetsky, Daniel R. A study of the inservice needs of teachers as perceived by teachers and principals in an urban school system. Ph.D. dissertation. University of Connecticut. 1979.

Describes differences in teachers' and principals' perceptions of teachers' inservice training needs and how to meet them.

614. Post, Thomas & others. Differences between teachers' attitudinal self-ratings and their principals' teacher ideal on a mathematics inventory. Research paper No. 14. Minnesota University. 1974. ERIC ED 148 635.

Principals hope that teachers give greater attention to needs of individual students than teachers report they think teachers should do.

615. Pritchard, Rosalind M.G. "The status of teachers in Germany and Ireland," Comparative Education Review 27 (1983): 341-50.

Describes attitudes of teachers in the Federal Republic of Germany and the Republic of Ireland toward teaching and aspects of their own teaching situations.

616. Rawn, Edwin L. & Valentine, Jerry W. "Principal comunication across grade levels: a comparative and predictive study," Planning and Change 11 (1980): 189-196.

Describes differences in attitudes of elementary and secondary teachers toward the communication skills of their principals; effective at communicating decisions but ineffective in communicating about affective topics.

617. Ray, Francis Edwin. The relationship of teacher effectiveness to teacher characteristics in a teacher-desegregated secondary school system. Ed.D. dissertation. University of Tennessee. 1971.

Describes greater differences in performance by principal rating than in teacher reported commitment toward desegregation, with overall positive commitment.

618. Reddick, Thomas & Peach Larry. A study concerning participation of public school teachers and principals regarding curriculum issues in middle Tennessee. ERIC ED 238 172.

Describes the attitudes of teachers and administrators toward curriculum, instructional methods, student evaluation and other aspects of schooling.

619. Reineke, Robert & Welch, Wayne. "Adequacy of science teaching conditions as perceived by administrators and teachers," Science Education 59 (1975): 229-233.

Finds differences between administators and teachers with teachers viewing load, facilities and support as less than satisfactory.

620. Richards, Geoffrey B. A study of the attitudes of school superintendents and teacher association presidents to identify an amendment to Maine

statutes. Ed.D. dissertation. George Peabody College for Teachers of Vanderbilt University. 1982.

Describes responses of superintendents and presidents of teachers' associations to alternatives to teacher dismissal for just cause, with limited agreement between the two groups of the appropriateness of several alternatives to just cause dismissal.

621. Richmond, Virginia P. & McCroskey, James C. Power in the classroom: two studies. ERIC ED 225 218.

Describes teachers' and students' perceptions of the uses of power in the classroom and the relationship of types of uses of power to student achievement.

622. Rizada, Benita Rupinta. Perceptions and attitudes of teachers and administrators toward mainstreaming educationally handicapped students in California public elementary schools. Ed.D. dissertation. University of the Pacific. 1981.

Describes attitudes toward mainstreaming and aspects of educational programs and support services available to assist regular teachers who are working with mainstreamed students.

623. Roberts, Charles Henry. An analysis of the attitudes of chief school administrators, principals, and classsroom teachers toward collective bargaining in Eastern Kentucky. Ph.D. dissertation. George Peabody College for Teachers of Vanderbilt University. 1980.

Describes differences in attitudes toward collective bargaining, with teachers, especially younger and untenured teachers, supporting collective bargaining and administrators opposing collective bargaining.

624. Rogers, Susan Marie. Parent and teacher attitudes toward education in a selected school system. Ed.D. dissertation. Boston College. 1983.

Describes teachers and parents as wanting the same relative emphasis on goals within the school system but greater attention to each of the goals, with a concern for development of intellectual curiosity among students.

625. Ruscello, Dennis M. & others. "Attitudes of educators toward speech-language pathology services

in rural schools," Language, Speech, and Hearing Services in the Schools 11 (1980): 145-153.

Describes consistencies in attitudes of teachers and administrators in rural schools to the services provided, and the need for services, for students with speech and language problems.

626. Russell, Jeffery Brent. Corporal punishment: a study of the attitudes of parents, students, and teachers in the Imperial Valley, California, toward its use as a disciplinary technique in the junior high school. Ed.D. dissertation. Brigham Young University. 1978.

Describes attitudes of three groups toward the appropriateness and effectiveness of corporal punishment in the school setting.

627. Saks, Diane. The reading attitudes of high achieving seventh grade students and their teachers' perceptions of those reading attitudes. ERIC ED 200 921.

Reports that teachers' perceptions of the attitudes of high achieving students toward reading are consistent with measured student attitudes.

628. Sanders, Willie Mae B. Perceptions of selected middle school teachers, administrators, and teacher educators regarding objectives for middle school teacher education. Ed.D. dissertation. East Texas State University. 1980.

Describes similarities in the three groups' perceptions of the need for teacher inservice education and for evaluation of current programs.

629. Sandrin, James V. Readiness for individualization of instruction: a school climate assessment procedure. ERIC ED 214 254.

Describes beliefs about innovation and individulized instruction among elementary and secondary teachers and student teachers.

630. Sapone, Carmelo V. "Appraisal and evaluation systems: perceptions of administrators, teachers," NASSP Bulletin 65 No. 442 (1981): 25-30.

Describes differences in administrators' and teachers' perceptions of the importance of the various components of a teacher evaluation system.

631. Sarlak, Morteza Gholi. Teaching preferences of teachers with operative and cooperative styles.

Ed.D. dissertation. New Mexico State University. 1983.

Describes the attitudes of experienced teachers and preservice teachers toward teaching styles, with females more authoritarian and males more cooperative; age and years of experience were also related to attitude.

632. Scarr, L.E. & others. Educating students today for a place in society tomorrow: the Lake Washington School District futures study. 1980. ERIC ED 214 270.

Describes differences and similarities in attitudes of parents, teachers and students toward issues that will be important in the future and the effectiveness of current educational programs in educating students to deal with those issues.

633. Schaefer, Julie Ann Eakes. Parent and teacher attitudinal differences on behaviors of urban middle-school male learning disabled students. Ph.D. dissertation. Texas Women's University. 1982.

Reports no differences between parents and resource room teachers in attitudes toward specific behaviors exhibited by students with behavior problems assigned to the resource room during a portion of the school day.

634. Schmelikin, Liora Pedhazu. "Perceptions of disabilities: a multidimensional scaling approach," Journal of Special Education 16 No. 2 (1982): 161-77.

Describes attitudes of regular and special education teachers toward handicapped individuals when the handicaps were and were not defined.

635. Schug, Mark C. "Elementary teachers' views on economic issues," Theory and Research in Social Education 11 No. 1 (1983): 55-64.

Describes secondary teachers as more liberal than elementary teachers in their economic views.

636. Schurr, K. Terry & others. Discrepancies in teacher and administrator preferences for inservice training topics. 1980. ERIC ED 186 401.

Compares teachers' and administrators' perceptions of the areas in which teachers need inservice education; teachers viewed topics related to student motivation to be more important than did administrators.

637. Scott, Dennis Lynn. A study of attitudes and procedural changes of counselors and teachers working with a computerized attendance information system. Ed.D. dissertation. University of Southern California. 1981.

Describes positive attitudes toward and actual use of the information resulting from a computerized student attendance system.

638. Seifert, Kelvin. The achievement of care: men who teach young children. ERIC ED 231 542.

Describes the attitudes toward teaching as a career of male and female teachers of young children; reports men having more complex career plans.

639. Sevcik, Bonita. Curriculum-based measurement: effects on instruction, teacher estimates of student progress, and student knowledge of performance. ERIC ED 236 196.

Describes the attitudes of teachers and students toward a system to evaluate student reading achievement.

640. Sherman, Thomas M. & Giles, Mary B. "The development and structure of personal control in teachers," Journal of Educational Research 74 No. 3 (1981): 139-42.

Reports a greater degree of personal control among more experienced teachers than less experienced teachers and student teachers.

641. Signer, Barbara. "How do teacher and student evaluations of CAI software compare?" Computing Teacher 11 No. 3 (1983): 34-36.

Describes attitudes of teachers and students toward computers and instructional software.

642. Sinclair, Robert L. Explorations in the perceived educational environment: contextual dimensions of elementary schooling. AERA presentation. 1972. ERIC ED 066 423.

Describes different perceptions of students and teachers of the school environment.

643. Sinning, H. Kent & others. Parental and staff expectations for the future achievement of learning disabled students. 1980. ERIC ED 217 640.

Describes differences in parents' and teachers' expectations for learning disabled students, with teachers having lower expectations than parents, and higher parental expectations for social than academic development.

644. Slaven, Richard Louis. A study of the attitudes of Ohio school leaders toward community involvement in teacher negotiations. Ph.D. dissertation. Ohio State University. 1979.

Reports no differences among school board members, superintendents and teacher association presidents in attitudes toward community involvement in negotiations; the school board serves as the community representative in such negotiations.

645. Smith, Bruce D. "Instructional planning: attitudes, decisions, and preparation time among secondary social studies teachers," Journal of Social Studies Research 7 No. 1 (1983): 1-22.

Reports similar attitudes among preservice and inservice teachers toward the curriculum, the allocation of instructional time and their own teaching.

646. Smith, John K. & LaPlante, Douglas A. "Student and teacher perceptions of fair versus unfair teacher activities and the problems of teacher legitimacy," High School Journal 64 (1980): 108-114.

Reports general consistency in teachers' and students' attitudes toward the fairness of various teacher behaviors and responses to students; differences existed in perceptions of appropriateness of teacher control of academic content and methods.

647. Spear, Randall Alva. Attitudes of teachers, administrators, school board presidents and state legislators on the issues concerning equity in school finance in Arkansas as identified in Educational Equity. Improving School Finance in Arkansas. Ed.D. dissertation. University of Arkansas. 1980.

Reports a low level of understanding of the issues involved in school finance but a general consensus that the issues identified in a state report are the relevant issues.

648. Spradling, Charles W. & Babcock, Susan. Resolving divergent expectations among the multiple publics of the public schools. ERIC ED 222 980.

Reports that teachers had more positive attitudes toward public school educational programs than do parents.

649. Stallworth, John T. Identifying barriers to parent involvement in the schools: a survey of educators. ERIC ED 227 540.

Describes attitudes of teachers and principals toward parent involvement and the barriers to such involvement.

650. Stephens, Thomas M. & Braun, Benjamin L. "Measures of regular classroom teachers' attitudes toward handicapped children," Exceptional Children 46 No. 4 (1980): 292-294.

Reports that elementary teachers and those who had had a course in special education were more willing to accept mainstreamed students than junior high school teachers and teachers who had not taken a special education course.

651. Stern, David & Bagley, Kate. "How participants in collective bargaining for public school teachers in California perceive the interests of teachers in relation to other groups," Journal of Collective Negotiations in the Public Sector 10 No. 1 (1981): 63-73.

Describes differences in attitudes toward collective bargaining and the specific issues being bargained for among administration and teachers.

652. Stevens, Robert Nichols. A comparative study of selected variables in special education and regular classroom teachers' attitudes toward the handicapped student. Ph.D. dissertation. Florida State University. 1981.

Describes differences in teachers' attitudes toward handicapped students related to teachers' personal philosophies and educational specializations.

653. Steward, William O. The opinions of administrators and teachers on the process of collective bargaining and the 1979-80 negotiated contract between the Chicago Board of Education and the Chicago Teachers Union. Ed.D. dissertation. University of South Dakota. 1980. ERIC ED 222 303.

Describes teachers' attitudes toward collective bargaining in general and the specific issues included in the negotiations of an individual collective bargaining agreement.

654. Stone, Judith Marie. A comparison of the attitudes of educators and their parents as measured by four constructs associated with child abuse. Ph.D. dissertation. Loyola University of Chicago. 1980.

Describes attitudes of teachers toward parenting and relationships between attitudes and early home experiences of those educators.

655. Strein, William. Fostering students' emotional growth: implications for preservice and inservice programs. ERIC ED 222 455.

Describes differences in the perceptions of inservice and preservice teachers toward their skills in fostering student emotional growth.

656. Stronck, David R. "The attitudes and needs of inservice science teachers," Science Education 58 (1974): 505-508.

Describes attitude of teachers and principals with some agreement and some disagreement about the science areas in which teachers need inservice education and the goals for science education.

657. Sugg, William Grady. A study of selected attitudes of superintendents, principals, and teachers and their relationship to the job satisfaction of principals and teachers. Ed.D. dissertation. George Peabody College for Teachers of Vanderbilt University. 1980.

Describes attitudes of supervisors and their effects upon attitudes of teachers whom they supervise and congruence in attitudes between teachers, principals and superintendents toward the nature of man.

658. Summerfield, John Andrew. A study of the sex role attitudes of superintendents and principals in California public schools. Ed.D. dissertation. University of San Francisco. 1979.

Describes superintendents as having less traditional attitudes toward female sex roles than the attitudes of principals.

659. Summers, Edward G. & others. "Information needs and uses in education," Canadian Journal of Education 9 No. 2 (1984): 121-38.

Describes differences between teachers, administrators and support personnel in sources of and uses made of information.

660. Sweeney, Jim & Pinckney, Robert. "Faculty management: the principal's most important role," Spectrum 1 No. 3 (1983): 3-6.

Reports attitudes of teachers and principaLs toward principals' responsibilities for management of others.

661. Swisher, Karen Gayton. A study of the attitudes of parents and teachers at Standing Rock Community Elementary School toward multicultural education. Ed.D. dissertation. University of North Dakota. 1981.

Describes some differences in attitudes toward multicultural education associated with personal characteristics, e.g., experience off reservation, degree of Indian blood.

662. Swisher, Karen. Attitudes of parents and teachers of American Indian children toward multicultural education. ERIC ED 225 764.

Describes teachers' and reservation parents' attitudes toward multicultural education for students in a reservation school.

663. Swisher, Karen. "Comparison of attitudes of reservation parents and teachers toward multicultural education," Journal of American Indian Education 23 No. 3 (1984): 1-10.

Describes attitudes of parents and teachers toward multicultural education in a reservation setting, with teachers more positive than parents.

664. Tamashiro, Roy T. The relationship between discipline problems and teachers', parents', and students' beliefs on discipline. ERIC ED 203 534.

Describes teachers' perceptions of discipline and discipline problems in their classrooms and compares those perceptions with the attitudes of students and parents.

665. Taylor, Rebecca Grier. "Views from the winners' circle," Music Educators Journal 69 No. 1 (1982): 43-46.

Describes attitudes of teachers and principals toward characteristics of effective art education programs.

666. Thomason, Julia T. A study of openness to new experiences of middle school teachers as compared

to elementary and secondary teachers. ERIC ED 214 274.

Reports no differences in attitudes toward new experiences among elementary, middle and high school teachers but differences across socioeconomic levels of communities served by the schools to which the teachers were assigned.

667. Thompson, Steven Ray. A survey and analysis of Pennsylvania public school personnel perceptions of staff development practices and beliefs with a view to identifying some critical problems or needs. Ed.D. dissertation. Pennsylvania State University. 1982.

Describes agreements and disageements among four categories of school personnel in the extent to which specific practices concerning inservice education programs were and should be followed.

668. Thornburg, Kathy R. "Attitudes of secondary principals, teachers, parents and students toward parent involvement in the schools," High School Journal 64 No. 4 (1981): 150-53.

Reports that teachers and administrators wanted more parental involvement in the schools than did parents and students.

669. Tibbett, Catherine Louise. A study of curriculum and instruction perceptions and attitudes of teachers and administrators in selected North Central Association accredited elementary schools in the state of Iowa. Ph.D. dissertation. University of Iowa. 1981.

Describes the attitudes of teachers and principals to selected curriculum and instructional concepts.

670. Tolar, Alexander, Scarpetti, William & Lane, Paul A. "Teachers' attitudes toward children's behavior revisited," Journal of Educational Psychology 58 (1967): 175-180.

Teachers describe different student behavior as abnormal than do psychologists who indicated same behaviors are normal; less experienced teachers differ from psychologists more than experienced teachers.

671. Toran, Ralph Anthony. An investigation of the current perceptions and ideal expectations of middle/junior high school principals and teachers

regarding principal's role in teacher evaluation. Ph.D. dissertation. Boston College. 1979.

Describes attitudes of teachers and principals toward the principal's role in teacher evaluation.

672. Triplett, Gene. Student's learning style: a comparative study of perceptions of principals, counselors, and teachers in the state of Ohio. Ph.D. dissertation. Miami University. 1980.

Study found no differences between members of the three groups in the perceptions of factors which may influence student learning style; respondents felt the issue of learning style needed to be considered for about one-third of all students.

673. Turrentine, Richard K. Educational goal priorities perceived by elementary principals and teachers. Ed.D. dissertation. University of Southern California. 1980.

Describes priorities of teachers and principals for elementary education, importance of goals relating to skills, values and affective domain, and differences between teachers and principals by sex, age, experience, school size and other factors.

674. Ulmer, David C., Jr. Implementing energy education focusing on attitudes and concerns. Ed.D. dissertation. University of Nebraska - Lincoln. 1983.

Describes teachers' attitudes as more positive than student attitudes but variations among aspects of teacher attitudes toward energy education.

675. Urdang, Meryl Sue. A causal model of inservice program characteristics and participant attitudes. Ed.D. dissertation. Rutgers University. 1982.

Describes more positive attitudes toward inservice programs among persons who volunteered to participate in the program than those who did not volunteer, and a relationship between attitudes toward past and toward present inservice education programs.

676. Usova, George M. "Comparing attitudes toward reading instruction among secondary principals, reading specialists, and content-area teachers," Reading Improvement 10 No. 2 (1979): 169-174.

Describes attitudes of teachers to reading instruction at the secondary level.

677. Van Cleaf, David W. A comparison of parents' attitudes with those of kindergarten teachers and principals concerning kindergarten objectives and preferences relating to behaviorist and cognitive-transactionist methods. Ph.D. dissertation. University of Nebraska - Lincoln. 1979.

Study found agreement between teachers and parents on objectives and cognitive-transactionist methods to achieve objectives but a greater number of parents support behaviorist instructional methods.

678. Van Cleaf, David W. Assessing preferences of kindergarten parents and staff toward behavioral and cognitively oriented kindergarten methods. 1979. _ERIC ED_ 180 606.

Describes preferences teachers and parents have for kindergarten programs; programs with a cognitive focus compose the first choice but more parents prefer teacher-directed than student-choice instructional methods.

679. Vancouver British Columbia School Trustees. Reactions of principals and teachers to the initial teaching alphabet. Vancouver Board of School Trustees (British Columbia). 1971. _ERIC ED_ 059 229.

Reactions of teachers and principals were found to be favorable to use of the Initial Teaching Alphabet.

680. Vernberg, Eric M. & Medway, Frederic J. "Teacher and parent causal perceptions of school problems," _American Educational Research Journal 18 No. 1_ 29-37.

Reports that teachers attribute most learning problems to parents and the home while parents attribute problems to the teacher and school.

681. Vidoni, Dennis O. & others. "Behavior problems of children as perceived by teachers, mental health professionals, and children," _Psychology in the Schools 20 No. 1_ (1983): 93-98.

Describes the attitudes of teachers, children and mental health professionals toward behavior problems; children's attitudes differed from those of the other two groups.

682. Voege, Richard B. Procedures for evaluating classroom teachers in certain school districts in the state of Washington. School Information and Research Service. Seattle, Washington. ERIC ED 044 437.

Presents interviews with evaluators and teachers who were developing criteria for the evaluation of teachers.

683. Walters, Judy Ann Daniels. An analysis of the attitudes of selected public school educators in Tennessee toward minimum competency testing. Ed.D. dissertation. East Tennessee State University. 1980.

Describes differences in teachers' attitudes and in relationships between attitudes and personal characteristics for male and female teachers.

684. Watson, Robert Victor. Community control of the schools: a case study of black public school teachers' and principals' attitudes in Buffalo. Ph.D. dissertation. State University of New York at Buffalo. 1980.

Describes attitudes of black teachers and principals toward community control and relates those attitudes to other cultural attitudes such as cultural nationalism.

685. Welch, Wayne W. & Lawrenz, Frances. "Characteristics of male and female science teachers," Journal of Research in Science Teaching 19 No. 7 587-94.

Describes differences in teachers' attitudes and in relationships between attitudes and personal characteristics for male and female teachers.

686. Wensel, Kenneth R. Comparative attitudinal study of students, teachers and parents of issues affecting Fenton High School. Ph.D. dissertation. University of Michigan. 1979.

Describes a general level of satisfaction but differences among the groups in perceptions about aspects of the educational program.

687. White, Florence Anne P. Attitudes toward education: involving administrators, teachers and parents in early childhood education programs. Ed.D. dissertation. University of Idaho. 1978.

Describes attitudes of parents, teachers and administrators related to degree of parent participation in early childhood education.

688. White, Janet A. & Fowler, John M. Energy education in the schools. ERIC ED 228 043.

Describes the attitudes of teachers and principals toward energy education, institutional objectives, available materials, barriers to inclusion within the curriculum.

689. Wilcox, Ray T. A comparison of secondary school teachers judged effective by principals, current students and graduates. AERA Presentation. 1976. ERIC ED 139 103.

Presents differences in teachers', principals' and students' ratings of the best teachers and the characteristics defined as good teaching qualities.

690. Williams, David L., Jr. & Stallworth, John T. A survey of educators regarding parent involvement in education: implications for teacher training. ERIC ED 220 048.

Describes parents, teachers and administrators as supportive of parent involvement in some, but not all, aspects of instructional programs.

691. Willie, Reynold & Kummerow, Jean M. "Age and interest in continuing teacher education," Educational Research Quarterly 6 No. 4 (1981): 30-37.

Reports differences in attitudes toward continuing professional education by teacher age.

692. Wilson, Joan Cobb. A comparison of the attitudes toward child rearing practices of teachers and parents of children in the day care setting. Ph.D. dissertation. University of Maryland. 1978.

Describes attitudes of preschool teachers and parents toward child rearing behavior.

693. Wilson, Joseph John. Related attitudes of Arizona teachers, superintendents and school boards toward collective negotiations. Ed.D. dissertation. Northern Arizona University. 1981.

Describes the attitudes of members of the three groups toward collective bargaining as a process and the relative roles of the three groups in the bargaining process.

694. Wilson, La Visa Cam. "A comparison of preservice and experienced teachers' perceptions of competence in teaching reading," Reading World 18 No. 2 (1978): 194-197.

Presents differences in preservice and experienced teachers in assessment of their reading instruction skills.

695. Wilson, Thomas Lee. A study of expressed attitudes toward teaching five controversial issues in public schools. Ph.D. dissertation. Kent State University. 1980.

Describes the attitudes of students, teachers, administrators and parents toward the teaching of controversial subjects, reporting more positive attitudes of teachers and students than administrators and parents.

696. Wisneski, Phillip D. & Wallbrown, Fred H. "The relevance of attitudinal variables for reading remediation," Reading Improvement 20 (1983): 278.

Describes several similarities in the attitudes of teachers and reading consultants toward reading and reading instruction.

697. Wolf, Alison. Evaluation of MCPS in-service training. ERIC ED 235 180.

Reports attitudes of teachers and principals in one county toward inservice programs and describes a continuing need for inservice education.

698. Wood, Carolyn M. The role of standardized achievement tests in the management of instruction: a survey of teacher and administrator practices and attitudes. ERIC ED 219 446.

Reports that administrators had more positive attitudes than teachers toward standardized tests and their use to assess student learning.

699. Wood, Robert W. "Controversial topics as perceived by South Dakota teachers and principals," Phi Delta Kappan 58 (1977): 501-502.

Most teachers and principals who responded to a questionnaire reported that they felt free to deal with controversial topics in the elementary classroom.

700. Woods, Jimmy Lavon. Attitudes of Louisiana public secondary principals and English teachers toward teaching the Bible as literature. Ed.D. dissertation. Northwestern State University of Louisiana. 1982.

Reports no significant differences in attitudes toward use of the Bible for literature instruction by teacher personal characteristics such as age and prior religious training but differences in attitudes among teachers who did and did not use the Bible.

701. Yaap, Sharon Spears. A survey of the attitudes and opinions of a secondary school district certificated staff toward the utilization of female administrators. Ed.D. dissertation. United States International University. 1980.

Describes differences in attitudes by position (teacher or administrator) and sex; female teachers more than male teachers perceived discrimination against females seeking entry to administrative positions.

702. Young, Jacqueline Ann. Collective bargaining and the public access movement in the schools: a study of the attitudes of parents, organized teachers and school management in Massachusetts schools. Ed.D. dissertation. Rutgers University. 1980.

Describes differences in attitudes of three groups toward increased public access to the process of collective bargaining, with teachers reporting class size as the only important collective bargaining issue.

703. Yvarro, Aurelio. Educational accountability: attitudes, perceptions and role expectations among principals, teachers, teacher-aides and parents. Ph.D. dissertation. Claremont Graduate School. 1979.

Describes attitudes of four groups toward educational accountability.

704. Yvon, Bernard R. & Downing, Davis A. "Attitudes toward calculator usage in schools: a survey of parents and teachers," _School Science and Mathematics_ _78_ (1978): 410-416.

Reports a negative feeling about the use of calculators for students in grades 3-6, moderately negative for grades 7-8 and positive for grades 9-12; general agreement between teachers and parents.

705. Zigarmi, Patricia, Betz, Loren & Jensen, Darrell. "Teachers' preferences in and perceptions of in-service education," _Educational Leadership_ _34_ (1977): 545.

Describes teachers' responses to a questionnaire identifying types of inservice they like and why.

III. ATTITUDES TOWARD STUDENTS

706. Adenika, T. Jean & Berry, Gordon L. "Teachers' attitudes toward the education of the black child," Education 97 No. 2 (1976): 102-114.

Presents results of a questionnaire on teachers' attitudes toward education of black children.

707. Algozzine, Bob & others. "A factor analysis of teachers' intervention choices for dealing with students' behavior and learning problems," Elementary School Journal 84 (1983): 189-97.

Describes teachers' more positive attitudes toward possible responses to classroom situations that involve actions by teachers rather than actions by others.

708. Algozzine, Bob. "The disturbing child: a matter of opinion," Behavioral Disorders 5 No. 2 (1980): 112-115.

Reports that regular classroom teachers rated student disruptive behavior in the classroom as more disturbing to them than did special education teachers.

709. Algozzine, Bob & others. "The influence of teachers' tolerances for specific kinds of behaviors on their ratings of a third grade student," Alberta Journal of Educational Research 29 No. 2 (1983): 89-97.

Reports that teacher tolerance is greater for immature than for unmanageable student behavior.

710. Aloia, Gregory F. "Influence of a child's race and the EMR label on initial impressions of regular-classroom teachers," American Journal of Mental Deficiency 85 No. 6 (1981): 619-23.

Reports that teachers' expectations for new students are influenced by student race and cultural group.

711. Aloia, Gregory F. & MacMillan, Donald L. "Influence of the EMR label on initial expectations of regular-classroom teachers," <u>American Journal of Mental Deficiency 88 No. 3</u> (1983): 255-62.

Describes attitudes of teachers toward handicapped mainstreamed students, concerning academic ability and classroom behavior.

712. Anderson, Linda M. & Prawat, Richard S. "Attributional analysis of teachers' affective reactions to student success and failure," <u>American Educational Research Journal 20</u> (1983): 137-52.

Describes teachers' beliefs about student learning and their affective responses to their perceptions that students have and have not mastered the course material.

713. Baer, G. Thomas & others. "Discipline in the classroom: perceptions of middle grade teachers," <u>Clearing House 57 No. 3</u> (1083): 139-42.

Describes attitudes of teachers toward student behavior problems in the classroom and teachers' responses to those behaviors.

714. Baldwyn Separate School. A gifted model designed for gifted students in a small, rural high school. <u>ERIC ED</u> 233 847.

Within a description of a program for gifted students, describes teachers' attitudes toward gifted secondary students.

715. Batty, Constance Wheat. Perceptions of elementary classroom teachers regarding the causes of the high incidence of reading retardation occurring among black pupils. Ed.D. dissertation. University of Massachusetts. 1980.

Describes teachers' views of reading problems of black students as caused by characteristics of the students, parents, community, but not school or teacher; indicates differences by race of teacher.

716. Beady, Charles H., Jr. & Hansell, Stephen. Teacher race and expectations for student achievement. 1980. <u>ERIC ED</u> 200 659.

Reports no differences between black and white teachers in their assessment of student achievement and ability but black teachers expected that more of their students would enter and complete college than did white teachers.

717. Beare, Paul L. The in school-in class program: a child advocacy/crisis teacher program for behaviorally disordered students in a rural school district. 1980. ERIC ED 195 123.

Describes a program to assist teachers to work with behaviorally disordered students in their classes and changes in attitudes of teachers after participation in the training program toward greater acceptance of students with behavior disorders.

718. Bell, Nancy J. & others. "Teachers' definitions of self-esteem when rating preschool children," Perceptual and Motor Skills 51 (1980): 292.

Reports that preschool teachers, when rating students on self-esteem, use criteria that are related to traditional images of male behavior, e.g., assertiveness.

719. Benz, Carolyn R. & others. Sex role expectations of classroom teachers, grades 1-12. 1980. ERIC ED 191 908.

Reports that teachers perceive high achieving students as having more of the qualities commonly associated with males and fewer of the qualities associated with females, regardless of sex of the student.

720. Biemiller, Andrew J. Characteristics of kindergarten children preceived as "thriving," "average," or "non-thriving" by their teachers. 1980. ERIC ED 200 307.

Describes differences in characteristics of students whom teachers classified into three groups, those doing well, average and not well; student differences occurred in social and problem solving skills.

721. Birchard, Bruce A. Attitudes, understanding, and interaction: students, teachers, and community leaders; perceptions of Indian education. The national study of American Indian education series IV. No. 12. final report. University of Illinois. Chicago. 1970. ERIC ED 048 962.

Describes attitudes of teachers toward Indian students and Indian students' and parents' attitudes toward formal education and community responses to school.

722. Birdin, Vinston E. A study of selected apprehensions of teachers toward working in schools predominately of the opposite race. Ed.D. dissertation. Virginia Polytechnic Institute and State University. 1978.

Describes black and white teachers' apprehensions of teaching in schools composed predominately of students of the opposite race.

723. Blood, Ingrid M. & Blood, Gordon W. "Classroom teachers' impressions of hearing impaired and deaf children," Perceptual and Motor Skills 54 No. 3 (1984): 877-78.

Describes teachers' ratings of selected characteristics of children with hearing difficulties.

724. Boersma, Frederic J. & Chapman, James W. "Teachers' and mothers' academic achievement expectations for learning disabled children," Journal of Psychology 20 No. 3 (1982): 216-21.

Reports that both teachers and parents had lower expectations for learning disabled than regular children.

725. Boucher, C. Robin. Teacher attributioning in decision making," Psychology in the Schools 18 No. 1 (1981): 115-20.

Reports that type and strength of information provided to teachers as well as the label given to a handicapped student influence teachers' expectations for students.

726. Brandt, Larry, Hayden, M. & Brophy, J. "Teachers' attitudes and ascription of causation," Journal of Educational Psychology 67 No. 5 (1975): 677-682.

Describes teachers' attitudes toward student achievement and perceptions of the factors associated with more and less student learning.

727. Brimacombe, Judy A. & others. "Teachers' perceptions of students who wear hearing aids: an empirical test," Language, Speech, and Hearing Services in the Schools 14 (1983): 128-35.

Describes differences in teachers' attitudes toward hearing impaired students with and without hearing aides.

728. Brophy, Jere E. & Rohrkemper, Mary M. Motivational factors in teachers' handling of problem students. ERIC ED 218 258.

Reports teachers' perceptions of problem students, possible responses to those students and teachers' characteristics associated with selected responses.

729. Brophy, Jere E. & Rohrkemper, Mary M. Teachers' thinking about problem students. 1980. ERIC ED 186 408.

Describes differences in teachers' perceptions of students' ability to control their behavior depending upon the extent to which the teacher assumed "ownership" of the behavior problem.

730. Brophy, Jere E. & Rohrkemper, Mary M. The influence of problem ownership on teachers' perceptions of and strategies for coping with problem students. 1980. ERIC ED 196 884.

Describes teachers' reported methods for coping with specific student behavior problems; methods selected by teachers varied with the degree that the teacher assumed responsibility for the student problem or resolution of the student problem.

731. Burdsal, Charles & others. "Behavioral dimensions in fourth, fifth, and sixth grade students as rated by teachers," Journal of Clinical Psychology 40 No. 1 (1984): 172-85.

Describes a wide range of teachers' perceptions of their students' behavior and personality characteristics.

732. Burns, R. Hugh & McCullen, Audrey. "Teachers look at classroom behavior problems - a survey," Mental Hygiene 55 No. 4 (1971): 504-506.

Reports teachers' descriptions of students' behavior problems in the school setting.

733. Byrd, Marguita L. & Williams, Hampton S. Language attitudes and Black dialect: an assessment. ERIC ED 213 062.

Describes attitudes of teachers toward students who speak black dialect and a relationship between those attitudes and teachers' definition of black dialect and teachers' race.

734. Caggiano, Rosemary. "The relationship between the values and attitudes of elementary school teachers

and pupils regarding pupil behaviors," Graduate Research in Education and Related Disciplines 6 (1970): 82-97.

Describes differences in teachers' and students' attitudes toward student behavior and the determination of which behavior should be rewarded or punished.

735. Camp, William G. "Indiana teachers look at student discipline," NASSP Bulletin 65 No. 441 (1981): 45-48.

Reports that teachers see mild discipline problems as more disruptive of teacher and student morale than more serious discipline problems.

736. Camp, William G. & Bourn, Lawton, P., Jr. Student discipline: an analysis of teacher and administrator perceptions. 1979. ERIC ED 173 971.

Describes attitudes of teachers toward behavior of students at the secondary level in Indiana.

737. Carnes, Leslie L. Discipline problems in secondary schools as viewed by teachers and students. Ph.D. dissertation. George Peabody College for Teachers of Vanderbilt University. 1980.

Describes differences in teachers' and students' expectations for the behavior of teachers and students.

738. Catalogna, Lenore, & others. An exploratory examination of teachers' perceptions of pupils' race. 1980. ERIC ED 185 197.

Reports that teachers differentiated students into an average of three racial categories; the sorting was most frequently based on color; teachers evaluated students differentially by race.

739. Christenson, Sandra & others. "Teachers' attributions for problems that result in referral for psychoeducational evaluation," Journal of Educational Research 76 No. 3 (1983): 174-80.

Describes teachers' perceptions of students with learning problems and their attribution of causes to factors outside the school.

740. Clark, E. Audrey. "Teacher attitudes toward integration of children with handicap," Education and Training of the Mentally Retarded 11 No. 4 (1976): 333-335.

Describes attitudes of regular classroom teachers toward students with handicaps and toward inclusion of those students in the regular classroom.

741. Clark, Frances Lee. The development of instrumentation to measure regular classroom teachers' attitudes toward mildly handicapped students. Ph.D. dissertation. University of Kansas. 1981.

Describes the development of an instrument and reports the attitudes of teachers toward handicapped students as measured by that instrument.

742. Clemens, Janette M. Reed. A comparative study of middle school and junior high school teacher attitudes toward transescent needs. Ph.D. dissertation. Indiana State University. 1983.

Describes differences and similarities in teachers' attitudes toward the social-emotional, physical and intellectual needs of students within the age range included in their schools.

743. Cohen, Libby. Stereotyping of learning disabled and remedial reading students by teachers. 1980. ERIC ED 187 045.

Reports that teachers assigned more positive attributes to students who were not than to students who were labelled as learning disabled or in need of remedial reading; elementary teachers had more positive attitudes toward normal students than secondary teachers.

744. Coleman, Margaret Cecil. Teacher attitudes toward various dimensions of behavior exhibited by emotionally disturbed students. Ph.D. dissertation. University of Texas at Austin. 1981.

Describes student aggressive interaction as prompting the most negative teacher attitudes and student peer avoidance as prompting the least negative teacher attitudes toward emotionally disturbed students.

745. Coleman, Margaret C. & Gilliam, James E. "Disturbing behaviors in the classroom: a survey of teacher attitudes," Journal of Special Education 17 No. 2 (1983): 121-29.

Decribes teachers as having the most negative attitudes toward aggressive student behavior and the least negative attitudes toward withdrawn student behavior.

746. Conner, Robert Edward. The relationship between student temperament and behavioral characteristics and teacher attitudes of attachment, concern, indifference and rejection. Ed.D. dissertation. University of Georgia. 1983.

Describes teachers' perceptions of young children toward whom they had attitudes of attachment, concern, non-concern and indifference.

747. Cooper, Harris M. "Controlling personal rewards: professional teachers' differential use of feedback and the effects of feedback on the student's motivation to perform," Journal of Educational Psychology 69 (1977): 419-427.

Indicates that teachers' expectations for student behavior are related to degree of teacher control; reports that lessened academic criticism of students is related to increased requests for assistance by low achieving students; students perceive a relationship between effort and results.

748. Cooper, Harris M. & others. "Teachers' beliefs about interaction control and their observed behaviors correlates," Journal of Educational Psychology 72 (1980): 345-354.

Reports that teachers perceive that they have more control over interactions with high-achieving than low-achieving students and that students from whom teachers expect low achievement are less predictable in their interactions.

749. Cramer, E. "What teachers want to know about reading," Curriculum Review 16 No. 5 (1977): 341-344.

Describes teachers' attitudes toward various common student reading problems.

750. Cruse, Jeannette Elaine. Attitudes of regular elementary school classroom teachers toward handicapped learners. Ph.D. dissertation. Pennsylvania State University. 1981.

Describes a relationship between attitude toward mainstreaming and personal characteristics, e.g., age and experience, and differences in teacher attitude toward mainstreaming and toward having a handicapped student in their class.

751. Curran, Thomas J. & Algozzine, Bob. "Ecological disturbance: a test of the matching hypothesis," Behavioral Disorders 5 No. 3 (1980): 169-174.

Reports that differences in teachers' tolerance for disruptive or immature behavior by students are associated with differences in teachers' characteristics.

752. Daly, John A. & Suite, Amy. "Classroom seating choice and teacher perceptions of students," Journal of Experimental Education 50 No. 2 (1981): 64-69.

Reports that teachers' attitudes toward students are influenced by student sex, grade level and seat selected in the classroom.

753. De Caro, J.J. & others. "A cross-cultural examination of parents' and teachers' expectations for deaf youth regarding careers," British Journal of Educational Psychology 53 No. 3 (1983): 358-63.

Describes the attitudes of teachers in England and Italy toward deaf students and their achievement prospects.

754. Dempsey, Arthur D. What is an elementary school child? Anglo, Black and Hispanic teachers' perceptions. ERIC ED 226 853.

Describe attitudes of teachers from different ethnic backgrounds toward elementary students.

755. Desforges, Charles. Teachers' thinking about children's thinking. ERIC ED 200 585.

Describes teachers' perceptions of student thinking and the ways that teachers match instructional tasks with student learning needs.

756. Dobson, Judith E. & Campbell N. Jo. "The relationship of teacher's philosophy of human nature and perception and treatment of behavioral problems," Humanist Educator 18 No. 1 (1979): 23-31.

Presents a relationship between teachers' beliefs of human nature and their reactions to student behavior problems.

757. Dobson, Russell & Brewer, Leon. The perception and treatment by teachers and principals of the behavioral problems of elementary school children. College of Education. Oklahoma State University. 1971. ERIC ED 057 533.

Describes differences in teachers' and principals' perceptions of the seriousness of student misbehavior; agreement on the value of parent-teacher conference.

758. Dominico, Janice Carol. Area vocational technical school teachers' expectations of mainstreamed handicapped students. Ph.D. dissertation. University of Pittsburgh. 1981.

Describes differences in teachers' attitudes toward and expectations for handicapped students by teachers' subject area and students' handicap.

759. Doswell, Walter Henry. Secondary teacher attitudes toward pregnant students and school-age parents. Ed.D. dissertation. Rutgers University. 1983.

Describes differences in teachers' attitudes toward pregnant students associated with teachers' personal characteristics, e.g., age, but not with experience with pregnant students.

760. Driscoll, Amy. Teachers' self-descriptions and descriptions of students to whom they're attached and whom they reject. ERIC ED 237 472.

Describes the attitudes of teachers toward students to whom they feel attachment and rejection and differences in those students.

761. Dudney, John Alfred. An analysis of administrators', guidance counselors' and teachers' perceptions of disruptive behavior in middle and junior high schools. Ph.D. dissertation. George Peabody College for Teachers of Vanderbilt University. 1980.

Describes agreement among three groups in perceptions of causes of disruptive behavior, such as boredom, and effects, such as increases in teacher time spent controlling the class.

762. Dzuiban, Charles & others. The national Teacher Corps program, 1966-1967, evaluation report. Atlanta Public Schools. Georgia. 1967. ERIC ED 019 110.

Reports that the attitudes of interns had a higher correlation with effective teaching than the attitudes of teachers.

763. Elijah, David. "Teacher expectations: determinants of pupils' reading achievement," Reading Improvement 17 (1980): 117-121.

Reports that teachers' assessments of students' reading readiness are accurate, when measured against a reading readiness test, and that teachers' expectations for student achievement are not readily altered.

764. Elijah, David & Legenza, Alice. "Teacher rankings, readiness tests, and socioeconomic status," Reading Improvement 17 (1980): 10-13.

Describes teachers' expectations for reading achievement for students as those expectations are related to students' measured reading readiness.

765. Emihovich, Catherine A. "The color of misbehaving: two case studies of deviant boys," Journal of Black Studies 13 No. 3 (1983): 259-74.

Describes differences in teachers' perceptions of and attitudes toward misbehavior by black and white students.

766. Epler, Doris M. Teachers' perceptions of predicted career success of students who choose nontraditional occupational careers. ERIC ED 226 113.

Describes teachers' perceptions of the likely success of students choosing nontraditional careers and relates those perceptions to teachers' characteristics.

767. Ervin, Douglas H. Teacher attitudes toward learning disabled elementary pupils as related to reading achievement. Ed.D. dissertation. University of South Carolina. 1983.

Reports some differences in attitudes toward learning disabled students between regular classroom and resource room teachers, and differences in grades given for pupil work.

768. Fair, J.W. & others. Teacher interaction and observation practices in the evaluation of student achievement. 1980. ERIC ED 190 527.

Describes the ways that teachers observe students to obtain information used to assess student skill levels and instructional needs and the relationship of observations to teachers' expectations for students.

769. Falkenhagen, Maria & Kelly, Inga K. "Teacher perception of stereotypes," Journal of American Indian Education 13 (1974): 9-13.

Describes stereotypes teachers see in juvenile fiction about American Indians in three areas: dress, living conditions and customs.

770. Flynn, Timothy M. "Validation of preschool teachers' recall of children's behavior," _Journal of Experimental Education 45 No. 2_ (1976): 46-51.

Describes four factors preschool teachers recall relative to student behavior.

771. Fogel, Loveen S. & Nelson, Rosemary O. "The effects of special education labels on teachers' behavioral observations, checklist scores, and grading of academic work," _Journal of School Psychology 21 No. 3_ (1983): 241-51.

Reports that labels for handicapped children influenced teachers attitudes but not assessments of student learning or behavior.

772. Forum, Rhea Ellen Stone. An assessment of classroom teachers' attitudes and knowledge of gifted and talented students. Ph.D. dissertation. University of Oregon. 1980.

Describes differences in teachers' knowledge about and attitude toward gifted students by teacher characteristics, e.g. educational level.

773. Foster, Glen & others. "Classroom teacher and teacher-in-training susceptibility to stereotypical bias," _Personnel and Guidance Journal 59_ (1980): 27-30.

Reports that teachers were influenced in their evaluations of pupils' behavior by the label assigned to the child, either normal or emotionally disturbed, when asked to assess students based on written descriptions.

774. Fowler, Michael Gregory. An analysis of the problems of Korean students in American secondary schools as perceived by Korean students and parents and the teachers in public schools. Ed.D. dissertation. University of Northern Colorado. 1978.

Presents students', teachers' and parents' attitudes about Korean students in American schools and associated problems.

775. Fuller, Mary Lou. Elementary school teachers' perceptions of the school behavior of children from intact and single parent families. Ph.D. dissertation. University of New Mexico. 1982.

Reports that teachers' attitudes are related to age and that teachers believe that more positive student behaviors are associated with students from intact homes than from single parent families.

776. Garza-Buentello, Maria T. A study of the relationship of Mexican teachers' attitudes to the mathematics achievement of their pupils. Ph.D. dissertation. Stanford University. 1983.

Describes differences and similarities in attitudes of Mexican teachers by teaching assignment, e.g., urban and rural schools, public and private schools.

777. Gillespie, David Craig & Stanbury, Gladys Mary. Hyperactivity: teacher knowledge, attitudes and practices. Ed.D. dissertation. United States International University. 1982.

Reports that teachers have limited knowledge about and no clear attitudes toward hyperactivity among students.

778. Gipps, Caroline. "Nursery nurses and nursery teachers II: their attitudes towards pre-school children and their parents," *Child Psychology and Psychiatry and Allied Disciplines* *23* *No. 3* (1982): 255-65.

Describes attitudes of preschool teachers toward students and their parents.

779. Grady, Mary L. "An assessment of teachers' attitudes toward disadvantaged children," *Journal of Negro Education* *40* (1971): 146-152.

Describes attitudes of teachers in one district toward disadvantaged and minority pupils; one-third felt they could do a better job with less culturally diverse classroom, one-third did not agree; related to cultural development and contact with cultural diversity.

780. Grant, Linda. Black females' "place" in desegregated classrooms. *ERIC* *ED* 224 844.

Describes differences in teachers' attitudes toward male and female black and white students in a desegregated classroom.

781. Graybill, Daniel & Gabel, Harris. "Relationship of teacher nominations for parent counseling to perceptions of children's behavior problems," *Southern Journal of Educational Research* *12* *No. 3* (1978): 151-160.

Reports that teachers viewed student behavior problems as a major factor in recommending counseling for the students' parents.

782. Green, Jon Christopher. Factors relating to the attitudes of regular education teachers toward integrating hearing impaired children. Ph.D. dissertation. University of Pittsburgh. 1981.

Reports that teachers' attitudes toward integration of hearing impaired children are influenced by teachers' characteristics, support available to the teacher and student in the regular classroom and students' characteristics.

783. Griffin, Mary Jane R. A study of classroom teachers' opinions of causes and possible remedies for low scoring by eighth grade students on the spring, 1978, Tennessee competency test. Ed.D. dissertation. University of Tennessee. 1980.

Describes teachers' atttitudes toward causes of student low scores, with parent permissiveness as major cause that teachers perceive for low scores.

784. Guerin, Gilbert R. "Regular teacher concerns with mainstreamed learning handicapped children," Psychology in the Schools 16 No. 4 (1979): 543-545.

Reports differences in teachers' attitudes toward retarded and handicapped mainstreamed students.

785. Haller, Emil J. & Davis, Sharon A. "Does socioeconomic status bias the assignment of elementary school students to reading groups?" American Educational Research Journal 17 (1980): 409-418.

Reports that teacher and student socioeconomic status are not associated with teacher assignment of students to reading groups in elementary classrooms.

786. Harasymiw, Stefan J. & Horne, M. "Teacher attitudes toward handicapped children and regular class integration," Journal of Special Education 10 (1976): 393-400.

Describes attitudes of regular classroom teachers toward handicapped children and more positive attitudes with training in special education.

787. Harasymiw, Stefan J. & others. Teacher and pupil disability attitude congruency. 1976. ERIC ED 125 209.

Describes attitudes of teachers and students toward students with disabilities.

788. Harvey, Mary R. "Public school treatment of low-income children: education for passivity," *Urban Education* *15* (1980): 279-323.

Reports that teachers respond differently to students from low income homes than they do to other students, expressing their lower expectations for the achievement of those students.

789. Hauptman, Elaine. Communication between special educators and the mainstream teachers. ERIC ED 231 173.

Describes the attitudes of regular classroom teachers toward handicapped students, mainstreaming and problems anticipated with mainstreaming.

790. Hazlett, Benjamin Addison. Relationships between elementary teachers' expressed attitudes toward students, quality of dyadic classroom interaction and student grades. Ed.D. dissertation. Oklahoma State University. 1982.

Reports a relationship between teachers' attitudes and dyadic interaction in the classroom and between both of those and student achievement as measured by grades.

791. Hedges, William D. Attitudes of parents, teachers, and students toward education and Florida high and low achieving high schools. 1980. ERIC ED 205 603.

Describes differences and similarities in attitudes of parents, teachers, and students toward the program in their high school, the achievement of students, and the use of minimum competency testing of students.

792. Hermes, Robert A. & Fleming, K. Paul. Analysis of teacher's perceptions of transient and nontransient sixth-grade students. 1978. ERIC ED 145 319.

Describes a slight difference in teachers' attitudes toward transient and nontransient students.

793. Hirshoren, Alfred & Burton, Thomas. "Willingness of regular teachers to participate in mainstreaming

handicapped children," Journal of Research and Development in Education 12 No. 4 (1979): 93-100.

Survey indicates greater teacher acceptance of behavior and of physically handicapped than of retarded pupils.

794. Hollomo, John W. Dealing with children's unacceptable classroom behaviors. 1976. ERIC ED 138 370.

Teachers listed nineteen unacceptable student behaviors and twelve techniques for dealing with such behavior.

795. Horak, Willis J. "Personal/professional characteristics and teachers' attitudes about science," Clearing House 56 No. 2 (1982): 78-81.

Describes attitudes of science teachers to their teaching as more closely related to their educational characteristics than to aspects of their work setting.

796. House, Peggy A. "Through the eyes of their teachers: stereotypes of gifted pupils," Journal for the Education of the Gifted 2 No. 4 (1979): 220-224.

Presents attitudes of teachers of gifted toward the gifted child; reports on some consistencies in perceptions.

797. Houtz, Jon C. & Shaning Dennis J. "Contribution of teacher ratings of behavioral characteristics to the prediction of divergent thinking and problem solving," Psychology in the Schools 19 No. 3 (1982): 380-83.

Describes students' characteristics to which teachers are sensitive that are associated with greater student problem-solving and divergent thinking.

798. Hutson, Barbara A. & Niles, Jerome A. Reading grouping as decision-making: selection and effects of cues. ERIC ED 222 875.

Describes teachers' perceptions of students' reading skills and effects on those perceptions of students' reading and social problems.

799. Jacobs, Jon C. "Teacher attitudes toward gifted children," Gifted Child Quarterly 16 No. 1 (1972): 3-6.

Suggests that teachers have a negative attitude toward gifted students.

800. Jenkinson, Josephine C. "Correlates of sociometric status among TMR children in regular classrooms," American Journal of Mental Deficiency 88 No. 3 (1983): 332-35.

Describes attitudes of parents, teachers and students toward mainstreamed handicapped students.

801. Johnston, William. A study to determine teacher attitude toward teaching special children with regular children. 1972. ERIC ED 065 950.

Teachers were amazed at the achievement levels of handicapped students.

802. Karper, William B. & Martinek, Thomas J. "The differential influence of instructional factors on motor performance among handicapped and non-handicapped children in mainstreamed physical education classes," Educational Research Quarterly 8 No. 3 (1983): 40-46.

Describes perceptions of teachers toward the behaviors and motivations of handicapped and non-handicapped students.

803. Keilbaugh, William S. "Attitudes of classroom teachers toward their visually handicapped students," Journal of Visual Impairment and Blindness 71 No. 10 (1977): 430-434.

Describes teachers' attitudes toward integration of visually handicapped students into regular classrooms.

804. Kelly, Thomas J. & others. "Behavioral disorders: teachers' perceptions," Exceptional Children 43 No. 5 (1977): 316-318.

Describes teachers' perceptions of and attitudes toward students with behavior disorders.

805. King, F.M. "Teacher attitudes toward acceleration," Education 88 No. 3 (1969): 203-207.

Describes teachers' positive attitudes toward the degree of original and independent work of students in accelerated secondary classes; teachers report spending extra time preparing class work for accelerated students.

806. Korynta, Carol Senger. Teacher attitudes toward the gifted: a survey of Grand Forks elementary schools.

Ed.D. dissertation. University of North Dakota. 1982.

Describes fewer stereotypical ideas about gifted children among teachers who have participated in inservice programs concerning gifted students and teachers assigned to schools with such programs than among other teachers.

807. Krebs, Richard L. "Teacher perceptions of children's moral behavior," Psychology in the Schools 6 (1969): 394-395.

Teachers perceive girls as more moral than boys but see no difference on cheating; the important test for teachers is actual student behavior.

808. Krenkel, Noele. Teacher attitude and interaction with gifted culturally different children. Ed.D. dissertation. University of Southern California. 1980.

Describes differences in teachers' attitudes and different patterns of behaviors toward gifted students depending upon teachers' attitudes.

809. Lamb, Pose. Attitudes of selected elementary teachers toward non-standard black dialect. AERA presentation. 1975. ERIC ED 106 379.

Describes attitudes of some elementary teachers toward non-standard black dialect and children who speak it.

810. Leach, David. "Teachers' perceptions and "problem" pupils," Educational Review 9 No 3 (1977): 188-203.

Presents teachers' perceptions of student behavior compared with actual student behavior.

811. LeBoef, Rodney Earl. An assessment of the effectiveness of a selected Texas independent school district curriculum council as perceived by classroom teachers and administrators of the district. Ed.D. dissertation. Texas A & M University. 1979.

Study found differences between administrators and teachers and by grade level of teachers in their views of effectiveness of the curriculum council; administrators saw the council as having a greater effect, teacher views were greater for elementary than senior and junior high school teachers.

812. Levine, Elinor R. What teachers expect of children from single-parent families. ERIC ED 219 692.

Describes teachers' negative attitudes toward or lower expectations for students from single-parent families.

813. Levitin, Teresa E. & Chananie, J.D. "Responses of female primary school teachers to sex-typed behaviors in male and female children," Child Development 43 No. 4 (1972): 1309-1316.

Teachers liked sex-typed behavior; male aggressive/female dependent behaviors were judged to be typical.

814. Lindsey, Jimmy D. & Frith, Greg H. Detrimental student behaviors as perceived by elementary teachers," Education 103 No. 3 (1983): 306-08.

Describes teachers' attitudes toward disruptive behavior; aggressive actions are viewed as the most disruptive of instruction.

815. Little, Linda F. & Thompson, Rock. "Truancy: how parents and teachers contribute," School Counselor 30 No. 4 (1983): 285-91.

Describes attitudes of parents and teachers toward habitually truant students; parents and teachers were overprotective and teachers rejective of such students.

816. McCullough, Michele Page. Teachers' knowledge of and attitudes toward black English and correction of dialect-related reading miscues. Ph.D. dissertation. University of Michigan. 1981.

Reports a relationship between teachers' attitude toward, but not knowledge about, black English and correction of student miscues related to dialectic differences between black and standard English.

817. McCurdy, Sarabeth H. A study of relationships between goals for the teaching of literature and teachers' attitudes towards the major categories of written student responses to literature. Florida State University. 1975. ERIC ED 117 755.

Describes English teachers' attitudes toward student responses to literature read in the classroom.

818. McGee, Rob & others. "Parents and teachers perceptions of behavior problems in seven year old

children," Exceptional Child 30 No. 2 (1982): 151-61.

Describes attitudes of teachers and parents toward childrens' behavior problems and the causes of the problems.

819. MacMillan, Donald L., Meyers, C. Edward & Yoshida, Roland K. "Regular class teachers' perceptions of transition programs for EMR students and their impact on the students," Psychology in the Schools 15 (1978): 99-103.

Teachers percieved decertified (former special education) students as having lower ability and achievement than regular students in low ability classes; saw no change in the instructional program when such students entered class; saw little or no support services.

820. McPartland, James & others. Student participation in high school decisions. A study of students and teachers in fourteen urban high schools. Summary and excerpts. Center for Study of Social Organization of Schools. Johns Hopkins University. Baltimore. 1971. ERIC ED 073 017.

Describes attitudes of students and teachers toward student involvement in school decisionmaking.

821. Martinek, Thomas J. & Karper, William B. "Multivariate relationships of specific impressions cues with teacher expectations and dyadic interactions in elementary physical education classes," Research Quarterly for Exercise and Sport 55 No. 1 (1984): 32-40.

Describes teachers' perceptions of and attitudes toward elementary students as associated with student characteristics, e.g. attractiveness.

822. Martins, Nelson Dias. The relationship between Portuguese bilingual/ESL teacher competency needs and attitude toward and knowledge of handicapped children. Ph.D. dissertation. University of Connecticut. 1982.

Reports that teachers' demographic characteristics had a stronger relationship to teachers' perceived competency needs than did teachers' attitudes.

823. Matthews, Horace. Attitudes and classroom behaviors of Virginia middle school English teachers

regarding black English and certain other usages. Ed.D. dissertation. University of Virginia. 1980.

Describes differences in teachers' attitudes by teaching location toward black English and less positive attitudes toward black English than toward other non-standard English usage.

824. Mazer, Gilbert E. "Effects of social-class stereotyping on teacher expectation," Psychology in the Schools 8 No. 4 (1971): 373-378.

Reports that teachers see differences between the behavior patterns of lower and middle class students.

825. Medway, Frederic J. "Causal attributions for school-related problems; teacher perceptions and teacher feedback," Journal of Educational Psychology 11 (1979): 809-818.

Teachers see students rather than teachers as responsible for student behavior problems and students who are perceived as lacking motivation are criticized more than those who are perceived to be motivated.

826. Metalitz, Beatrice R. A comparison of teacher attitude toward two methods of identifying children with learning problems; informal observation and structured observation. Ph.D. dissertation. Walden University. 1976.

Kindergarten teachers believe they can identify children with learning disabilities with informal observation as well as they can with structured observation techniques.

827. Milburn, Joanne Fellows. Special education and regular class teacher attitudes regarding social behaviors of children: steps toward development of a social skills curriculum. Ph.D. dissertation. Ohio State University. 1974.

Describes teachers' attitudes toward student social behaviors; reports some differences between special education and regular classroom teachers.

828. Miller, Arten & Asher, William. "Gender differences as a factor in teachers' perceptions of students: a comment," Perceptual and Motor Skills 56 No. 3 (1983): 856-58.

Reports that teachers' perceptions of students are biased by student sex.

829. Minner, Sam. "The influence of educational labels and behavioral descriptions on secondary vocational educators," Journal for Vocational Special Needs Education 4 No. 2 (1982): 4, 7.

Reports that teachers viewed as less competent a student labelled as handicapped than a regular student.

830. Moore, Helen A. "Hispanic women: schooling for conformity in public education," Hispanic Journal of Behavioral Sciences 5 No. 1 (1983): 45-63.

Describes teachers as perceiving assertiveness and leadership as related to educational success.

831. Myers, Betty & others. Perceived problems of teachers of reading: fact and paradox. 1975. ERIC ED 167 951.

Describes teachers' perceptions of the frequency of occurrence and degree of difficulty of reading problems.

832. Nabors, Pearlie Profit. The attitude of Louisiana elementary school teachers toward promotion and nonpromotion as a factor in raising the reading and mathematical achievement level of elementary school pupils. Ed.D. dissertation. Northeast Louisiana University. 1983.

Describes differences in achievement levels of promoted and nonpromoted students and describes the attitudes of teachers toward the nonpromotion of students.

833. Natriello, Gary & Dornbusch, Sanford M. Academic instruction of behavior control: an experimental study of teacher responses to classroom problems. 1980. ERIC ED 209 337.

Reports that teachers identified more and more important standards for student social behavior, behavior that did not disrupt the classroom, than academic behavior that indicated failure to learn.

834. Nelson, Jack L. Ideological dimensions of political restraint and censorship. ERIC ED 225 928.

Describes views of teachers and teacher education students about academic freedom and censorship.

835. Nelson-Le Gall, Sharon & Scott-Jones Diane. Teachers and young childrens perceptions of task persistence. ERIC ED 230 278.

Describes teachers' and students' views of student task persistence and the student characteristics associated with persistence.

836. Neumann, Karl F. & others. Factor analysis of student learning styles. APA presentation. 1978. ERIC ED 167 853.

Presents teachers' preceptions that students group themselves in four learning styles: rigid-inhibited, undisciplined, acceptance-anxious and creative.

837. Nicely, Robert F., Jr. & others. "Teachers attitudes toward gifted children and programs--implications for instructional leadership," Education 101 (1980): 12-15.

Reports that teachers with greater knowledge of gifted students and special programs for gifted students are more receptive to having such students in their classes than teachers with more limited knowledge.

838. Pagen, John. Teacher and student attitude interactions and their effects in a program for the culturally deprived. Ed.D. dissertation. Wayne State University. 1967.

Describes a disparity between students' and teachers' perceptions of student self concept.

839. Palmer, Douglas J. "Regular classroom teachers' attributions and instructional prescriptions for handicapped and non-handicapped pupils," Journal of Special Education 13 No. 3 (1979): 325-337.

Describes teachers' attributions and educational prescriptions for normal, educational handicapped and retarded pupils.

840. Parish, Thomas & others. "Stereotypes concerning normal and handicapped children," Journal of Psychology 102 (1979): 63-70.

Describes attitudes of teachers toward a number of labels for students.

841. Pellegreno, Dominick D. & Williams, Wendell C. "Teacher perceptions and classroom verbal interaction," Elementary School Guidance and Counseling 7 No. 4 (1973): 270-275.

Teachers' perceptions of students' roles are related to teachers' interactions with students.

842. Peterson, H.A. "Teacher and peer acceptance of four student behavior types," _California Journal of Educational Research_ _19_ _No. 1_ (1968): 16-27.

Describes differences in teachers' attitudes toward secondary students classified as adaptive academic, adaptive social, maladaptive active and maladaptive passive, with most positive teacher responses toward students in the first category.

843. Peterson, Sarah & Ayabe, Carol. Kindergarten entrance age requirements: Mesa Public Schools research and evaluation technical memo. _ERIC ED_ 231 520.

Describes teachers' attitudes toward early entry to kindergarten; teachers are opposed.

844. Pflaum, Susanna W. & others. "The influence of pupil behaviors and pupil status factors on teacher behaviors during oral reading lessons," _Journal of Educational Research_ _74_ _No. 2_ (1980): 99-105.

Reports that teachers respond more to student behaviors than to student status characteristics in reacting to students during oral reading lessons.

845. Powers, Shirley Gloria. Orientation of school administrators, classroom teachers, and community members toward gifted and non-gifted students' attributes in relation to methods of evaluating achievement. Ph.D. dissertation. American University. 1980.

Describes attitudes of three groups toward gifted, reporting an attitude that at the secondary level no distinctions should be made in the scholastic level of courses.

846. Prawat, Richard S. & Jarvis, Robert. "Gender differences as a factor in teachers' perceptions of students," _Journal of Educational Psychology_ _72_ (1980): 743-749.

Reports that teachers' assessments of students were more related to student achievement than students' sex.

847. Price, Nora Wright. Elementary school teachers' perceptions of responsible and irresponsible behavior in children. Ph.D. dissertation. University of Alabama. 1967.

Describes teachers' perceptions of a responsible child; has good work habits, tries, shares, is helpful, uses time wisely and lives up to group standards.

848. Prowst, Richard S. "Teacher perceptions of student affect," _American Educational Research Journal 17 No. 1_ (1980): 61-73. Research Series No. 44. Institute for Research on Teaching. Michigan State University. 1979. _ERIC ED_ 173 326.

Describes teachers' descriptions of classroom events related to student affective and noncognitive behavior in terms of interpersonal and intrapersonal adjustment and individuals versus groups.

849. Reiser, Ann Lea. A descriptive study of classroom teachers' perspectives of students experiencing difficulties in reading. Ph.D. dissertation. Michigan State University. 1979.

Describes perceptions of teachers of students with reading difficulties and of the teacher's role and responses to students.

850. Reynolds, Bill J. & others. "Elementary teachers' attitudes toward mainstreaming educable mentally retarded students," _Education and Training of the Mentally Retarded 17 No. 3_ (1982): 171-76.

Describes positive attitudes of teachers toward mainstreamed students and no relationship between the attitudes and teachers' characteristics, e.g., years of experience and experience with mainstreamed students.

851. Richey, Linda S. & others. Teachers' attitudes and expectations for siblings of learning disabled children. 1980. _ERIC ED_ 203 613.

Reports that teachers expected the siblings of learning disabled students to have lower achievement and more classroom behavior problems than other students.

852. Robinson, Linwood. Selected correlates of teachers' attitudes toward minority-group students in urban classrooms. Ph.D. dissertation. University of Connecticut. 1979.

Reports differences in teachers' attitudes and teachers' characteristics and teaching preferences but no differences related to teachers' training or characteristics of the classroom.

853. Roper, Birdie Alexander. School desegregation and teacher attitudes toward the nonstandard black

dialect. Ph.D. dissertation. Claremont Graduate School. 1980.

Describes no differences in attitudes toward the non-standard dialect of black pupils among teachers in integrated and predominantly black schools.

854. Roscoe, Bruce Kraig. Attitudes of regular classroom teachers toward the integration of students with visual impairments into regular education programs. Ph.D. dissertation. University of North Carolina at Greensboro. 1980.

Describes attitudes of regular classroom teachers toward visually impaired students, favoring integration into regular classrooms but different standards of performance.

855. Roubinek, Darrell LeRoy. A comparison of the attitudes of elementary school teachers and school psychologists toward the behavior of elementary school children. Ed.D. dissertation. Oklahoma State University. 1971.

Describes a change in teachers' attitudes toward problem children, with a greater concern for aggressive behavior than in 1928; school psychologists' attitudes have become more like teachers'.

856. Rubenzer, Ronald L. & Twaite, James A. "Attitudes of 1,200 educators toward the education of the gifted and talented: implications for teacher preparation," _Journal for the Education of the Gifted_ _2_ _No. 4_ (1979): 202-213.

Describes teachers' attitudes toward education of gifted children and perceptions of the characteristics of such children.

857. Rubin, Rosalyn A. & Balow, Bruce. "Prevalence of teacher identified behavior problems: a longitudinal study," _Exceptional Children_ _45_ _No. 2_ (1978): 102-111.

Presents teachers' ratings of behavior of students across the grades from kindergarten to grade 6.

858. Russell, Alan & Lin, Low Guat. "Teacher attention and classroom behavior," _Exceptional Child_ _24_ _No. 3_ (1977): 148-155.

Describes teachers' responses to the best and worst behavior of seventh grade students.

859. Schanberger, Mary C. An investigation of interrelationships of ratings by classroom teachers and school psychologists of selected physical, learning, and behavioral characteristics of children. Ed.D. dissertation. University of Maryland. 1967.

Did not find extensive agreement between teachers and school psychologists in evaluation of behavior of students.

860. Schlosser, Linda & Algozzine, Bob. "Sex, behavior, and teacher expectancies," Journal of Experimental Education 48 (1980): 231-236.

Reports that teachers viewed less favorably behavior exhibited by boys or girls that is associated with the other sex, based on teachers' responses to descriptions of student behavior.

861. Schwartz, Ruth Roth. A study of the handling of verbal nonstandard grammar by English teachers in an innercity secondary school. Columbia University. 1974. ERIC ED 113 753.

Presents teachers' reactions to student non-standard dialect - reactions differed for oral and written student responses.

862. Scott, Marvin B. "The effect of teacher perception of personality factors on the cognitive and affective learning of black students," Journal of Negro Education 45 (1976): 89-93.

Describes students' personality factors rated important by groups of white and black teachers and students in a teacher education program.

863. Scott, Marvin B. & Ntegeye, Margaret Gibbs. "Acceptance of minority student personality characteristics by black and white teachers," Integrated Education 18 (1980): 110-112.

Describes differences in teachers' assessments of the personality characteristics and behaviors of disadvantaged students in urban schools.

864. Sherwood, Charles F. A paradigm for teacher education in reading instruction based upon the perceptions of selected elementary teachers in Dade County, Florida. 1972. ERIC ED 078 355.

Describes no differences in the attitudes of teachers teaching white, black and Cuban students but teachers of black students report a greater need to understand the emotional development of their students.

865. Sherwood, Charles F. The effect of faculty desegregation on teachers' attitudes toward their pupils. 1972. <u>ERIC ED</u> 086 710.

No difference found in teachers' attitudes toward students whether teaching in a segregated or desegregated faculty.

866. Shiver, Denise Eva. Attitudes of preservice and inservice teachers toward gifted, handicapped, gifted-handicapped, and normal students and the relationship to personal and professional belief systems. Ph.D. dissertation. Texas A & M University. 1981.

Describes attitudes of teachers toward classes of students as related to aspects of teacher personality; teachers have more negative attitudes toward handicapped than toward gifted students.

867. Silverman, Ellen-Marie & Van Opens, Katherine. "An investigation of sex-bias in classroom teachers' speech and language referrals," <u>Language, Speech and Hearing Services in the Schools 11</u> (1980): 169-174.

Describes differences in teachers' willingness to refer students for speech and language problems based on sex of the student.

868. Simmons, Barbara. "Sex role expectations of classroom teachers," <u>Education 100</u> (1980): 249-53.

Reports that teachers report different expectations for the behaviors of boys and girls, with boys expected to exhibit more aggressive behavior and girls more emotional behavior.

869. Smart, Rosemary & others. "Teacher factors and special class placement," <u>Journal of Special Education 14</u> (1980): 217-229.

Describes attitudes of regular classroom teachers toward mainstreaming and handicapped students and relates those attitudes to teachers' characterstics.

870. Smith, Waldran P. The attitudes and beliefs of teachers concerning the education of American Indian children in the Southwest. American Indian Education Papers. No. 1. Department of Anthropology. Arizona University. Tucson. 1970. <u>ERIC ED</u> 051 957.

Describes the attitudes of teachers toward the education of Indian children.

871. Solano, Cecelia H. Teacher and pupil stereotypes of gifted boys and girls. APA presentation. 1976. ERIC ED 137 667.

Stereotypes indicated that gifted boys were positively viewed, gifted girls negatively viewed; views changed with contact for girls, not much change when information alone was presented to teachers.

872. Stake, Jayne E. & Katz, Jonathan F. "Teacher-pupil relationships in the elementary school classroom: teacher-gender differences," American Educational Research Journal 19 No. 3 (1982): 465-71.

Reports that male and female teachers respond differently toward and have different attitudes toward male and female students.

873. Starks, Mary Louse. Classroom problem behavior: teachers' and pupils' perceptions. Ph.D. dissertation. University of Michigan. 1974.

Describes elementary teachers' and students' views of classroom behavior problems; students viewed their own behavior as teachers viewed it, but saw that behavior as not as serious.

874. Stone, Brenda G. "Relationship between creativity and classroom behavior," Psychology in the Schools 17 (1980): 106-108.

Reports no relationship between student scores on a measure of creativity and classroom misbehavior as reported by teachers and other students.

875. Stone, Samantha J. A study of teacher attitudes that affect the quality of education for exceptional students. Ed.D. dissertation. University of Tennessee. 1980.

Describes teachers' attitudes toward handicapped students, with more positive attitudes associated with age and more teaching experience; teachers generally viewed themselves as not adequately trained to work with handicapped students.

876. Tanners, Henry. Teachers' perceptions of children's behavior as important for referral to school psychologists. Ph.D. dissertation. University of Iowa. 1972.

Some consistency across grades, students' sex and school in the factors that teachers report cause them to make a referral to a school psychologist.

877. Taylor, Ronald L. & others. "The effects of labels and assigned attributes on teacher perceptions of academic and social behavior," _Education and Training of the Mentally Retarded_ _18_ (1983): 45-51.

Describes differences in teachers' attitudes toward students associated with the labels assigned to the students.

878. Thomas, Clifton D., Jr. A study of teacher-pupil attitudes and the impact such relationships have on academic proficiency. Ph.D. dissertation. University of Southern Mississippi. 1972.

Reports that teachers' image of the ideal student is relatively stable and not related to the grades assigned to actual students.

879. Thurlow, Martha L. Criteria for identifying LD students: definitional problems exemplified. _ERIC ED_ 236 841.

Describes teachers' agreement and disagreement with criteria used to define learning disabled students.

880. Thurman, Richard L. & others. "An analysis of teacher rating differences between first-grade and mentally retarded children: were expectancy biases involved?" _Educational Research Quarterly_ _7_ _No. 1_ (1982): 7-14.

Describes special education teachers as rating their students lower in mathematical ability than did regular classroom teachers.

881. Tisdale, Pamela C. & Flower, Robert E. Incidence of behavior disorders in children in South Carolina: teachers' perceptions. 1980. _ERIC ED_ 198 085.

Describes teachers' perceptions of the frequency of behavior disordered children within their classes; teachers perceived that the needs of those children, and of the teachers who worked with those children, were not being met.

882. Touliatos, John, & Lindholm, Byron W. "Teachers' perceptions of behavior problems in children from intact, single parent, and stepparent families," _Psychology in the Schools_ _17_ (1980): 264-269.

Reports that teachers perceive that students from homes with different patterns of families, e.g., single-parents, had different patterns of behavior adjustment or behavior problems.

883. Trenholm, Sarah & Rose, Toby. "The compliant communicator: teacher perceptions of appropriate classroom behavior," Western Journal of Speech Communication 45 No. 1 (1981): 13-26.

Describes teachers' views of students' behavior associated with students' communication competencies.

884. Vaac, Nicholas A. & Kirst, Nancy. "Emotionally disturbed children and regular classroom teachers," Elementary School Journal 77 (1977): 309-317.

Describes attitudes of regular elementary teachers toward emotionally disturbed children; they should be taught in special classes, are not acceptable to other children and would have a negative effect on the classroom program.

885. Von Rosenberg, Barbara. Perceptions of teachers concerning competencies and related needs for integration of special education students into the regular classroom. Ed.D. dissertation. Baylor University. 1979.

Describes competencies viewed as important by teachers and resource room teachers for classroom teachers who are integrating special education students into their classrooms - different views of each group; teachers need more training in several aspects.

886. Washington, Valora. "Racial differences in teacher perceptions of first and fourth grade pupils on selected characteristics," Journal of Negro Education 51 No. 1 (1982): 60-72.

Reports that black and white teachers perceive black students more negatively than they do white students.

887. Weathers, Janet Lynn. The effect of assertive communication and presence of audience on students' and teachers' perceptions of the rules which should guide a student in a disagreement with a teacher. Ph.D. dissertation. University of Southern California. 1979.

Describes attitudes of teachers and students toward student behavior when the student disagrees with the teacher.

888. Webb, J. "What do teachers think of teaching," _Illinois Education_ _54_ (1966): 313.

Describes responses of a sample of teachers of gifted students toward professional attitudes and aspects of teaching.

889. Wechsler, Henry, Suarez, Amorita C. & McFadden, Mary. "Teachers' attitudes toward the education of physically handicapped children: implications for the implementation of Massachusetts chapter 766," _Journal of Education_ _157_ (1975): 17-24.

Describes attitude of teachers toward handicapped children and the degree of success expected from integration into regular class as related to the degree of the child's handicap, with more positive attitudes from teachers with experience teaching handicapped students.

890. Weinberg, Dorothe R. Teachers' perceptions of students: traditional, progressive, and emerging communal orientations. APA presentation. 1977. _ERIC ED_ 148 972.

Teachers' perceptions of students were related to teaching location; older teachers had more traditional, suburban teachers had more progressive, inner city teachers had more communal perceptions.

891. West, Mina Georgi. Is the learning disabilities label a biasing factor in teachers' perceptions? 1980. _ERIC ED_ 188 425.

Reports no observed differences in the classroom behavior of learning disabled and other students and no bias in the reported attitudes of teachers toward those mainstreamed students.

892. White, Amos J.J., Jr. A study of student and teacher perceptions as resources for curriculum development. Ph.D. dissertation. Ohio State University. 1978.

Students' perceptions of student needs are related to teachers' perceptions of student needs.

893. White, Regina Mandel & others. "An investigation of responsible versus less responsible students," _Illinois School Research and Development_ _19_ _No. 1_ (1982): 18-25.

Reports that teachers perceive as more responsible those students who behave in ways teachers find acceptable and follow teachers' directions.

894. White, W.F. Affective dimensions of teachers of disadvantaged children in six majority Negro school districts. 1969. ERIC ED 028 833.

Describes teachers' attitudes toward children and toward themselves as teachers of disadvantaged children.

895. Wong, Morrison G. "Model students? teachers' perceptions and expectations of their Asian and white students," Sociology of Education 53 (1980): 236-247.

Reports differences in teachers' attitudes toward and expectations for the achievement of Asian and white students, with higher expectations for Asian students.

896. Ysseldyke, James E. An analysis of current practice in referring students for psychoeducational evaluation: implications for change. ERIC ED 228 823.

Reports the factors which teachers consider in referring students for evaluation and teachers, attributions of causation relative to student problems.

897. Ysseldyke, James E. Classroom teachers attributions for students exhibiting different behaviors. ERIC ED 236 848.

Describes teachers' perceptions of students who are exhibiting behavior problems and teachers' attributions of causes for those behaviors.

898. Zucker, Martine & Snoddy, James E. "Needs, attitudes and behaviors of teachers relative to stress situations of children," Journal of Alcohol and Drug Education 28 No. 1 (1982): 32-42. ERIC ED 181 009.

Reports that elementary teachers are aware of the stresses and conflicts in the home lives of their students but feel that they have little training in how to intervene.

IV. ATTITUDES TOWARD TEACHING

899. Adams, Ronald D. & Martray, Carl R. Correlates of teacher perceived problems. 1980. <u>ERIC</u> <u>ED</u> 195 567.

Describes problems that teachers report encountering, related to their teaching and professional roles, during the first several years of teaching.

900. Adams, Ronald D. & Martray, Carl. Teacher development: a study of factors related to teacher concerns for pre, beginning, and experienced teaching. <u>ERIC</u> <u>ED</u> 200 591.

Describes teachers' concerns about teaching as varying by teaching level, experience and personality characteristics and concerns are related to others' perceptions of teachers' effectiveness.

901. Alday, Armando Cruz. Patterns of attitudes, perceptions, and behaviors among junior high school teachers participating in a strike. Ph.D. dissertation. University of Arizona. 1981.

Describes teachers' attitudes toward a strike in one school district, including attitudes toward other strikers, the administration, the causes of the strike, and teacher professionalism.

902. Algozzine, Bob. Teachers intervention choices for children exhibiting different behaviors in school. <u>ERIC</u> <u>ED</u> 224 192.

Describes teachers' attitudes toward student misbehavior and preferences for interventions which directly involve teachers.

903. Anders, Patricia L. & Mitchell, Judy Nichols. Comparing elementary and secondary teachers: reading attitudes, awareness, and abilities.

National Reading Conference presentation. 1978. _ERIC_ _ED_ 166 666.

Describes similarities and differences in elementary and secondary teachers' attitudes toward reading instruction, reading habits and willingness to teach reading.

904. Anderson, Harry E. & others. Relative importance of reading readiness factors as perceived by various teacher groups. 1967. _ERIC_ _ED_ 015 106.

Describes differences among elementary, secondary and non-teachers in ranking factors they consider important to reading readiness.

905. Anderson, James G. Teachers of minority groups: the origins of their attitudes and instructional practices. New Mexico State University. Las Cruces. 1969. _ERIC_ _ED_ 026 192.

Presents results of a questionnaire given to math teachers identifying their views on compensatory education, bilingual education, student ability and effort and type of students they enjoy teaching; responses were related to type of professional training.

906. Anemoyanis, Vivian K. Teachers' attitudes toward the Aspira consent decree and perceptions of teachers and supervisors of teachers' classroom behavior in bilingual and non-bilingual programs. Ph.D. dissertation. Fordham University. 1979.

Presents teachers' attitudes toward the bilingual education requirement and finds no difference in descriptions by bilingual and non-bilingual teachers of their teaching behavior.

907. Appleberry, James B. & Hoy, Wayne K. "The pupil control ideology of professional personnel in 'open' and 'closed' elementary schools," _Educational_ _Administration_ _Quarterly_ _5_ (1969): 74-85.

Finds differences in pupil control ideology; teachers in open schools are more humanistic than teachers in closed schools.

908. Arth, Alfred A. & others. Seeking the profile of an elementary educator: phase III. 1971. _ERIC_ _ED_ 086 659.

Reports a finding of different personality and belief variables among elementary, middle and secondary teachers.

909. Ashton, Patricia T. A study of teachers' sense of efficacy. *ERIC ED* 231 833.

Describes teachers' attitudes toward their effects on student learning and the effects of aspects of the teaching situation that influence their sense of efficacy.

910. Ashton, Patricia T. A study of teachers' sense of efficacy: final report volume I. *ERIC ED* 231 834.

Describes teachers' attitudes toward teaching and their sense of the extent to which they can influence student learning.

911. Ashton, Patricia T. A study of teachers' sense of efficacy: final report volume II. *ERIC ED* 231 835.

Describes attitudes of teachers with a high and low sense of efficacy and presents data collection instruments.

912. Austin, Erma Jewel Miller. Attitudes toward and participation in in-service education in the state of Oklahoma. Ed.D. dissertation. Oklahoma State University. 1981.

Describes limited teacher involvement in but considerable interest in involvement in planning for inservice education, and teachers' attitudes toward aspects of inservice education.

913. Awender, Michael A. "Teachers and decisions," *Alberta Journal of Educational Research 26* (1980): 113-119.

Reports that teachers perceive that they have limited involvement in school decision making and would like to be consulted about specific types of decisions, e.g., curriculum, discipline, home-school relations.

914. Baca, Joseph Donald. A comparison study of differences in perception of Mexican American students between Anglo and Mexican American secondary school teachers in Dona Ana County (New Mexico). 1972 *ERIC ED* 065 218.

Presents differences in teachers' attitudes toward Mexican American students by teachers' ethnic background.

915. Baer, G. Thomas & others. "Middle grade reading instruction: preferences and grouping practices," *Clearing House 55 No. 8* (1982): 341-44.

Describes a discrepancy between teachers' perceptions of ideal teaching behavior and their actual teaching behavior.

916. Baker, Eva L. "Reinforcers for teacher behavior reported in cued and uncued situations," *Journal of Teacher Education* *22* (1971): 205-209.

Describes teachers' reports about types of district actions which would result in teachers implementing new behaviors which take increased work; fewer and/or smaller classes, clerical assistance, more money, released time.

917. Balderson, James H. The bureaucratization of teacher behavior scale and the measurement of school organizational structure. AERA presentation. 1977. *ERIC ED* 139 841.

Teacher behaviors combine bureaucratic and professional input, based on results of a self-report questionnaire.

918. Barber, Patricia Ann. Job satisfaction of elementary and secondary teachers. Ed.D. dissertation. Rutgers University. 1980.

More experienced and elementary teachers had higher job satisfaction than secondary and less experienced teachers; intrinsic factors were more influential than extrinsic factors in teacher job satisfaction.

919. Barrick, Joan T. Current usage of microcomputers in the Oklahoma public school classroom as perceived by teachers. Ed.D. dissertation. Oklahoma State University. 1983.

Reports that most teachers were not using microcomputers but that the majority had a favorable attitude toward their use and were interested in learning to use them.

920. Bean, Thomas W. "Can we update experienced teachers' beliefs and practices in reading?" *Reading Horizons* *20* (1980): 183-187.

Reports that teachers enrolled in a graduate course in psycholinguistics change their attitudes toward aspects of reading instruction and reported changes in teaching practices.

921. Beckerman, Marvin M. The relationship between selected characteristics of teachers and attitudes toward educational innovations. Ph.D. dissertation. Syracuse University. 1971.

Describes generally accepting attitude of teachers toward educational innovations - not related to background characteristics.

922. Behrens, Katherine A.M. Perceptions of principals, resource room teachers and regular class teachers regarding mainstreaming the hearing impaired. Ph.D. dissertation. Fordham University. 1979.

Describes attitudes of the three groups of educators toward mainstreaming and the teacher skills necessary for successful instruction.

923. Bennett, Clifford T. "Citizenship traditions in the Commonwealth of Virginia," _Journal of Social Studies Research 4_ (1980): 17-21.

Reports that teachers did not have a strong sense of the purpose and goals of social studies instruction and the appropriate content for elementary social studies.

924. Bentz, W. Kenneth, Hollister, William G. & Edgerton, J. Wilbert. "An assessment of the mental health of teachers: a comparative analysis," _Psychology in the Schools 8_ (1971): 72-76.

Describes the mental health of teachers in comparison with community leaders and finds that teachers as a group have a high level of mental health.

925. Berg, Roger. "Resisting changes: what the literature says about computers in the social studies classroom," _Social Education 47 No. 5_ (1983): 314-16.

Reports that teachers have concerns about the use of computers in the classroom and the inadequacy of the teachers' training.

926. Besag, Frank. "Professional characteristics and attitudes of teachers: sex, race, and teaching area differences," _Urban Education 5 No. 3_ (1970): 268-286.

Describes teachers' attitudes and differences by sex, race and teaching areas.

927. Biklen, Sari Knopp. Autonomy in the lives of women elementary schoolteachers. _ERIC ED_ 215 964.

Describes the attitudes of female elementary teachers toward teaching as a profession, teaching in their school, and the attitudes of parents towards teachers.

928. Biklen, Sari Knopp. Teaching as an occupation for women: a case study of an elementary school. ERIC ED 234 049.

Describes the attitudes of female teachers toward their work, teaching as a career and teaching as it affects the rest of their lives.

929. Bitter, Gary G. "Calculator teacher attitudes improved through inservice education," School Science and Mathematics 80 No. 4 (1980): 323-26.

Reports that teachers expressed more positive attitudes toward the use of calculators in mathematics classes after participating in an inservice workshop on the use of calculators.

930. Blackbourn, Richard. The relationship between teachers' perceptions of supervisory behaviors and their attitudes toward the supervisory conference following classroom observation. ERIC ED 242 076.

Describes teachers' attitudes toward evaluation and toward supervisory conferences; principal's behavior as collaborative or directive had the strongest influence on attitude.

931. Blaga, Jeffrey James. A study of teachers' perceptions and utilization of simulations in public secondary social studies classrooms in Ohio. Ph.D. dissertation. Ohio State University. 1978.

Describes teachers' attitudes toward and use of simulation techniques.

932. Blase, Joseph J. "Teachers' perceptions of moral guidance," Clearing House 56 No. 9: 389-93.

Reports that teachers view their teaching responsibilities to include providing for student moral education.

933. Bloom, Robert B. "Morally speaking, who are today's teachers?" Phi Delta Kappan 57 (1976): 624-625.

Describes responses of black and white teachers toward values instruments, with black teachers exhibiting stronger traditional American values than white teachers, such as courage, honesty, independence.

934. Boag, Noel & Massey, Don. "Teacher perspectives on program change," Theory and Research in Social Education 9 No. 3 (1981): 37-59.

Describes the attitudes and perceptions of two teachers as they implement a new social studies curriculum.

935. Boger, R.P. Head Start teachers' ethnic group membership and attitude toward child behavior, some relationships. 1967. ERIC ED 011 884.

Negro and Mexican-American teachers were more positive in their attitude about the possibilities of Head Start: Anglo teachers were less dominative and authoritarian toward the children than were Mexican-American teachers.

936. Bond, Carole L. & Dietrich, Amy. Survey of teacher attitudes toward the role of the resource program. ERIC ED 221 988.

Describes regular classroom teachers as believing that communication with resource teachers about handicapped students was important but as less willing to take responsibility for such communication.

937. Boyd, Jillian Rae. Sexuality attitudes of Iowa secondary teachers. Ph.D. dissertation. Iowa State University. 1981.

Describes teachers' attitudes toward their own sexuality (positive), toward their ability to teach about sexuality (positive) and toward district support for teaching about sexuality (negative).

938. Broaden, Shirley Mae. The allocation of instructional time to students in elementary schools that seek to individualize instruction. 1980. ERIC ED 193 229.

Within a study of teachers' instructional decisions and allocation of instructional resources, describes teachers' perceptions of students and the relationship of those perceptions to instructional decisions.

939. Brown, Cynthia Gruber. Attitudes: propensity to exit by teacher type in a large urban school district. Ph.D. dissertation. University of California. Los Angeles. 1983.

Describes differences among teachers who remain in teaching and those who leave associated with demographic characteristics and attitude toward aspects of teaching assignments.

940. Bruner, Anna L. Stress producing conditions in the secondary classroom. ERIC ED 213 699.

Describes the attitudes of secondary teachers toward aspects of their work environment, e.g., administrative support for discipline, the amount of paperwork, the frequency of interruptions of instructional activities.

941. Bruner, Anna L. & Felder, B. Dell. "Problems teachers encounter: how difficult is teaching? what is the principal's role?" NASSP Bulletin 67 No. 461 68-72.

Describes the problems that teachers believe cause stress, including classroom management and administrator inefficiency.

942. Buchmann, Margret. Justification in teacher thinking: an analysis of interview data. ERIC ED 228 193.

Describes the attitudes of elementary teachers toward the school day, their role in the classroom, and their perceptions of affective teaching.

943. Buczek, Michael Leon. The effects of reduced class size on pupil attitudes, pupil self-concept, and teacher morale. Ph.D. dissertation. University of Toledo. 1981.

Reports no differences in teachers' morale between teachers with twenty-five or more students and teachers with fifteen or fewer students.

944. Burcham, Stanley Preston. Job attitudes of teachers with coaching and non-coaching responsibilities in selected school districts in the state of Illinois. Ph.D. dissertation. Southern Illinois University at Carbondale. 1982.

Reports no differences in overall job satisfaction but differences in responses to specific aspects of job satisfaction between teachers with and without coaching responsibilities.

945. Burden, Paul R. Teachers' perceptions of the characteristics and influences on their personal and professional development. 1980. ERIC ED 198 087.

Describes teachers' perceptions of the factors that have influenced the development of their careers, their satisfaction with their career development and the options available to them, and the type of school in which they would like to teach.

946. Burden, Paul R. Personal and professional conflict: stress for teachers. ERIC ED 218 272.

Describes teachers' perceptions of their work environments, teaching careers, and factors associated with stress.

947. Burton, John Robert. Teachers' attitudes toward consumer issues and their appraisal of the educational relevance of these issues. Ph.D. dissertation. University of Connecticut. 1970.

Indicates some differences in teachers' attitudes toward consumer issues by subject field.

948. Butler, August Phillip. A study of teachers' knowledge of and attitudes toward mainstreaming as related to the educational placement of educationally handicapped students within the classroom. Ph.D. dissertation. George Peabody College for Teachers of Vanderbilt University. 1980.

Describes attitudes of regular classroom and physical education teachers toward handicapped children and limited knowledge about such children.

949. Butts, David P. & Raun, Chester E. A study of teacher attitude change. Science Education Center. Texas University. Austin. 1967. ERIC ED 021 806.

Presents teachers' attitude changes when using a new science curriculum; primary teachers change more than intermediate; teachers with little college science change more than those with more; previous teaching experience and school location are not related to changes.

950. Bybee, Rodger W. "Science educators' perceptions of the ideal science teacher," *School Science and Mathematics* *78* (1978): 13-22.

General agreement among male and female elementary and secondary teachers and college science teachers about characteristics of ideal science teacher; describes adequacy of personal relations with students and enthusiasm in working with students as most important qualities.

951. Carlton, P.W. The attitudes of certificated instructional personnel toward professional negotiation and "sanctions". University of Oregon. Eugene. 1967. ERIC ED 014 801.

Males and classroom teachers more favorably inclined than females and principals toward collective bargaining, sanctions and strikes.

952. Carter, Pamela & DiBella, Robert. Follow-up of 1980-81 graduates at the Ohio State University's college of education teachers certification program. Technical report No. 7 ERIC ED 222 462.

Describes attitudes of teachers toward their teacher education program and toward problems encountered in their first year of teaching.

953. Chabassol, D.J. "A comparison of variables which predict success in male teachers at the elementary and secondary levels," Canadian Education and Research Digest 7 (1967): 327-333.

Study found some differences among successful elementary and secondary teachers; elementary teachers were more inhibited, hesitant and reflective, neither group was possessive of students, there was greater hostility among elementary teachers.

954. Chapman, David W. "Career satisfaction of teachers," Educational Research Quarterly 7 No. 3 (1982): 40-50.

Reports that teachers' job satisfaction is related to their sense of personal achievement within their jobs.

955. Choppin, Bruce H. & others. Test use project. ERIC ED 211 593.

Describes teachers' attitudes toward and uses of information from student achievement tests.

956. Clark, William Austin. An identification of the gap between the scientific culture and the humanistic culture in the secondary school. Ph.D. dissertation. University of Connecticut. 1970. ERIC ED 057 039.

Describes differences in attitudes between science and humanities teachers.

957. Clayton, S.C. Sr. Anne M. The relationship between teacher beliefs and classroom evidences of teacher behavior in open education as compared in IGE (Individually Guided Education) and non-IGE schools. Ed.D. dissertation. Rutgers University. 1974.

Compares factors for IGE and non-IGE teachers; beliefs and practices related for non-IGE, no correlation for IGE; years of experience and belief in open education negatively correlated for non-IGE; IGE teachers' beliefs more open than non-IGE.

958. Clifford, George D. A description of teachers' perceptions of critical factors in a change program. Ed.D. dissertation. Temple University. 1982.

Reports differences in perceptions of important aspects of an innovative program between high and low implementors of the program but no association between teachers' demographic characteristics and extent of implementation of the innovative program.

959. Coman, Peter Noel. An examination of the relationship between preferred and observed classroom management behaviors of elementary school teachers. Ed.D. dissertation. University of Houston. 1978.

Reports a relationship between teachers' attitudes toward and use of management behavior in the classroom.

960. Cookson, Peter W., Jr. The educational attitudes of private school educators. 1980. ERIC ED 201 048.

Describes the attitudes of private school teachers and administrators toward students, the goals of education, and the important characteristics of effective teachers and administrators.

961. Criscuolo, Nicholas P. & others. "What reading strategies make sense to content area teachers," Reading World 19 No. 3 (1980): 265-271.

Describes attitudes of middle and secondary school teachers toward teaching reading and toward strategies for teaching reading in the content areas.

962. Cruz-Rodriguez, Aristides. The application of Herzberg's theory of motivation to work to public elementary school teachers in Puerto Rico. Ph.D. dissertation. New York University. 1980.

Describes teachers' attitudes toward work, satisfaction with responsibilities but not with salary.

963. Cunningham, Sandra. "Off to a good start with microcomputers," Educational Computer 1 No. 3 (1981): 38-39.

Describes the attitudes of teachers and administrators toward the use of computers for instruction during their first year of use.

964. Damer, Linda Kay. A study of attitudes of selected public school music teachers toward the integration of handicapped students into music classes. Ed.D. dissertation. University of North Carolina at Greensboro. 1979.

Describes attitudes of music teachers toward handicapped students and the participation of those students in the teachers' classrooms.

965. Davis, Billie Clare. An investigation of perceptions of goals related to multiethnic curriculum by black, Hispanic, and non-Hispanic white elementary school teachers. Ed.D. dissertation. Universtiy of Miami. 1979.

Reports significant differences in the perceived importance of and attainment of various goals of multiethnic education for teachers from three ethnic backgrounds.

966. Davis, Todd M. "Teachers and their tools," Reading Improvement 19 No. 2 (1982): 129-34.

Describes complex attitudes of teachers toward two methods of reading instruction, meaning-based and phonics.

967. Davis, Walter Navarro. A study of the role perceptions and occupational behaviors of elementary and secondary reading teachers. Ed.D. dissertation. American University. 1976.

Study found differences in six of nine categories between elementary and secondary teachers; secondary teachers have a different role perception and opportunities to fill that role.

968. Dean, Raymond S. "A comparison of preservice and experienced teachers' perceptions of the school psychologist," Journal of School Psychology 18 (1980): 283-289.

Preservice and experienced teachers agreed on the importance of the school psychologist but experienced teachers had more negative perceptions of the actual functioning of school psychologist.

969. Deever, R. Merwin & Berg, George E. Role expectations of elementary teachers as perceived by principals and teachers in low-income schools. Research Reports in Educational Administration. Volume VI. Bureau of Educational Research and Services. Arizona State University. Tempe. 1980. <u>ERIC</u> <u>ED</u> 181 585.

Study found some difference in role perceptions between white and minority teachers, teachers and principals.

970. DeLuca, Frederick P. & Dawns, Gary E. "Measuring the differences between teaching preferences of teacher-centered and student-centered teachers," <u>Journal of Research in Science Teaching</u> <u>16</u> (1979): 153-158.

Study did not find much difference in attitude between the two types of teachers.

971. Diamond, C.T. Patrick. On a different level: two pedagogies of written expression. 1980. <u>ERIC</u> <u>ED</u> 197 369.

Describes teachers' perceptions of the task of writing and the relation of specific approaches and activites for writing instruction to two models of writing and of writing instruction.

972. Dickie, Robert Francis. An investigation of differential attitudes toward the physically handicapped, blind persons, and attitudes toward education and their determinants among various occupational groups in Kansas. Ed.D. dissertation. Michigan State University. 1967.

Describes attitudes of regular and special education teachers, laborers, and managers and executives toward handicapped individuals.

973. Dieter, Don. How outstanding teachers view themselves as persons. 1976. <u>ERIC</u> <u>ED</u> 115 500.

Describes perceptions of self held by outstanding secondary biology teachers.

974. Dillon-Peterson, E. Sameness drives me up a wall. <u>ERIC</u> <u>ED</u> 218 220.

Reports the attitudes of four teachers toward their work, their teacher education and experiences as beginning teachers.

975. Dingwall, Wyman Walter. An analysis of differences in beliefs about the teaching-learning process

between elementary, junior high and high school teachers in one school district. Ed.D. dissertation. University of Northern Colorado. 1976.

Describes attitudes of elementary, junior high and high school teachers; similar across groups, greater difference between groups.

976. Dobson, Russell L. & Dobson, Judith E. The congruency of teachers' beliefs and practices. ERIC ED 242 678.

Describes a system whereby teachers can record and analyze their own beliefs about education and their own teaching.

977. Donielson, Susan Janan. Choice in teachers' inservice: effects on learning and attitude. Ed.D. dissertation. Drake University. 1983.

Describes no differences in changes in attitudes and knowledge among teachers participating in three different inservice programs.

978. Dorr-Bremme, Donald W. "Assessing students: teachers' routine practices and reasoning," Evaluation Comment 6 No. 4 (1983): 1-12.

Describes teachers' uses of tests and the information acquired from testing for instructional decision making.

979. Dorsey, Dawn Ellen. Teacher stress and attitudinal militancy in New Jersey schools. Ph.D. dissertation. Fordham University. 1980.

Describes teachers' reports of stress associated with working environment and personal safety; describes teachers as militant in attitude but reports no relationship between stress and militant attitude.

980. Dotts, Wayne. "Black and white teacher attitudes toward the disadvantaged and poverty," Education 99 No. 1 (1978): 48-54.

Study indicates teachers' attitude does not differ by race.

981. Draud, Jon E. The effects of organizational structure of middle schools and junior high schools on the attitudes of teachers and students toward the school. Ed.D. dissertation. University of Cincinnatti. 1978.

Describes teachers' and students' attitudes and presents differences in teachers' attitudes at middle and junior high schools.

982. Duffy, Gerald & Anderson, Linda. Conceptions of Reading Project. Final report. <u>ERIC</u> <u>ED</u> 218 583.

Describes teachers' theories of reading and reading instruction and the relationship of those theories on teachers' behaviors.

983. Dunn, Marvin & others. Successful teaching of disadvantaged children: from the perspective of 94 Title I elementary school teachers who were identified as being the most effective in their school. 1980. <u>ERIC</u> <u>ED</u> 205 488.

Describes teachers' assessments of the characteristics, behaviors, and attitudes of successful teachers of disadvantaged students in inner-city schools, emphasizing the importance of planning and organization.

984. Dunton, Dennis Duane. A study of demographic characteristics and stated attitudes towards work of new and reentry teachers in selected Illinois districts. Ed.D. dissertation. University of Illinois at Urbana-Champaign. 1983.

Describes some differences by teachers' sex and teaching level in attitudes toward schools, and reasons for leaving and returning to teaching; women left for family reasons and returned for financial reasons; men left for further education, returned for the joy of teaching.

985. Dupuis, Mary M. & Askov, Eunice N. "Content area differences in attitudes toward teaching reading," <u>The</u> <u>High</u> <u>School</u> <u>Journal</u> <u>62</u> (1978): 83-88.

Describes differences in teachers' knowledge about and attitude toward teaching reading in the high school content areas, with English teachers revealed as having limited skills to assist other teachers to teach reading.

986. Ellis, Joseph R. Differences in professional role performance difficulties reported by first year male and female public school teachers. <u>ERIC</u> <u>ED</u> 229 347.

Describes the difficulties related to their jobs experienced by first year male and female teachers.

987. Ellis, Joseph R. & Ellis, Deloris J. Professional role performance difficulties reported by first

year home economics teachers in Illinois public schools. <u>ERIC</u> <u>ED</u> 228 217.

Describes teachers' perceptions of the problems they encountered during their first year of teaching, including role conflicts.

988. Ellis, William E. "Biology teachers and border state beliefs," <u>Society</u> <u>20</u> <u>No.</u> <u>2</u> (1983): 26-30.

Reports that biology teachers teach evolution and are opposed to the mandatory teaching of creationism and citizens' interference in curriculum decisions.

989. Engstrom, Dorothy Anne. Professional sharing patterns and attitudes among elementary classroom teachers. Ph.D. dissertation. Iowa State University. 1982.

Describes teachers' sharing of teaching ideas and emotional support, with variations depending upon years of experience, perceptions that such sharing is experienced within the building and similarities of teaching assignment.

990. Evans, Walter. Race and teacher perception of organizational climate. Ed.D. dissertation. University of Massachusetts. 1978.

Indicates that the race of teachers and principals is not related to their perceptions of school climate.

991. Farber, Barry A. Stress and burnout: implications for teacher motivation. <u>ERIC</u> <u>ED</u> 222 483.

Describes factors which teachers associate with burnout and aspects of their work which increase and prevent burnout.

992. Faunce, R.W. Attitude and characteristics of effective and not effective teachers of culturally disadvantaged children. Minneapolis Public Schools. Minnesota. 1969. <u>ERIC</u> <u>ED</u> 039 289.

Describes differences between effective and not effective teachers in their acceptance of physical deprivation, acceptance of culture of disadvantaged, non-punitive acceptance and willingness to teach disadvantaged students.

993. Fields, Jacqueline P. & Kumar, V.K. "How teachers use the group I.Q. test scores," <u>Journal</u> <u>of</u> <u>School</u> <u>Psychology</u> <u>20</u> <u>No.</u> <u>1</u> (1982): 32-38.

Describes the majority of teachers as reporting that they make use of the information from standardized tests.

994. Flores, Alfredo R. A study of Mexican American and Anglo teachers' attitudes and behaviors toward Mexican American children. Ed.D. dissertation. Northern Illinois University. 1974.

Study found no differences by ethnicity and years of experience in attitudes toward Mexican American students.

995. Flowers, John D. & McMilan, Frank M. Regular classroom and special education teachers' attitudes toward exceptional children. Augusta College. Georgia. 1979. ERIC ED 182 946.

Describes differences in attitudes, with classroom teachers having more positive attitudes than special education teachers toward exceptional children, especially speech defective and mentally retarded children.

996. Floyd, Mary A. An investigation of public school teachers' knowledge about, attitude toward, and willingness to use microcomputers as instructional tools. Ph.D. dissertation. Pennsylvania State University. 1983.

Reports limited knowledge of but positive attitude toward the use of microcomputers among teachers in rural Pennsylvania.

997. Flynn, F. Dennis. Teacher perception of curricula in transitional and non-transitional junior high schools. Ed.D. dissertation. University of Southern California. 1979.

Describes teachers' attitudes about student needs and curriculum at black, white and transitional schools.

998. Flynn, James R., Gacka, Richard C. & Sundean, David A. "Are classroom teachers prepared for mainstreaming?" Phi Delta Kappan 59 (1978): 562.

Describes attitudes of teachers and special education teachers toward aspects of mainstreaming such as the extent that the district will provide materials and support.

999. Fraser, Ken P. "Supervisory behavior and teacher satisfaction," Journal of Educational Administration 18 (1980): 224-231.

Describes teachers' perceptions of supervision as it occurs and as they would like it to occur in their schools and relates those perceptions to teachers' satisfaction with their teaching situation.

1000. Gaetino, Joseph Q. Teacher attitudes toward early retirement incentive plans. Ed.D. dissertation. Pennsylvania State University. 1980.

Describes teachers' attitudes toward early retirement, finding that sex and job satisfaction were strong predictors of teachers' attitudes and that more experienced teachers and younger teachers dissatisfied with their job preferred an early retirement option.

1001. Garman, Lynne G. & Plant, Walter T. Sex-role stereotypes and educators' descriptions of mature personality. 1974. ERIC ED 109 519.

Suggests that educational descriptions of mature males and females differ, following sex-role stereotype patterns.

1002. Gehrke, Nathalie J. An analysis of teachers' perceptions of their school environment. ERIC ED 213 677.

Describes teachers' perceptions of their school building as a teaching environment and reports that teachers seldom consciously use the school environment for instructional purposes.

1003. Ghubrial, Thabet K.H. Teachers' perceptions of selected societal fundamentals of curriculum in American schools and Egyptian schools: a comparative study. Ph.D. dissertation. University of Pittsburgh. 1979.

Describes the attitudes and perceptions that teachers from two countries have toward fundamental aspects of the curriculum.

1004. Gillan, Robert E. The middle school questionnaire. 1978. ERIC ED 160 617.

Describes different attitudes of teachers toward aspects of middle school teaching by certification for middle school vs. elementary or secondary certification.

1005. Gillespie, Barbara O.W. An identification of the level of teacher competence needed to teach writing in selected subject areas of the secondary school. Ed.D. dissertation. University of La Verne. 1979.

Describes differences among teachers by subject taught in perceptions of writing competencies as important.

1006. Girardi, Joseph Leo. A study of the relationships between pupil control ideologies and rated teacher effectiveness in public and parochial intermediate schools. Ph.D. dissertation. Syracuse University. 1980.

Describes differences in beliefs about pupil control between teachers rated as effective by their peers and other teachers but not between teachers rated effective by principals and other teachers.

1007. Gist, Ronald Colonel. Organizational structure and teacher job satisfaction. Ed.D. dissertation. University of Denver. 1979.

Study found some relationship between opennes of elementary school, teacher job satisfaction and teacher sense of competence motivation, with competence motivation more important than openness of school.

1008. Glasman, Naftaly S. & Paulin, Pauline J. "Possible determinants of teacher receptivity to evaluation," _Journal of Educational Administration 20 No. 2_ (1982): 148-71.

Describes teachers' attitudes toward evaluation in relation to their attitudes toward aspects of their teaching and their teaching situation.

1009. Goldenberg, Irene. "Social class differences in teacher attitudes toward children," _Child Development 42 No. 5_ (1971): 1637-1640.

Middle and lower class teachers have different attitudes toward and relations with students.

1010. Gordon, C. Paul & Gallimore, Ronald. "Teacher ratings of behavior problems of Hawaiian-American adolescents," _Journal of Cross-Cultural Psychology 3 No. 2_ (1972): 209-13.

Reports that teachers' ratings of behavior problems differed little across situations and cultures.

1011. Graham, Steve & others. "Educational personnel's perception of mainstreaming and resource room effectiveness," _Psychology in the Schools 17 No. 1_ (1980): 128-134.

Describes different perceptions of the value of mainstreaming between regular classroom and resource room teachers.

1012. Grand, Gerald & others. "The teacher's predicament," Teachers College Record 84 No. 3 593-609.

Describes teachers' attitudes toward their responsibilities, support available, and changes in teachers' authority.

1013. Granelli, Bryan Francis. Psychologist facilitativeness, teacher/psychologist relationship and reason for seeking consultation: correlates of teacher preference for consultant style. Ph.D. dissertation. Fordham University. 1982.

Describes variations in teachers' preferences for types of consultation services depending upon the nature of the problem for which they were considering use of consultation services.

1014. Green, James Harlen. Attitudes of special educators versus regular teachers toward the physically handicapped and toward education. Ph.D. dissertation. Michigan State University. 1967.

Describes attitudes of regular and special education teachers toward handicapped students, but found no relationship between attitudes and traditional or progressive values held by teachers.

1015. Griffith, Albert R. & London, Clement B.G. "A career study of inner-city teachers," Journal of Non-White Concerns in Personnel and Guidance 8 (1980): 167-183.

Black teachers had the same commitment toward teaching as white teachers, believed thay had less opportunity for advancemant, and more often chose service as their motivation for their career choice.

1016. Griffith, Albert R. & London, Clement B.G. "Student relations among inner city teachers: a comparative study by teacher race," Education 101 (1980): 139-147.

Describes attitudes and beliefs of white and black teachers toward students and teachers' relations with students.

1017. Guskey, Thomas R. Teachers' beliefs in their own control of factors influencing the academic achievement of students. AERA presentation. 1980. ERIC ED 187 766.

Describes teachers' assumption of responsibility for student learning, with greater responsibility by female than male teachers but no differences by grade taught or years of experience.

1018. Hall, Horace Don. A study of current practices and teachers' attitudes regarding staff development programs as mandated by House Bill 1706 for the state of Oklahoma. Ed.D. dissertation. Oklahoma State University. 1983.

Describes positive attitudes among teachers toward inservice education and the aspects of the inservice education program in Oklahoma and reports that teachers perceive credit for participation as the most important aspect of the program.

1019. Halliwell, Gail L. Kindergarten teachers and curriculum construct systems. ERIC ED 201 385.

Describes three teachers' views of teaching and curriculum within their classes, documenting variations in teachers' conceptions of teaching and curriculum.

1020. Hammond, Sallie Mae B. A study of the relationship between use of sick and personal leave and selected factors for teachers in the public schools of Petersburg, Virginia. Ed.D. dissertation. George Washington University. 1982.

Describes differences in use of leave associated with some but not other teacher characteristics, e.g., sex and age were but teaching level was not related to use of leave.

1021. Hange, Jane. Teachers in their fifth year: an analysis of teaching concerns from the perspective of adult and career development. ERIC ED 214 906.

Describes teachers' attitudes toward teaching as a career, their own teaching situations and aspects of teachers' personal lives that support and conflict with a commitment to teaching.

1022. Haroontunian, Berj & Yarger, Gwen P. Teachers' conceptions of their own success. ERIC ED 200 518.

Reports that teachers define success in teaching as related to students behavior rather than strictly to student learning; teachers' views differed from external definitions of success in teaching.

1023. Harty, Harold. Statistical report and observations on attitudes toward S-APA installation from fourth and fifth grade teachers in ERIE's pilot schools prior to an initial workshop session. Eastern Regional Institute for Education. Syracuse, New York. 1970. ERIC ED 049 948.

Experienced teachers were more knowledgeable about and had a more favorable attitude toward the use of equipment for Science-A Process Approach (S-APA) science.

1024. Haubrich, Vernon F. Cross-cultural approaches to behavior and learning. 1965. ERIC ED 010 781.

Teachers' attitudes and values prevent their teaching of students of different cultures.

1025. Haughey, Margaret & Murphy, Peter James. Changing times: rural teachers comment on the quality of their work life. ERIC ED 238 649.

Reports that the majority of rural teachers surveyed in British Columbia were dissatisfied with the quality of their working situations.

1026. Hayes, Mary Vidolin. A survey of teacher attitudes toward in-class versus pull-out compensatory reading programs. ERIC ED 228 619.

Reports that teachers favored pull-out programs and had negative attitudes toward in-class programs for compensatory reading instruction.

1027. Heckman, Michael Gary. Job satisfaction of substitute and regular classroom teachers. Ed.D. dissertation. Northern Illinois University. 1980.

Describes differences in areas of job satisfaction between regular and substitute teachers.

1028. Helge, Swen & Pierce-Jones, John. The relationship between specific and general teaching experience and teacher attitudes toward project Head Start. Part of the final report. Child Development Evaluation and Research Center. Texas University. Austin. 1968. ERIC ED 025 323.

Teachers with no experience and six or more years of experience had the most positive attitudes toward Head Start, insight into problem areas and more easily incorporated new experiences with deprived students.

1029. Helvie, Marilyn Jeanne. A comparison of teacher attitudes and teacher involvement toward work stoppages with respect to a strike action in the state of Illinois. Ed.D. dissertation. Northern Illinois University. 1983.

Reports differences in teachers' attitudes toward strike activities in general and actual participation in a work stoppage.

1030. Henderson, Judith E.T. An investigation of practitioner evaluation and agreement regarding effective language arts instruction. 1968. ERIC ED 034 780.

Teachers and principals agree on level of competence of elementary and junior high teachers in language arts; supervisors demonstrate less agreement.

1031. Hendrickson, Dean & Virant, Milt. A study of needs for further learning as seen by teachers of secondary school mathematics. 1977. ERIC ED 141 353.

Teachers perceive that the learning need is greatest in area of instructional process in contrast to math content.

1032. Hetzel, Donna Cameron. A comparison of British and Connecticut elementary teachers' opinions on their educational aims and priorities and on their views of the role of the teacher. Ph.D. dissertation. University of Connecticut. 1977.

Describes attitudes of Connecticut teachers compared with British teachers.

1033. Hewiston, Mal. "Participative decision making for teachers - placebo or panacea?" Australian Journal of Education 22 No. 2 (1978): 189-205.

Reports that the relation between teacher involvement in decision making and job satisfaction may be negative.

1034. Hoffman, James V. & Kugle, Cherry L. A study of theoretical orientation to reading and its relationship to teacher verbal feedback during reading instruction. ERIC ED 203 304.

Describes a limited relationship between teachers' beliefs about reading instruction and teachers' instructional behavior.

1035. Holleman, Herbert Leon. A key respondent investigation of teacher attitudes about teacher evaluation in the Durham County schools. Ed.D. dissertation. University of North Carolina at Chapel Hill. 1981.

Describes teachers' attitudes toward evaluation, reporting confusion about the purposes of evaluation and interests in evaluation involving more evaluator time in the classroom.

1036. Holloway, William H. & others. Policy analysis: an assessment of public school educators' concerns in relation to P.L. 94-142. 1980. <u>ERIC</u> <u>ED</u> 191 168.

Describes teachers in Kansas as at an early stage in the adoption of an innovation, the mainstreaming of handicapped children, in response to Public Law 94-142, and describes their concerns about this innovation and the adequacy of their training.

1037. Holly, Mary Louise. Reflections on classroom life: an empirical base for professional development. progress report No. 3. <u>ERIC</u> <u>ED</u> 243 865.

Describes seven elementary teachers' perceptions of teaching and their classrooms.

1038. Holmes, Margaret McCann. Teachers' perspectives on open education: a case study. Ph.D. dissertation. University of Wisconsin - Madison. 1980.

Describes two different views of open education held by teachers in the process of implementing an open curriculum.

1039. Holtzman, Wayne, Jr. Effects of locally conducted research on policy and practice regarding bilingual inservice teacher education. <u>ERIC</u> <u>ED</u> 201 254.

Reports on teachers' perceptions of their needs for training to adequately meet the needs of children speaking a language other than English.

1040. Hoot, James L. "Teaching aging in the public schools: results of an exploratory study," <u>Educational</u> <u>Gerontology</u> <u>7</u> <u>No.</u> <u>4</u> (1981): 331-37.

Reports that most teachers do not teach about aging but report that they would be receptive to including aging in the curriculum if materials were available.

1041. Hopkins, Thomas Robert. Navajo and non-Navajo teachers: a comparison of characteristics. Ed.D.

dissertation. George Washington University. 1971. ERIC ED 127 064.

Study found some differences between Navajo and non-Navajo teachers in responses toward Navajo children but no difference in goals for education.

1042. Hoyle, John R. Learning environments: space and perceptions. 1975. ERIC ED 117 815.

Describes teachers' views of classroom space and approaches to classroom organization and climate.

1043. Hudson, Beverly S. An assessment of the attitudes of secondary level teachers toward incorporating reading skill with content; report from the project on conditions of school learning and instructional strategies. technical report No. 329. Research and Development Center for Cognitive Learning. University of Wisconsin, Madison. 1975. ERIC ED 105 446.

Reports that teachers are aware of the need for instruction but feel inadequate to teach reading in content areas in secondary schools.

1044. Hudson, James Michael. An investigation of the cognitive/content needs and the professional education needs of junior high/middle school teachers of English. Ed.D. dissertation. Auburn University. 1980.

Describes needs that teachers report they have for further training, most of them in the professional area.

1045. Hunt, Madgie Mae. A study of teachers' perceptions regarding implementation of career education in the classroom. Ed.D. dissertation. University of Montana. 1979.

Describes perceptions of junior high and elementary teachers toward career education activities and effects on students.

1046. Instructor. "How do elementary teachers grade themselves?" Instructor 93 No. 1 (1983): 104-06, 107.

Describes the results of a survey of teachers' perceptions of their own teaching, the curriculum, the support services, and teaching as a career.

1047. Ismail, Mohamed. A comparative study of the perceptions of secondary science teachers and science educators of competencies needed by science teachers. Ph.D. dissertation. University of Nebraska - Lincoln. 1979.

Study found no difference between teachers and teacher educators in rating of seven of eight clusters of competencies; the groups differed on student needs; found agreement between ratings of importance of competencies and level of acquisition of competencies.

1048. James, Kelvin C. Teacher perceptions of factors in the school environment which influence innovative science teaching. Ed.D. dissertation. Columbia University. 1978.

Describes factors teachers perceive to be related to changes in science teaching.

1049. Jarratt, Loren George. A comparison of South Dakota teacher perceptions of job related stress. Ed.D. dissertation. University of South Dakota. 1983.

Reports no association between teachers' perceptions of stress associated with the job of teaching and teacher characteristics, e.g., sex, years of teaching experience, level of teaching assignment.

1050. Jensen, A.R. Parent and teacher attitudes toward integration and busing. Research resume No. 43. California Teachers Association. Burlingame, California. 1970. ERIC ED 041 092.

The majority of teachers favored integration and busing, with older teachers less favorable, and with differences by racial group.

1051. Johnson, Bruce K. Film and video utilization study. ERIC ED 235 797.

Describes teachers' attitudes toward and use of instructional films within their classrooms.

1052. Jones, Dan R. & Harty, Harold. "Instructional and classroom management preferences of secondary school science teachers," Science Education 62 (1978): 1-9.

Describes attitudes of secondary science teachers with greater preferences for inquiry instructional approaches and humanistic management.

1053. Jones, Richard John. Comparative career orientations of beginning male mathematics, science, social studies, and English teachers.

Ed.D. dissertation. Pennsylvania State University. 1971.

Study found no differences in career plans of male beginning teachers from several subject areas.

1054. Kanowith, V. Teacher attitudes and the Spanish bilingual program. 1980. <u>ERIC ED</u> 190 713.

Reports that attitudes of teachers teaching within and outside a bilingual education program but in a school with a large Hispanic enrollment were contraditory in terms of attitudes toward program procedures, goals and philosophy.

1055. Kavale, Kenneth & Rossi, Constance. "Regular class teachers' attitudes and perceptions of the resource specialist program for educable mentally retarded pupils," <u>Education and Training of the Mentally Retarded</u> <u>15</u> (1980): 195-198.

Describes attitudes of teachers toward a supportive program of assistance to mainstreamed students by resource room teachers, with middle school teachers having a greater number of questions about the program.

1056. Kennon, Adah F. & Sandoval, Jonathan. "Teacher attitudes toward the educable mentally retarded," <u>Education and Training of the Mentally Retarded</u> <u>13</u> (1978): 139-145.

Survey found no differences in attitudes toward educable mentally retarded students among special education and regular classroom teachers but differences by ethnic group and by experience with EMR students among regular teachers.

1057. Kerlinger, Fred N. "The factor structure and content of perceptions of desirable characteristics of teachers," <u>Educational and Psychological Measurement</u> <u>27</u> (1967): 643-656.

Describes characteristics of effective teachers as perceived by teachers in terms of orientation to people, tasks and functional flexibility.

1058. Keyes, Jeff Nunnally. Student behavior problems: perceptions of junior high students, teachers, and administrators. Ph.D. dissertation. George Peabody College for Teachers. 1977.

Perceptions of student behavior differ in beliefs about the seriousness of specific problems by group and by sex within group.

1059. Kimbell, Carolyn S. A study of teacher morale as affected by teacher transfer caused by declining enrollments. Ed.D. dissertation. Northern Illinois University. 1980.

Study found higher morale among teachers awaiting transfer then among teachers already transferred.

1060. Kimpston, Richard D. Social studies teachers' perceptions of knowledge, attitudes, and skills goals: implications for curriculum change and faculty development. 1976. ERIC ED 124 481.

Study found differences among elementary (student socialization) and secondary (content, knowledge) teachers' goals for social studies; both groups were satisfied with the curriculum.

1061. King, Charles Thomas. Professional development needs as perceived by full-time teachers not pursuing advanced study and factors affecting their acceptance of programs designed to meet those needs. Ph.D. dissertation. Michigan State University. 1978.

Describes teachers' attitudes toward staff development needs and programs.

1062. Kingston, Michael Lewis. A comparison of more effective and less effective teachers of reading. Ph.D. dissertation. University of Illinois at Urbana-Champaign. 1979.

Describes attitudes of teachers toward reading instruction; slight differences between more and less effective teachers, no difference in strength of attitude or consistency of attitude and behavior.

1063. Klein, A.E. "Relations of level and amount of teaching experience to educational attitudes," Proceedings of the Annual Convention of the American Psychological Association 5 No. 2 (1970): 641-642.

Elementary teachers hold more favorable attitudes toward progressivism than secondary teachers.

1064. Klein, M. Frances. Teacher perceived sources of influence on what is taught in subject areas. 1980. ERIC ED 214 885.

Describes the factors that teachers perceive as influencing the extent to which the teachers have an influence on decisions within the school; factors include state education policies, teachers' characteristics and interests, and district policies.

1065. Kleine, Paul F. & Smith, Louis M. Educational innovators then and now. ERIC ED 225 230.

Describes the attitudes of teachers involved in an innovative school program and their recollections of that program.

1066. Kleinfeld, Judith & McDiarmid, G. Williamson. Effective schooling in rural Alaska: information for the Rural Effective Schools Project. ERIC ED 232 813.

Describes attitudes of teachers in rural Alaska toward teaching methods, their students' aspects of their work situations and relations with central administrations.

1067. Klugman, Edgar & others. Too many pieces: a study of teacher fragmentation in the elementary school. 1979. ERIC ED 178 515.

Reports teachers' opinions toward fragmentation of classroom, e.g., students in and out, lack of administrative support, administrative interruptions and too wide span of ability within classes; frustration.

1068. Kneale, Shirley Mary. Teachers' perceptions of the organizational climate, the conditions of decisional participation, and leader behavior in each of four selected elementary schools. Ed.D. dissertation. University of Southern Mississippi. 1979.

Describes consistent teacher interest in participation in school decision making regardless of organizational style of the school, with organizational climate varying among the four elementary schools studied.

1069. Knoop, Robert. The alienated teacher: a profile. ERIC ED 214 905.

Reports that job-related variables accounted for more career alienation than were accounted for by teachers' personal characteristics.

1070. Knoop, Robert. Job involvement of teachers. 1980. ERIC ED 208 508.

Reports that teachers' sense of involvemnt in their job is related most strongly to motivation, satisfaction with present teaching situation and marital status, with other factors related less strongly.

1071. Koci, Janet Ilene L. A study of the needs of regular education teachers in implementing Public Law 94-142. Ed.D. dissertation. University of Houston. 1980.

Describes concerns of teachers relative to implementing provisions of P.L. 94-142 - teachers reported greater ability to handle handicapped students when they had had an inservice program.

1072. Kohr, Richard L. A survey of teacher attitudes and classroom practices. AERA presentation. 1977. ERIC ED 139 839.

Describes results of self reports where elementary teachers reported more positive attitudes toward students, parents, staff and administrators with fewer problems; newer teachers reported greater innovation and greater problems in school.

1073. Kornblau, Barbara. "The teachable pupil survey: a technique for assessing teachers' perceptions of pupil attributes," *Psychology in the Schools* 19 No. 2 (1982): 170-74.

Describes characteristics teachers perceive to be associated with the ideal teachable student and discusses the research methodology.

1074. Kortmeyer, Gloria F.C. Expectations of sixth and seventh grade teachers concerning selected language arts competencies of students. Ph.D. dissertation. University of Minnesota. 1979.

Reveals differences between 6th and 7th grade teachers in competencies in language arts expected of students at the end of grade 6; few differences by years of teaching and type of community.

1075. Krchniak, Stefan & Helsel, A. Raymond. Professional and bureaucratic orientations of teachers and organizational socialization. Southern Illinois University. Edwardsville. 1971. ERIC ED 046 899.

Student teachers are more employee-oriented than experienced teachers; females have more professional status orientation than males.

1076. Krohn, Eric Wilson. Perceived organizational structure and the pupil control ideology and job satisfaction of elementary and secondary school teachers. Ph.D. dissertation. University of North Carolina at Chapel Hill. 1979.

Describes a relationship between teachers' perceptions of school climate and their attitude toward pupil control and job satisfaction.

1077. Kruse, Mary Louise. The effects of increasing teacher competencies as related to improved secondary student reading scores. 1975. ERIC ED 198 776.

Teachers were reported to favor student-centered approaches to reading instruction at the secondary school level.

1078. Lawrenz, Frances. "Changing science teacher perceptions of their teaching skills and their school conditions," Science Education 64 No. 1 (1980): 43-51.

Describes teachers' perceptions of their teaching skills and teaching conditions; a comparison with data from four years before indicates more positive attitudes in present study.

1079. Lawrenz, Frances. "Science teachers' perceptions of their teaching skills and their school conditions," Science Education 54 No. 4 (1974): 489-496.

All teachers rated their satisfaction with their skills and teaching conditions from satisfactory to good.

1080. Lebowitz, Ruth. "Women elementary-school teachers and the feminist movement," Elementary School Journal 80 No. 5 (1980): 239-45.

Describes teachers' attitudes toward teaching as a profession and toward the goals and language of the feminist movement.

1081. LeCoultre, Margie H. Female and male teachers' perceived participation and satisfaction in the decision-making process of selected East Tennessee school systems and the potential for collective action. Ed.D. dissertation. University of Tennessee. 1979.

Teachers differed by sex in perceived level of participation in and satisfaction with decision making and willingness to participate in collective action; females were more dissatisfied but not more willing to participate in collective action.

1082. LeCrone, Charles Mauzey. The relationship of teacher and supervisor competitive-cooperative attitudes and principal ratings of successful supervision. Ed.D. dissertation. University of Illinois at Urbana-Champaign. 1983.

Reports slight differences in cooperativeness but no competitiveness in supervision relationships among the school districts.

1083. Leithwood, Kenneth A. & others. Describing teacher decision making. ERIC ED 220 464.

Describes factors which teachers consider important in making curriculum decisions, including students' abilities.

1084. Lewandowski, Jean A.D. Nebraska social studies teachers' perceptions about in-service education experiences and self-initiated professional development activities. Ed.D. dissertation. University of Nebraska - Lincoln. 1980.

Describes methods teachers report that they use to learn to improve classroom instruction: reading, college courses, resource persons, travel, in-service education, tv and movies, etc.

1085. Lincoln, Eugene A. Differences in teachers' perceptions of the effectiveness of techniques of teaching and learning in inner-city, outer-city, and suburban schools. ERIC ED 209 219.

Describes teachers' views of the effectiveness of teaching techniques; views vary by teachers' race.

1086. Little, Judith Warren. The power of organizational setting: school norms and staff development. ERIC ED 221 918.

Describes teachers' attitudes toward the school as a work place and aspects of the working environment and the effects of teachers' attitudes on staff development programs.

1087. Logan, John W. & Erickson, Lawrence. "Elementary teachers' reading inservice preferences," Reading Teacher 33 No. 3 (1979): 330-334.

Describes survey results of teachers' preferences for topics for inservice training in reading.

1088. Lorenz, Jens Holger. "Attributions used by mathematics teachers in assessing achievement,"

Journal for Research in Mathematics Education 11 (1980): 63-66.

Describes initial hypotheses about teachers' attitudes toward mathematics instruction and teachers' theories of student acquisition of mathematics knowledge.

1089. Lovett, Gladys J. Instructional problems in reading as seen by teachers of disadvantaged vs non-disadvantaged children. ERIC ED 229 724.

Describes teachers of disadvantaged students as perceiving that they encounter more instructional and classroom management problems than do teachers of non-disadvantaged students.

1090. Lubomudrov, Carol. Relationships between level of moral cognitive development, teachers' understanding of educational issues and teaching practices. ERIC ED 214 925.

Describes teachers' views of teaching and the relationships between those views and teachers' classroom management and teaching behaviors.

1091. Lugo, Elizabeth. A survey of bilingual-bicultural program teachers' perceptions of the importance of competencies, training needs, and attitudes toward bilingual education. Ph.D. dissertation. University of Florida. 1981.

Describes teachers' attitudes toward bilingual education but no relationship between attitudes and perceptions of the need for further training related to bilingual education.

1092. Lyston, Jack P. & Liss, Jody A. "Attitudes of content area teachers towards teaching reading," Reading Improvement 15 (1978): 294-300.

Describes attitudes of subject matter teachers toward reading instruction in junior high schools, with differences in attitude by subject area.

1093. McArthur, John T. The first five years of teaching: their effect on pupil control ideology and commitment to teaching. 1980. ERIC ED 191 799.

Describes the effects of teacher characteristics, e.g., sex and teacher training, on the pupil control ideology and commitment to teaching of students in their last year of teacher education and their first year of teaching.

1094. McBeath, Gerald A. Rural teachers and community schools in Alaska. ERIC ED 233 841.

Describes attitudes of teachers in rural Alaska toward education, their teaching situation, their students and the communities within which they lived.

1095. McBride, Oliver Allan. Teachers' perceptions of teaching practices and factors they perceive as having an influence upon implementation of those practices. Ed.D. dissertation. University of Virginia. 1977.

Describes attitudes teachers have toward teaching behaviors and factors they see related to the use of those behaviors.

1096. McClure, John E. & Barcikowski, Robert S. A study of attitude factors for secondary school teachers and teacher education students. AERA presentation. 1972. ERIC ED 062 308.

Study describes differences in attitudes between groups of teachers and teachers in training.

1097. McCoy, Linda Jones. Attitudes of remedial reading, learning disabilities, and classroom teachers toward job roles. Ed.D. dissertation. University of Kansas. 1978.

Describes attitudes of three groups toward their own and each other's job roles.

1098. McDonald, David G. Structural coupling and school outcomes: job satisfaction, student attitudes and perceptions of school, student achievement in reading, student achievement in mathematics, and perceived organizational effectiveness. Ph.D. dissertation. University of Kansas. 1982.

Describes teachers' job satisfaction, reporting high morale and no relationship between organization of the school and teacher morale.

1099. MacDonald, Roderick A. A study of the intrinsic reward structure of the classroom for the teacher. Ed.D. dissertation. University of Toronto, Canada. 1978.

Describes teachers' reports of satisfaction with teaching based on satisfaction from classroom interaction with students.

1100. McElhone, James Walter. A study to determine the attitudes of Wyoming teachers toward inservice education. Ph.D. dissertation. University of Wyoming. 1979.

Describes dissatisfaction of Wyoming teachers with inservice programs in which they had participated and aspects of teachers' attitudes which might be used to develop more satisfactory inservice programs.

1101. Maddux, Cleborne D. & others. A survey of Texas public school teachers. 1980. ERIC ED 212 559.

Describes teachers' perceptions of teaching as a profession, their own work situations and patterns of career development, and their indication of willingness to enter teaching as a career, as well as work experiences outside of teaching.

1102. Manera, Elizabeth S. & Wright, Robert E. "Stress factors in teaching," *Action in Teacher Education* 2 (1980): 51-56.

Reports that teachers perceive several factors as associated with increased job stress, including relations with students, other teachers and supervisors and time management.

1103. Markill, Clark. Exceptional students in regular classes: interviews with 43 North Dakota elementary teachers. Minot State College. North Dakota. 1976. ERIC ED 117 912.

Describes teachers' attitudes toward handicapped students and the task of integrating them into regular classrooms.

1104. Markson, Maxine Beth. Life experiences and teaching maturity: a study of teacher concerns. Ed.D. dissertation. University of Massachusetts. 1979.

Describes teachers' perceptions of successful staff development procedures; those procedures differ for teachers at three career stages.

1105. Marston, Rip & Leslie, David. "Teacher perceptions from mainstreamed versus non-mainstreamed teaching environments," *Physical Educator* 40 No. 1 (1983): 8-15.

Reports that teachers with mainstreamed students in their classroom had more positive attitudes toward mainstreaming than other teachers.

1106. Mayes, Beatrice H. A study of the experimental beliefs and open-mindedness of teachers of first grade reading. 1972. ERIC ED 072 416.

Study found slight differences in the beliefs of teachers teaching Distar and using a basal method of reading instruction.

1107. Meinke, Dean L. & others. Perceived stress events by teachers. ERIC ED 222 448.

Teachers reported that student behavior in the classroom was a major component of teacher stress.

1108. Mendez, Luis Manuel. A comparative analysis of teaching styles in open and traditional classrooms. Ph.D. dissertation. University of Alabama. 1979.

When teachers rated themselves, there were no differences between teachers in traditional and open schools on ratings of creativity, dynamism, organized demeanor and warmth and acceptance.

1109. Menlo, Allen. A comparison of school-related perceptions, attitudes, and values of teachers in three countries. AERA presentation. 1978. ERIC ED 164 438.

Describes attitudes of teachers in cities of the United States, West Germany and England toward aspects of daily work, colleagues and students and goals for student development.

1110. Meyer, H.J., Likwak, E. & Warren, D. "Occupational and class differences in social values: a comparison of teachers and social workers," Sociology of Education 41 (1968): 263-281.

Describes differences in values by teachers' ethnic group and school setting.

1111. Meyers, Robert E. Relationships of teacher orientations and effectiveness under inductive and deductive teaching methods. 1968. ERIC ED 106 176.

Reports no differences among teachers using deductive and inductive teaching methods.

1112. Miller, Harry B. & Hering, Steve. "Teacher's ratings - which reading group is number one?" The Reading Teacher 28 No. 4 (1975): 389-391.

Teachers reported a preference for teaching reading to the more able reading group, but no preference for teaching boys or girls.

1113. Milner, Joseph O. "Towers and trenches: polar perceptions of the English curriculum," English Education 15 No. 1 (1983): 31-35.

Describes the attitudes of English teachers toward the curriculum, teacher preparation and English instruction.

1114. Miskel, Cecil & others. "A test of the inequity theory for job satisfaction using educators' attitudes toward work motivation and work incentives," Educational Administration Quarterly 11 No. 1 (1975): 38-54.

Describes job satisfaction among groups of educators in relation to inequity theory.

1115. Miskel, Cecil J. & others. Public school teachers' work motivation, organizational incentives, job satisfaction, and primary life interests. Kansas University. Lawrence, Kansas. 1972. ERIC ED 072 000.

Describes teachers' attitudes toward several aspects of their lives.

1116. Moffett, Bryon. "A statement from the field - what good teachers say and do about teaching elementary school social studies," Social Studies Review 22 No. 3 (1983): 69-79.

Reports that teachers prefer not to teach social studies and feel inadequately trained to teach social studies.

1117. Molner, Sheila R.F. The analysis of teachers' task contributions to decision-making interaction: differences in three content areas and two types of teaching teams. Stanford Center for Research and Development in Teaching. Stanford University. California. 1972. ERIC ED 063 256.

Describes differences among groups of teachers in participation in group decision-making.

1118. Monroe, Eula Ewing. An exploratory study of inservice needs in reading education of elementary school classroom teachers. Ph.D. dissertation. George Peabody College for Teachers of Vanderbilt University. 1980.

Describes needs teachers report they have for inservice education in reading education including correcting reading difficulties, providing for the superior reader, developing comprehensive skills, identifying strengths and weaknesses of individuals.

1119. Moody, Dwight L. Perceptions of middle grade teachers concerning the knowledge and skill competencies of real and ideal middle grade teachers. Ed.D. dissertation. University of Toledo. Ohio. 1979.

There are differences in the skills and knowledge which middle grade teachers report that real teachers have and that the ideal teacher should have.

1120. Moore, Judy & Fine, Marvin G. "Regular and special class teachers' perceptions of normal and exceptional children and their attitudes toward mainstreaming," Psychology in the Schools 15 (1978): 253-259.

Teachers of learning disabled (LD), educable mentally handicapped (EMH) and regular students view three groups as different; LD and EMH teachers are more supportive of mainstreaming; all teachers were more supportive of mainstreaming LD than EMH students.

1121. Morbeck, Judith Uresti. In-service education needs of senior high school regular classroom teachers relative to mainstreaming learning disabled students. Ed.D. dissertation. University of Idaho. 1980.

Describes teachers' reports of needs for inservice education relative to mainstreaming, and the absence of hierarchy of needs.

1122. Morgan, Marylou & others. "Teacher attitudes and practices in open and traditional spaces: a comparison," CEFP Journal 14 No. 5 (1976): 7-9.

Describes teachers' attitudes and behaviors and students' behaviors in open and traditional elementary classrooms.

1123. Morris, Elizabeth Anne. Job satisfaction and dissatisfaction of teachers in urban and suburban secondary schools in Birmingham, Alabama. Ed.D. dissertation. University of Alabama. 1979.

Describes aspects of job satisfaction of teachers, and some differences between urban and suburban teachers.

1124. Morris, Monica B. The public school as workplace: the principal as a key element in teacher satisfaction. ERIC ED 214 899.

Describes the characteristics of schools where teachers reported higher and lower job satisfaction; size and principal characteristics were associated with level of teacher satisfaction.

1125. Morrison, Beverly A.L. Parent involvement and teacher morale in selected elementary schools. Ed.D. dissertation. University of Florida. 1980.

Schools with high teacher morale also had high parent involvement; schools with low teacher morale had low parent involvement; no consistency for schools in the middle of the range.

1126. Mosses, H. & Delaney, D. "Dimensions of pressures faced by teachers: a factor analytic study," SPATE Journal 8 (1970): 122-128.

Describes pressures which teachers report including classroom teaching, community and professional responsibilities, relationships with administrators and others.

1127. National Education Association. "Teacher opinion poll: teacher qualifications," National Education Journal 54 (1965): 10.

Ninety percent of classroom teachers reporting considered themselves qualified for their teaching position.

1128. National Education Association. "NEA survey investigates teacher attitudes, practices," Phi Delta Kappan 62 (1980): 49-50.

Describes results of a survey of teachers' attitudes toward students, teaching and the context in which teachers work.

1129. NEA Research Division. "Corporal punishment: teacher opinion," NEA Research Bulletin 48 (1970): 48-49.

Approximately two-thirds of teachers approve of corporal punishment with similar results for elementary and secondary teachers; a greater number of men than women favor corporal punishment.

1130. Natriello, Gary & Cohn, Marilyn. Beyond sanctions: the evolution of a merit pay system. ERIC ED 238 140.

Describes a merit pay system in operation in one school system and positive attitudes toward the system.

1131. Newberry, Janet McIntosh. "The barrier between beginning and experienced teachers," Journal of Educational Administration 16 No. 1 (1978): 46-56.

Reports hesitation of beginning teachers to ask for help and experienced teachers to offer it.

1132. Newman, Katherine K. "What's on older teachers' mind?" Principal 60 No. 4 (1981): 26-29.

Describes the prospectives of older teachers toward their careers and retirement.

1133. Newman, Katherine K. Middle-aged experienced teachers' perceptions of their career development. Ph.D. dissertation. Ohio State University. 1978. ERIC ED 171 697.

Describes ten teachers' perceptions of their careers after 2-3 decades of teaching and perceived changes in attitudes and relations with students.

1134. North Carolina State Department of Public Instruction. A survey of teachers and principals: grade 3. State assessment of educational progress in North Carolina, 1973-1974. Division of Research. North Carolina State Department of Public Instruction. Raleigh, North Carolina. 1975. ERIC ED 106 294.

Reports results of a survey incicating areas in which teachers seek help.

1135. Novak, John M. & Bennett, Allan C. Informally inviting moral development: teacher perception and behavior regarding the handling of moral transgressions. ERIC ED 230 519.

Describes teachers' attitudes toward moral development of students and actions in their classrooms designed to encourage moral development.

1136. Oakes, Jennis. 208 English teachers. 1980. ERIC ED 214 881.

Describes a sample of teachers, including their background, perceptions of their training and current teaching situations, professional activities and attitudes toward teaching; describes differences by subject taught.

1137. O'Hara, Mary Rita. The teacher and group development. 1965. ERIC ED 013 787.

Reports teachers' attitudes toward group process as both negative and neutral with group process identified as equivalent to grouping for instruction; saw discipline as a problem resulting from group process.

1138. O'Kech, Jack Green. A comparative analysis of mathematical knowledge and mathematical attitude between urban and suburban elementary school teachers. Ed.D. dissertation. Texas Southern University. 1978.

Describes knowledge and attitudes of teachers, with no differences between urban and suburban teachers except for new teachers, teachers with eleven or more years of experience, and science teachers, all in favor of suburban teachers.

1139. Okey, James R. & Yearny, Russel H., Jr. The relationships among science educators' research priorities and demographic variables. Presentation at the National Association for Research in Science Teaching. 1977. ERIC ED 139 632.

Presents science educators' ratings of their priorities for science teaching.

1140. Olander, Herbert T. & Farrell, Mary Elizabeth. "Professional problems of elementary teachers," Journal of Teacher Education 21 (1970): 276-280.

Describes problems which teachers report: almost half deal with provisions for individual children.

1141. Oliver, Ronald Lee. The analysis of teacher lateral mobility within selected public school districts. Ph.D. dissertation. Kansas State University. 1980.

Study found differences between elementary and secondary teachers in reasons given for transfer among schools.

1142. Orlov, Marsha Slugman. Factors associated with career change in teachers during young adulthood and middle age. Ed.D. dissertation. University of Virginia. 1983.

Describes factors which contribute to teachers' decisions to leave the teaching profession, with younger teachers and those from higher socio-economic levels having a greater likelihood of leaving.

1143. O'Rourke, Bill. "'Lion tamers and baby sitters': first-year English teachers' perceptions of their undergraduate teacher preparation," English Education 15 No. 1 (1983): 17-24.

Describes the attitudes of first year teachers toward their teaching situations, the curriculum and their preparation.

1144. O'Rourke, William J. "Research on the attitude of secondary teachers toward teaching reading in content classrooms," Journal of Reading 23 (1980): 337-339.

Reports a survey showing most junior and senior high teachers had no training in teaching reading; English teachers had more positive attitudes toward teaching reading than did mathematics, science and social science teachers.

1145. O'Sullivan, Denis. "Teachers' views on the effects of the home," Educational Research 22 (1980): 138-142.

Describes similarities in views of teachers in middle and working class schools on effects of home characteristics on student achievement.

1146. Otto, Wayne & Smith, Richard. Junior and senior high school teachers' attitudes toward teaching reading in the content areas. 1968. ERIC ED 026 226.

Teachers in junior and senior high schools recognize the need for continued reading instruction for which they are responsible; felt they needed more training.

1147. Owen, Jerry Monroe. A survey of teacher perspectives and practice of selected individualized instructional elements in middle-level schools. Ed.D. dissertation. University of Colorado at Boulder. 1980.

Describes teachers' perceptions of values of the elements of individualized instruction; found differences by subject taught and between valued behaviors and actual behaviors.

1148. Pajals, Edward & Blumberg, Arthur. Teachers' attachment to work. AERA presentation. 1979. ERIC ED 171 665.

Suggests that teachers are not job oriented in their central life interests; they differ from other professions in this respect.

1149. Palmer, Henry B.A. "Minicalculators in the classroom - what do teachers think?" Arithmetic Teacher 25 No. 7 (1978): 27-28.

Describes teachers' attitudes and concerns about the use of calculators in classrooms.

1150. Panda, Kailas C. & Bartel, Nettie R. "Teacher perception of exceptional children," Journal of Special Education 6 (1972): 261-266.

No differences reported among teachers with and without experience with special education children in attitude toward the children; attitudes did differ by type of handicapping condition.

1151. Parkay, Forrest W. Inner-city high school teachers: their perceptions of classroom life as revealed through a content analysis of projective stories. ERIC ED 206 772.

Describes attitudes of high school teachers toward their work environment and reports differences by teacher sex and race.

1152. Parsons, G. Llewellyn. The influence of supervisory roles. Memorial University. St. John's (Newfoundland). 1972. ERIC ED 091 826.

Reports teachers' perceptions of the influences of others on their teaching.

1153. Paulin, Pauline. The politics of evaluation at the local level: a view through teachers' perspectives. ERIC ED 207 224.

Describes teachers' attitudes toward teacher evaluation systems and their desire for participation in the design of evaluation systems.

1154. Payne, Tyrone & others. Small groups for instruction: an investigation of teacher viewpoints. ERIC ED 214 282.

Describes teachers' attitudes toward the use of small groups and the relationship between teachers' attitudes to the use of small groups for instructional purposes and effective classroom management.

1155. Perkes, V.A. "Correlates of teacher satisfaction in junior and senior high schools," California Journal of Educatonal Research 19 No. 5 (1968): 222-225.

Junior high teachers indicated greater dissatisfaction than senior high teachers about their interactions with students.

1156. Peterson, Anne R. Career patterns of secondary school teachers: an exploratory interview study of retired teachers. Ph.D. dissertation. Ohio State University. 1979.

Reports teachers' perceptions about and patterns of career development.

1157. Peterson, Anne R. Teachers' changing perceptions of self and others throughout the teaching career: some perspectives from an interview study of fifty retired secondary school teachers. AERA presentation. 1979. _ERIC_ _ED_ 173 337.

Teachers report changes over their careers in commitment to teaching, level of job morale, aging factors, levels of tolerance, and a change in attitude toward students, parents, colleagues and administrators.

1158. Peterson, Robert M. Work concepts in the schools: a survey of educators' opinions about work. 1978. _ERIC_ _ED_ 181 263.

Reports that current Colorado teachers' perceptions of quality work in teaching situations are similar to perceptions in the past; perceptions have not changed as people report a decline in the role of work in people's lives.

1159. Phelan, William T. Declining enrollment and the professional colleagueship of teachers. _ERIC_ _ED_ 241 526.

Describes teachers' attitudes toward seniority and evaluations as the major criterion on which to base lay-off decisions when districts must reduce the number of teachers.

1160. Phelan, William T. "Staffing policies in times of retrenchment: teacher opinions," _Peabody_ _Journal_ _of_ _Education_ _60_ _No._ _2_ (1983): 37-48.

Describes teachers' attitudes toward seniority and evaluation results as the basis for lay-off decisions when districts face reductions in professional staff.

1161. Phelan William T. Teachers under duress: some effects of declining enrollment and district staffing policies. _ERIC_ _ED_ 214 245.

Describes attitudes of teachers toward declining enrollments, reduction in force procedures and teachers' participation in development of those policies.

1162. Phihal, Jane. Intrinsic rewards of teaching. ERIC ED 200 599.

Describes teachers' views of the rewarding aspects of teaching as associated with their enjoyment of teaching which is in turn related to student achievement.

1163. Phihal, Jane. Types of intrinsic reward of teaching and their relation to teacher characteristics and variables in the work setting. ERIC ED 219 578.

Reports that teachers receive two types of rewards from teaching, rewards based on interactions with students and rewards associated with student learning.

1164. Pinkney H.B. & Esposito, James P. "Organizational climate of desegregated elementary schools: black and white teachers' perceptions," Journal of Educational Research 69 (1976): 226-231.

Black and white teachers differ in their perceptions of some organizational climate factors but differences are not related to the race of the principal.

1165. Poll, Carol. It's a good job for a woman (and a man): why males and females choose to be elementary school teachers. American Sociological Association presentation. 1979. ERIC ED 183 562.

Describes differences by sex in when and why males and females decide to become elementary teachers.

1166. Pontiac City School District. School staff attitudes and job satisfaction. Pontiac City School District. Michigan. 1976. ERIC ED 120 326.

Describes teacher's attitudes toward their jobs and factors which they viewed as positive and negative.

1167. Pook, Mary Ellen P. A study of the relationship of teacher job satisfaction and the level of implementation of recommended middle school practices. Ph.D. dissertation. University of Colorado at Boulder. 1980. ERIC ED 215 430.

Describes teachers' satisfactions with their jobs and working conditions and relates those to characteristics of middle schools.

1168. Price, Lafayette. A comparison of elementary school personnel perceptions of principals and teachers in high and low achieving schools in an urban school system. Ph.D. dissertation. University of Michigan. 1980.

Describes the same expectations for students among teachers in high and low achieving elementary schools, but greater intimacy, consideration, non-hinderance and productivity among teachers in high achieving schools, based on teacher reports.

1169. Quinsaat, Marilyn G. Implementing computer technology in a classroom setting: an anecdotal report of long term use. ERIC ED 224 464.

Describes the attitudes and experiences of one teacher in using a computer for classroom instructional activities.

1170. Rafky, Davie M. & Beckerman, Marvin. Teachers' acceptance of innovations: self-interest, altruism, and professionalization. 1971. ERIC ED 079 267.

Reports that self-interest is the primary motive through which elementary teachers implement innovations.

1171. Ramsay, Russell. Teachers' perceptions of the design and implementation of teacher evaluation systems in Tennessee public schools. Ed.D. dissertation. University of Tennessee. 1980.

Describes teachers' perceptions of characteristics of a system to evaluate teachers.

1172. Rasmussen, Roger. A study of alternatives in American education, volume III: teachers' responses to alternatives. ERIC ED 216 425.

Describes the attitudes of teachers toward alternative programs for students, the role of and problems with parental choice of programs, and aspects of alternative programs toward which teachers had positive attitudes.

1173. Rice, G. Elizabeth & Higgins, Norman. The role of standardized testing in the teacher's evaluation strategy. ERIC ED 222 498.

Describes teachers' attitudes toward student testing and uses of information from such testing.

1174. Richardson, John C. The effects of teacher race, segregation/desegregation, student race, and student sex on teacher-reported student behavior. Ed.D. dissertation. University of Kentucky. 1971.

Teachers' reports on student behavior are related to teachers' race; black teachers report more deviant student behavior; males, desegregation and student race (black) lead to more reported deviant behavior.

1175. Richman, Charles L. & others. Teacher attitudes concerning the nature of intelligence. Wake Forest University. 1979. ERIC ED 167 923.

Older teachers and those from private schools have greater belief in genetic I.Q. than younger and public school teachers.

1176. Riley, Daniel Eric. An analysis of teacher participation in decision-making in Iowa public schools. Ph.D. dissertation. University of Iowa. 1980.

Teachers wanted more involvement than they perceived they had in decision making at the classroom, school and district levels.

1177. Ringawa, Marcel M. Bilingual/bicultural teacher needs and attitudes: the mismatch between teacher training and teacher needs as documented in a Massachusetts community. Ed.D. dissertation. University of Massachusetts. 1980.

Describes needs and attitudes of bilingual teachers in one school district, identifying teaching needs related to instructional methodology, assessment and culture and community.

1178. Rist, Marilee C. "Our nationwide poll: most teachers endorse the merit pay concept," American School Board Journal 170 No. 9 (1983): 23-27.

Reports that the majority of teachers favor pay increases for effective teachers.

1179. Roberts, Arlie Jane. A study of the use of electronic media by secondary language arts teachers in the Denver metropolitan area. Ed.D. dissertation. University of Kansas. 1978.

Describes teachers' attitudes toward and use of electronic media for instructional purposes.

1180. Robertson, Kristine L. A descriptive study of teacher attitudes toward mainstreaming the special-needs child in the Poway Unified School District. Ed.D. dissertation. United States International University. 1983.

Describes positive teacher attitudes toward mainstreaming, teachers' ability to work with mainstreamed students, and the support services available to them in integrating mainstreamed students into their classrooms.

1181. Robinson, Daniel C. An investigation of the extent to which members of a single occupation (elementary teacher) show different or identical interests depending upon whether they are male or female or members of black or caucasian racial groups. Ph.D. dissertation. Iowa State University. 1978.

Study presents differences by sex and race in teacher interests.

1182. Robitaille, David F. & Sherrill, James M. "The teaching of mathematics in British Columbia," Canadian Journal of Education 5 (1980): 14-26.

Describes the attitudes and characteristics of mathematics teachers; they identified instruction in conceptual skills and algebraic manipulation as the most important content areas.

1183. Rose, Stephen Andrew. A study of current practices of Ohio public secondary social studies teachers engaged in values education. Ph.D. dissertation. Ohio State University. 1979.

Describes attitudes and self-reported behaviors that teachers identify related to values education.

1184. Rubio, Carmelo Albert. An interpretive inquiry into the world of the teacher. Ed.D. dissertation. University of North Carolina at Greensboro. 1979.

Describes perspectives of four teachers on teaching and teachers within their school system.

1185. Rundberg, Carol Williams. A study of usefulness, influence and accurate perceptions in relation to participant satisfaction with parent-teacher conferences. Ed.D. dissertation. University of Massachusetts. 1979.

Describes perceptions of parents and teachers toward parent-teacher conferences.

1186. Russell, Jerry Morris. Characteristics, attitudes, and practices of teachers in planning and implementing instructional strategies. Ed.D. dissertation. East Tennessee State University. 1979.

No differences between teachers in a city and a county school system in perceived value of written lesson plans, time reported spent preparing lesson plans or characteristics of teachers who used lesson plans.

1187. Rutherford, William L. & Weaver, Susan W. "Preferences of elementary teachers for preservice and in-service training in the teaching of reading," Journal of Educational Research 67 (1974): 271-275.

Teacher preferences for inservice vary by grade level and years of experience but are similar by site.

1188. Ryans, David J. Similarities and differences in teacher characteristics among ethnic groups represented in the United States. 1973. ERIC ED 078 041.

Presents differences in teachers' attitudes by ethnic group.

1189. Salmon-Cox, Leslie. "Teachers and standardized achievement tests: what's really happening?" Phi Delta Kappan 62 No. 9 (1981): 631-34.

Reports that teachers use information from their own observations more frequently than results of standardized tests for student assessment.

1190. Samuels, Barbara G. Young adult novels in the classroom? ERIC ED 227 893.

Describes teachers using some but not much of the literature written for young adults.

1191. Sanders, Ann & George, Archie. Concerns about the adoption of the learning resources center program in a rural school district. 1980. ERIC ED 190 291.

Describes the attitudes of teachers toward an innovation in a rural elementary school; the teachers had limited knowledge of the purpose of the innovative program and its relation to other school programs.

1192. Sanders, Annette & Watkins, J. Foster. "Organizational climate changes over time: another look," Capstone Journal of Education 1 (1980): 21-27.

Describes attitudes of teachers and principals toward their schools and work situations, comparing those attitudes to attitudes expressed by teachers and principals prior to desegregation of the schools.

1193. Schaefer, Charles. "An exploratory study of teachers' descriptions of the 'ideal' pupil," Psychology in the Schools 10 No. 4 (1973): 444-447.

Study indicates there is consensus between regular teachers and teachers of emotionally disturbed students in describing the ideal pupil.

1194. Schaeffer, Donald Thomas. An investigation into the differences between male and female elementary teachers in their perceptions of problems in pupils. Ed.D. dissertation. University of Maryland. 1968.

Describes differences by teacher sex in perceptions of student problems, and differences by student sex.

1195. Schibect, R.A. "Do teachers rate science attitude objectives as highly as cognitive objectives?" Journal of Research in Science Teaching 18 No. 1 (1981): 69-72.

Reports that science teachers view cognitive objectives as more important than affective objectives for student learning.

1196. Schubert, Nancy A. Educators' perception of the degree that their students learn according to selected principles of learning. ERIC ED 222 491.

Reports that teachers were aware of learning principles, applied them in their teaching and that attitudes toward student learning were associated with teacher sex and teaching assignments.

1197. Schubert, Sister Agnes L. Professional behaviors and teaching attitudes of mathematics teachers in public and nonpublic high schools. Ph.D. dissertation. Ohio University. 1974.

Describes preparation and values of teachers, with some differences between private and public schools.

1198. Schwartz, Daniel Erlund. Teacher attitudes following racial staff integration in Los Angeles and measures to modify these attitudes. Ed.D. dissertation. University of Southern California. 1981.

Describes differences in attitudes toward their present teaching assignment by whether teachers volunteered for reassignment or were assigned and whether they moved from or to inner-city schools.

1199. Schwartz, Terry Ann & others. Teacher dissatisfaction and alienation as related to mainstreaming in education. 1980. ERIC ED 191 194.

Reports that the majority of teachers surveyed felt that they had not received adequate information about their responsibilities related to the mainstreaming of handicapped students or training to teach such students.

1200. Seerman, Gael J., Brophy, J., Crawford, W. & Evertson, C. "Traditional attitudes and teacher consistency in producing student learning gains in the early elementary grades," Journal of School Psychology 14 No. 3 (1976): 192-201.

Reports consistent effect of some teachers showing more traditional attitudes than other teachers in the same school.

1201. Seyfarth, John T. & others. Influences on work preferences of team teachers in selected Individually Guided Education (IGE) schools. AERA presentation. 1975. ERIC ED 104 839.

Teachers' attitudes toward innovation related to severity of problems in implementing the innovation.

1202. Shaw, James Donald. Leadership behavior, teacher morale, and unexpected teacher absenteeism in selected elementary schools in an urban school district. Ed.D. dissertation. University of Florida. 1980. ERIC ED 221 929.

Reports relationships between teachers' morale, perceptions of the quality of educational leadership within their schools and levels of absenteeism in those schools.

1203. Shaw, Paul C. & Funderburk, Charles. "Teachers' political attitudes: alienation, dogmatism, and commitment to democratic values," Urban Education 10 No. 4 (1976): 366-378.

Describes teachers' political attitudes, with consistency across urban/rural and teacher race; supportive of the social order.

1204. Shaw, Rex Frederick. Teachers' professional preparation, experience, and work setting as determinants of their knowledge and attitude toward mental retardation and mainstreaming. Ed.D. dissertation. Columbia University. 1980.

Study reports a relationship between attitude toward mental retardation and mainstreaming but not between knowledge and attitudes among regular or special education teachers.

1205. Shelton, Jean Ann. Teacher knowledge of and attitudes toward Public Law 94-142. Ph.D. dissertation. Southern Illinois University at Carbondale. 1979.

Describes no differences in attitude but differences in knowledge about P.L. 94-142 between regular classroom and special education teachers.

1206. Shrigley, Robert L. "Science supervisor characteristics that influence their credibility with elementary school teachers," Journal of Research in Science Teaching 17 (1980): 161-166.

Reports that teachers perceive some characteristics of science supervisors as more credible than others and that some supervisors inspire greater teacher interest in science education.

1207. Sikula, John P. & others. "Do teachers differ in their values?" Education and Urban Society 4 No. 4 (1972): 459-466.

Reports different value profiles for teachers by geographic (urban/suburban) and grade level of teachers identified as successful.

1208. Silver, Paula F., Podemski, Richard S. & Engin, Ann W. "Attitudes toward sex role differentiation in education: implications for Title IX implementation," Journal of Research and Development in Education 10 (1977): 26-35.

Describes generally "liberal" attitudes of educators toward sex role differentiation, little support for traditional sex role distinctions, females more "liberal" and more suportive of change than males; similar responses for administrators.

1209. Smith, Dolores Abu. Perceptions of school effectiveness in teaching the basic skills: by parents, students, and certificated staff - a comparative study, 1974 and 1978. Ph.D. dissertation. University of Southern California. 1979.

Describes attitudes of parents, students and teachers toward success in teaching basic skills with differences by socioeconomic level.

1210. Smith, Frederick R. & Feathers, Karen M. "Teacher and student perceptions of content area reading," Journal of Reading 26 No. 4 (1983): 348-54.

Reports that teachers and students see reading as of limited importance in content area courses.

1211. Smith, R.A. & Fox, F.H. Expressed attitude of teachers toward negotiations: a factor analytic study. AERA presentation. 1971. ERIC ED 048 628.

Teachers have a greater interest in determining negotiating items related to professional duties than relating to working conditions.

1212. Smith, Richard J., Otto, Wayne & Harty, Kathleen. "Elementary teachers' preferences for pre-service and in-service training in the teaching of reading," Journal of Educational Research 63 (1970): 445-449.

Describes teachers' reported attitudes toward inservice and their perceptions of needs for training in reading.

1213. Smith, Thomas E. "The image of high school teachers: self and other, real and ideal (should teachers be seen and not heard?)," Journal of Educational Research 59 (1965): 99-104.

Reports differences in images of "ideal teachers" among teachers and non-teachers with teachers identifying a more passive role and non-teachers a more active role.

1214. Smith, Tom E.C. "Attitudes of principals and teachers toward mainstreaming handicapped children," Journal for Special Educators 16 (1979): 89-95.

A survey found agreement among regular and special education teachers in terms of categories of children who should be mainstreamed; against mainstreaming trainable mentally retarded.

1215. Sobelman, Marilyn. The relationship of secondary school teachers' subject specialization, teaching level, and reaction to selected teaching situations. 1971. ERIC ED 075 170.

Study identified differences between English and social studies/math and science teachers in responding to a teaching situation reaction test.

1216. Sparks, Dennis C. "A biased look at teacher job satisfaction," Clearing House 52 No. 9 (1979): 447-449.

Reports teachers' attitudes toward aspects of their jobs and work situations.

1217. Sponseller, Doris B. & Fink, Joel S. "Early childhood education: a national profile of early childhood educators' views," Education and Urban Society 12 No. 2 (1980): 163-173.

Describes attitudes of early childhood educators, showing support for education outside the home and differences between educators in public and private institutions.

1218. Stallard, Sandra Faye. Perceptions of selected teachers regarding knowledge and skill competencies needed for teaching black students. Ph.D. dissertation. University of Virginia. 1979.

Describes the several skills and knowledge that successful teachers of black students believe are necessary e.g., knowledge of culture, history, language, learning problems and learning strengths of black students.

1219. Stanton, Jack Le Roy. Preferences and opinions of regular teachers in mainstreaming exceptional children in classes of nonexceptional children in school districts of Kern County which host county-operated classes. Ed.D. dissertation. University of Southern California. 1980.

Describes teachers' interests in the concept of mainstreaming, preferences for lower class size when handicapped children are mainstreamed, and perceptions that they have the necessary training.

1220. Starkey, John D. & others. Discipline: are older teachers more liberal than younger ones? 1972. ERIC ED 074 053.

Presents beliefs in discipline according to the age of the teachers.

1221. Staton-Spicer, Ann Q. The measurement and further conceptualization of teacher communication concern. ERIC ED 272 384.

Reports that teachers' concerns about communication are related to their attitudes toward teaching as a career and anxiety about their teaching.

1222. Staton-Spicer, Ann Q. & Bassett, Ronald E. An investigation of the communication concerns of preservice and inservice elementary school teachers: a developmental conceptualization. Speech Communication Association presentation. 1978. ERIC ED 168 066.

Describes a range of concerns and differences between pre and inservice teachers.

1223. Stavros, Denny. Report on the results of a survey of Northwestern High School staff. High School Improvement Project. 1982. ERIC ED 230 663.

Describes teachers' attitudes toward their school and aspects of the program and teaching environment.

1224. Steber, James M. A study of the perceptions of teaching effectiveness by supervisors and classroom teachers at three levels of schooling: elementary, intermediate, and senior high school. Ed.D. dissertation. Rutgers University. 1977.

Bias of principals in rating teachers differs by level of school as does the relationship between principal and teacher rating; no difference by level of teacher ratings and teacher effectiveness.

1225. Stennett, R.G. & Earl, L.M. Open area elementary schools: survey of teachers attitudes and opinions. ERIC ED 238 834.

Describes the attitudes of teachers teaching in open education classrooms toward aspects of open education; attitudes differed for different aspects of open education.

1226. Steward, Judith R. & Love, W.A., Jr. "The teacher's response to technology and the individualization of instruction," *Educational Technology* 10 (1970): 56-61.

Describes attitudes of teachers in one innovative high school - high level of satisfaction with school, feeling that they work harder, lack role clarity, have a different preference for developing curriculum materials and individualized instruction.

1227. Strein, William & Murphy, James P. "Fostering student emotional growth: teacher self-assessments," Humanist Educator 20 No. 3 (1982): 124-33.

Describes teachers as having a positive view of their ability to foster student emotional growth.

1228. Stunard, Sonja-Lou Linnea. Job satisfaction and teacher attitudes of regular classroom and special education teachers. Ph.D. dissertation. University of Illinois at Chicago Circle. 1982.

Reports differences in job satisfaction and attitudes toward students by teaching assignment, with teachers in regular classrooms and resource special education teachers having more positive attitudes toward students than special education teachers.

1229. Tamir, P. & Jungwirth, E. "Teaching objectives in biology: priorities and expectations," Science Education 56 No. 1 (1972): 31-39.

Describes teachers' priorities for biology education and differences between those using new and experimental (BSCS) curricula.

1230. Tanner, Paul Morton. Attitudes toward high school sex education of sex educators, other teachers and the adult public in three Oregon school districts. Ph.D. dissertation. University of Minnesota. 1979.

Describes attitudes of several groups toward issues of sex education.

1231. Tellenback, Sten. Teacher stress: complex model building with LISREL. ERIC ED 229 332.

Describes factors which teachers report as associated with stress and methods to identify such factors.

1232. Thompson, Bruce. Teacher thought regarding instructional preference. 1980. ERIC ED 196 918.

Describes teachers' perceptions of ideal teaching as related to their educational philosophies and models of teaching and found consistent patterns of teachers' ideal teaching models.

1233. Thompson, Virginia Lee. Attitudes of regular classroom teachers toward mainstreaming in relationship to the availability and perceived adequacy of counseling services. Ph.D. dissertation. George Washington University. 1981.

Reports no relationship between teachers' characteristics, e.g., age and courses taken, and attitude toward mainstreaming, but a relationship between attitude toward adequacy of counseling services for handicapped students and attitude toward mainstreaming.

1234. Tighe, M.A. & Koziol, S.M., Jr. "Practices in the teaching of writing by teachers of English, social studies, and science," English Education 14 No. 2 (1982): 76-85.

Describes teachers' perceptions of writing instruction and of their own writing instruction activities.

1235. Tinajero, Josefina V. Oral language competencies found in language assessment or achievement tests as related to teachers' perceptions of their importance, time-treatment, and received training. Ed.D. dissertation. Texas A & I University. 1980.

Reports discrepancies among what teachers felt should be taught and what they felt prepared to teach and what they felt was assessed in competency tests.

1236. Tolar, A. & Lane, P.A. "Educational backgrounds of teachers who differ in attitudes toward child behavior," Psychological Reports 21 No. 1 (1967): 179-180.

Describes differences in teachers' perceptions of child behavior; more experienced teachers' views of normal child behavior are more like the views of clinical psychologists than are the views of less experienced teachers.

1237. Tompkens, Patricia A.L. An examination of stress and anxiety in teachers of handicapped and non-handicapped children. Ph.D. dissertation. University of Texas at Austin. 1980.

Study found no difference in levels of anxiety and stress among regular classroom teachers and teachers of handicapped children.

1238. Truesdell, Lee Ann M. A comparison of teacher perceptions of generic teaching skills for early childhood and elementary classroom teachers. Ph.D. dissertation. Florida State University. 1978.

Describes ratings of teacher competencies by elementary and secondary teachers, and early and upper elementary teachers.

1239. Tucker, Oscar DePriest. The perceptions of students, teachers, and administrators regarding unwed, pregnant students in the public secondary schools of the state of Alabama. Ph.D. dissertation. University of Alabama. 1980.

Describes differences in perceptions by race and urban/rural location of school but not by group membership in perceptions of unwed mothers in school.

1240. Tye, Kenneth A. Changing our schools: the realities. ERIC ED 218 241.

Describes teachers' attitudes toward their schools, school policies and procedures, and their own careers as they relate to the possibilities for change in schools.

1241. Usova, George M. "Analysis of attitudes toward reading among secondary content-area teachers," Clearing House 52 No. 1 (1978): 22-24.

Study found differences in teachers' attitudes toward reading instruction by subject (English, history, mathematics).

1242. Van Schaack, Herbert & Glick, I. David. A qualitative study of excellence in teaching and the search for excellence in teaching: an annotated bibliography. ERIC ED 213 660.

Describes the attitudes toward teaching and behaviors of teachers selected as being effective teachers through the National Teacher of the Year program.

1243. Van Wagner, Suzanne Kay. Perceptions of practicing middle school teachers holding the Michigan middle school endorsement regarding middle school teacher competencies. Ph.D. dissertation. Michigan State University. 1979.

Describes beliefs of middle school teachers toward a set of teaching competencies and their reports of the extent to which they use those competencies.

1244. Volsch, Lucretia R.P. Perceptions of regular and special education teachers regarding the influence of selected variables of school performance. Ed.D. dissertation. Northern Illinois University. 1980.

Describes differences among regular and special education teachers by level taught in perceptions of influence of school factors on the school performance of students.

1245. Wallich, Lynn R. School climate: an organizational development view. 1980. ERIC ED 201 043.

Describes the morale of teachers and administrators before and after a program directed to changing several characteristics of school climate thought to be related to teacher morale, such as discipline procedures, inservice training, and communication.

1246. Washington, Valora. Desegregation attitudes, perceptions and classroom behavior of black and white teachers of second grade: group profiles and interrelationships in integrated settings. Ph.D. dissertation. Indiana University. 1978.

Describes characteristics and attitudes of black and white teachers in desegregated schools.

1247. Wayson, W.W. Source of teacher satisfaction in slum schools. 1967. ERIC ED 012 267.

Describes differences in perceptions of teachers who remain in and leave slum schools with those who stay stressing the warm personal relationships they have there.

1248. Weber, Wilford A. Teacher perceptions of effective classroom management strategies. ERIC ED 204 311.

Reports the strategies for classroom management that teachers report are related to effective teaching.

1249. Weinstock, H.R. & Turner, H.E. Philosophical orientation, logical consistency, and teaching attitudes of urban and suburban teachers. AERA presentation. 1970. ERIC ED 040 128.

Describes differences in philosophical orientation by teaching site and age.

1250. Whitcombe, J.E. An investigation of the position of women in primary and secondary teaching in New Zealand. 1980. ERIC ED 211 540.

Describes differences between male and female teachers in career development, career aspirations, factors external to teaching that influence career decisions.

1251. Wilkerson, Elvedine. A comparative study of teacher attitudes regarding the forced desegregation of urban elementary school faculties. Ed.D. dissertation. Temple University. 1979.

Describes no differences in teachers' attitudes by years of teaching and whether school transfers were forced or voluntary but differences in black and white teachers in attitudes toward desegregation.

1252. Wilkes, Sam T. & Blackbourn, Joe M. The revalidation of an instrument to measure zones of indifference of teachers to directives issued by administrators. ERIC ED 240 166.

Describes areas of teachers' indifference to directives by principals and the development of a measurement instrument.

1253. Wilkins, Glenn Calvin. An attitudinal survey of selected elementary school teachers concerning in-service training in educational media. Ed.D. dissertation. Louisiana State University and A & M College. 1979.

Describes attitudes of teachers toward staff development needs regarding the use of media for instructional purposes.

1254. Williams, Jean Alexander. An analysis of teacher attitudes toward mainstreaming as perceived by elementary teachers of selected schools in northeastern Ohio. Ph.D. dissertation. Kent State University. 1981.

Describes limited relationships between teachers' characteristics, e.g., age and educational level, and attitudes toward mainstreaming of handicapped students.

1255. Williams, Robert C. An analysis of the attitudes of junior high school teachers toward the placement of the exceptional child in the regular classroom. Ed.D. dissertation. University of Southern Mississippi. 1982.

Reports a relationship between teachers' attitudes toward specific handicaps and attitudes toward mainstreaming, but not relationship between attitudes toward mainstreaming and teacher personal characteristics, e.g., age, race, teaching experience.

1256. Williams, Sheri S. "Colorado PTSA studies the home-school partnership," PTA Today 8 No. 7 (1983): 31-32.

Describes the attitudes of teachers toward communication with parents.

1257. Winn, Deanna Daines. Selected personality characteristics and demographic data of in-service teachers as they relate to clinical supervision. Ed.D. dissertation. Utah State University. 1981.

Reports differences in attitude and personality characteristics of teachers who did and did not volunteer to participate in an innovative clinical supervision program.

1258. Witmer, J.M. The teacher's guidance role and functions as reported by elementary teachers. American Personnel and Guidance Association presentation. 1968. ERIC ED 030 890.

Describes teachers' perceptions of their guidance functions, e.g., using information from cumulative records, identifying exceptional children, helping children explore the world of work and cope with learning and adjustment problems, developing special aptitudes.

1259. Wolf, Richard Paul, Jr. Role expectations and instructional improvement. Ed.D. dissertation. Colorado State College. 1969.

Teachers perceive that they share with principals the responsibility for improvement of instruction.

1260. Wright, Benjamin D. & Stone, Mark H. Measurement as an instrument of learning. ERIC ED 238 441.

Describes teachers' attitudes toward the use of computers for instruction and changes associated with the use of computers.

1261. Wright, David P. Teachers' perceptions of their own influence over school policies and decisions. 1980. ERIC ED 214 886.

Reports that teachers in a sample of schools thought they had the most influence in matters relating to instruction, such as curriculum, communication with parents and control of pupil behavior.

1262. Wright, William Francis. A study to determine the effectiveness of the semantic differential as a means for measuring attitudes of teachers toward public school supervisory personnel. Ed.D. dissertation. Florida Atlantic University. 1980.

Reports differences in teachers' attitudes related to supervisory methods and teachers' demographic characteristics; major focus of work is on development of the measurement technique.

1263. Yeh, Jennie P. A reanalysis of test use data. 1980. ERIC ED 205 590.

Describes teachers' uses of test information for instructional decision making and the teacher characteristics associated with use of test information.

1264. Yeh, Jennie P. & others. Teachers and testing: a survey of test use. ERIC ED 218 336.

Describes teachers' attitudes toward and use of information from standardized and teacher made tests and the influences of teaching assignment and years of experience in attitudes.

1265. Young, J.E.M. "A survey of teachers' attitudes toward certain aspects of their profession," Canadian Education and Research Digest (1967). ERIC ED 012 712.

Results of a survey of teachers with one to two years of experience; most liked aspects: working with pupils, holidays and hours, variety of work; least liked aspects: clerical duties, parent-teacher conflicts, correcting work; best teacher well organized.

1266. Zahorik, John A. "Learning activities: nature, function, and practice," Elementary School Journal 82 No. 4 (1982): 309-18.

Describes teachers' attitudes toward specific student learning activities and their likelihood of success.

1267. Zahorik, John A. & Kritek, William J. Using direct instruction. 1980. ERIC ED 231 768.

Describes teachers' instructional behaviors and relates those behaviors to attitudes toward student learning needs and pupil control ideology; some elements of "direct instruction" were used more frequently than were others.

V. INFLUENCES ON ATTITUDES

1268. Adams, Ronald D. "Teacher development: a look at changes in teacher perceptions and behavior across time," Journal of Teacher Education 33 No. 4 (1982). ERIC ED 214 926.

Describes changes in teachers' attitudes toward schools and teaching over time, noting the specific needs of beginning teachers.

1269. Agnew, Jimmie Dell. "Confidence levels of earth science teachers," Journal of Geological Education 31 No. 3 (1983): 197-99.

Describes factors which contribute to science teachers' confidence in their ability to teach earth science; preservice and inservice education were perceived by teachers as important.

1270. Aikens, Louis Langston. The relationship of teachers' perceived administrative style to evaluations of their principals' administrative efficiency on functions requiring interpersonal relations. Ph.D. dissertation. Bowling Green State University. 1978.

Reports that teachers' ratings of principals' effects are related to teachers' characteristics.

1271. Allen, Barton S., Jr. The relationships among principals' attitudes toward unions, principals' role activities, and principals' and teachers' perceptions of management style. Ed.D. dissertation. Fordham University. 1979.

Describes teachers' perceptions of principals' style in relation to principals' attitudes toward unions and the principals' union activities.

1272. Althoff, Rosemary Helen. The effects of an inservice training procedure on the attitudes of regular education teachers toward mainstreaming of handicapped students. Ed.D. dissertation. Wayne State University. 1981.

Describes attitudes of teachers toward inservice education related to mainstreaming, reporting changes resulting from inservice training.

1273. Amodeo, Luiza B. & Martin, Jeanette. A study of the effects of multicultural training on the factual knowledge of stereotypic attitudes of elementary and secondary teachers. ERIC ED 213 686.

Describes the effects of an inservice education program on teachers' knowledge about and attitudes toward Hispanic students.

1274. Anderson, Kristen Marie. Effects of day care and nursery school settings on teacher attitudes. Ph.D. dissertation. Stanford University. 1981.

Describes differences in teachers' attitudes and expectations between teachers in the two settings, associated with differences in teachers' characteristics.

1275. Anderson, Shirley Seaton. Head Start teacher attitudes toward mainstreaming as related to knowledge. Ph.D. dissertation. George Peabody College for Teachers of Vanderbilt University. 1982.

Reports changes in teachers' knowledge about handicapping conditions and positive attitudes toward mainstreaming resulting from participation in an inservice education program.

1276. Anderson, Susan Joy. The effects of variations of specificity and elaboration of feedback on rating ability and attitude toward the assessment of teacher performance. Ph.D. dissertation. University of Georgia. 1981.

Describes a change in the attitudes of teachers toward evaluation of teaching performance resulting from participation in an inservice program designed to teach teachers to use a performance assessment instrument.

1277. Aquino, Charles C. "Teacher attitudes toward audiovisual instruction as they are influenced by selected factors within the teaching environments," A.V. Communication Review 18 (1970): 187-195.

Teacher interest is related to the amount of audiovisual materials and accessibility of AV equipment, i.e., enough materials to browse and select.

1278. Arikado, M.S. "Status consensus as it relates to team teacher satisfaction," Alberta Journal of Educational Research 21 No. 2 (1975): 104-109.

Describes teachers' satisfaction with team teaching as related to the degree of team consensus.

1279. Askov, Eunice N. & Dupuis, Mary M. Impact of content area reading inservice education on teachers: a follow-up study conducted one year later. 1980. ERIC ED 188 140.

Reports that, one year after an inservice education program on reading instruction, teachers retained their positive attitudes toward reading instruction in the content areas that resulted from the inservice program.

1280. Askov, Eunice N. & Dupuis, Mary M. Teacher change: impact of an inservice program in content area reading. ERIC ED 211 966.

Describes teachers' attitudes toward teaching reading in other subject area courses and changes in those attitudes resulting from an inservice education program.

1281. Asselin, Susan B. "Peer tutoring inservice program: effects on home economics teachers' knowledge and attitudes," Home Economics Research Journal 11 No. 4 (1983): 352-58.

Describes changes in teachers' attitudes toward mainstreamed students resulting from participation in an inservice program.

1282. Attles, LeRoy. Teacher attitudes toward the mentally retarded as a function of teacher's level of personal security. Ed.D. dissertation. Rutgers University. 1980.

Study found that teachers' attitudes toward the mentally retarded are related to contact with the mentally retarded and teachers' feelings of personal security.

1283. Austin, Harry Loyd. The relationship of degree, sex, experience, subject and grade level with teacher perceived problems in selected urban secondary schools. Ed.D. dissertation, University of Kansas. 1979.

Indicates that differences in teachers' perceptions of problems are related to characteristics such as experience, degree level and teaching level; e.g., greater time problems with higher grade level students.

1284. Axelberd, F.J. "Attitudes of elementary school teachers toward counseling and guidance in the elementary schools," Journal of Experimental Education 37 No. 3 (1969): 1-4.

Teachers in schools with guidance programs have more favorable attitudes toward elementary school guidance programs than teachers in schools without such programs.

1285. Ayers, Jerry B. & Richey, David Dean. Influencing teacher attitudes and knowledge about child maltreatment. ERIC ED 238 883.

Describes changes in teachers' attitudes toward a knowledge of child abuse resulting from participation in an inservice program.

1286. Ayers, Macy N. Beginning teachers' attitudes and their relationship to selected variables. 1972. ERIC ED 073 166.

Changes between preservice and first year of teaching in attitude related to openness of the school where the teacher is teaching.

1287. Bailey, Susan C. Educational attitudes and classroom teaching behaviors of teachers in selected models of licensure. Ph.D. dissertation. Fordham University. 1976.

Describes teachers' attitudes toward teaching; they differ by the type of system the teachers followed to get a teaching license.

1288. Bajorat, William Henry. An analysis of attitudinal differences between teachers involved in Science - A Process Approach. Ed.D. dissertation. University of Florida. 1980.

Study found no differences in background characteristics or educational philosophy between teachers who favored and those who opposed Science - A Process Approach.

1289. Baker, Larry Dean. Effect of an in-service training program in "sex-roles and education" on educator attitudes. Ed.D. dissertation. University of Arkansas. 1980.

Describes educators' attitudes toward sex roles and changes in those attitudes resulting from participation in a course in sex roles.

1290. Baldwin, James Edward. Role perception and teacher morale: a study of their relationship in secondary schools. Ed.D. dissertation. Brigham Young University. 1979.

Congruence between teacher and principal perception of principal role is related to higher teacher morale.

1291. Banks, Eunice Jean Myatt. The effects of attitudes of teachers toward the achievement level of educable mentally impaired students in a local school district. Ph.D. dissertation. University of Michigan. 1983.

Reports no relationship between teacher demographic characteristics, e.g., age, years of experience with handicapped students, and teacher attitudes toward handicapped students.

1292. Baptiste, H. Prentice & others. The impact of racial membership on teacher/administrator attitudes towards multicultural education. 1980. ERIC ED 184 987.

Reports that teachers' and administrators' attitudes toward multicultural education were associated with race of the educator; white administrators had the least positive attitudes toward multicultural education.

1293. Baylor, John Gibson. The influence of an introductory microcomputer course on educators' attitudes toward computers. Ed.D. dissertation. University of Southern Mississippi. 1982.

Describes a training program in the use of microcomputers for teachers and changes in behavior and attitudes resulting from participation in the program.

1294. Bean, Thomas W. "The effect of a mini-conference on teacher beliefs about the reading process," Reading Horizons 22 No. 2 (1982): 85-90.

Reports changes in teachers' attitudes toward reading instruction resulting from participation in an inservice program.

1295. Beard, Gary Don. Assessment of attitudes of teachers involved in team teaching in the elementary school compared to team size. Ed.D. dissertation. University of Northern Colorado. 1978.

Describes attitudes of teachers in teams toward the teams and problems related to team size.

1296. Beare, Paul L. The effect of a combined crisis teacher and child advocacy program on teacher attitude, student school morale and student school attendance behaviors. Ph.D. dissertation. University of Missouri-Columbia. 1979.

Reports no differences in teachers' attitudes toward teaching potential dropouts between teachers who did and did not participate in a training program.

1297. Becker, Sidney Graves. The effectiveness of inservice training using simulation, videotape and participatory lecture in changing attitudes and increasing diagnostic abilities of elementary teachers involved in mainstreaming mildly handicapped children. Ph.D. dissertation. Union Graduate School (Ohio). 1979.

Describes no differences in teachers' attitudes and diagnostic skills when working with mildly handicapped students as a result of participation in an inservice program; the evaluation data resulted in changes in the materials used for the inservice program.

1298. Beezer, Bruce Gerald. The influence of pupil socio-economic status and teacher characteristics on teacher role performance. Ed.D. dissertation. University of Arizona. 1970.

Describes differences in the amount of emphasis teachers report toward different teacher roles by teacher age, years of experience, and socioeconomic level of students.

1299. Behrman, Edward Henry. Teacher-student relations as a predictor of teachers' job satisfaction. Ed.D. dissertation. University of Pennsylvania. 1976.

The teacher-administrator relationship has a greater effect on teacher job satisfaction than teacher-peer and teacher-student relationships; teacher-student relationship has greater influence when teachers and students are poorly matched socially and racially.

1300. Bennett, Darlene B. Teacher practices and attitudes on pupil retention in Louisiana elementary schools.

Ed.D. dissertation. Northwestern State University of Louisiana. 1981.

Reports that promotion or nonpromotion is affected by teachers' attitudes toward nonpromotion, grade level and school structure, but not years of experience.

1301. Berchin, Arthur. Congruency of values among teachers, principals, and parents and its relationship to the goal-attaining process. AERA presentation. 1971. ERIC ED 132 447.

Describes differences in values among teachers, parents and principals but no differences by the degree of school attainment of school goals.

1302. Bergesom, Teresa Marion. A comparison of two methods of improving math attitudes in intermediate teachers and counselors. Ph.D. dissertation. University of Washington. 1982.

Describes a program to train teachers in spatial visualization skills and limited changes in teachers' attitudes resulting from participation in the program.

1303. Berrigan, Carol Rizzo. Effects of an inservice education workshop on the attitudes of regular classroom teachers toward disabled students. Ph.D. dissertation. Syracuse University. 1979.

Describes a program for training teachers and reports an increase in positive attitudes toward disabled students among teachers who participated in the program.

1304. Bethel, Lowell J. "The effects of a NSF institute on inservice teachers' views of science and attitudes toward environmental science education," Science Education 66 No. 4 (1982): 643-51.

Reports that participation in an inservice program had a positive effect on teachers' attitudes toward science and science education.

1305. Bethel, Lowell J. & Hord, Shirley M. A case study of change: inservice teachers in National Science Foundation environmental science education program. ERIC ED 200 589.

Describes positive changes in attitudes of teachers toward science teaching resulting from participation in an inservice education program.

1306. Bhella, Surjit K. "Principals leadership style: does it affect teacher morale?" Education 102 No. 4 (1982): 369-76.

Describes differences in teachers' attitudes toward teaching situations associated with teachers' sex and principal's attitudes.

1307. Bilsky, Dorothy Gartner. An analysis of the relationship of teachers' job satisfaction and teachers' union attitudes in a large midsouthern city. Ed.D. dissertation. Memphis State University. 1982.

Describes differences in teachers' attitudes toward the goals and methods of collective bargaining by teacher characteristics, e.g., age, race, level of satisfaction with their teaching position.

1308. Blankenship, Jacob W. "Biology teachers and their attitudes concerning BSCS," Journal of Research in Science Teaching 3 (1965): 54-60.

Describes differences in attitudes between teachers teaching and not teaching BSCS biology.

1309. Blase, Joseph J. "A social-psychological grounded theory of teacher stress and burnout," Educational Administration Quarterly 18 No. 4 (1982): 93-113.

Reports that decreases in teachers' involvement in their work are associated with increases in teacher burnout.

1310. Bogaty, Boris E. An investigation of teacher expectancies of instructional materials. research report No. 2. Northwest Regional Special Education Instructional Materials Center. University of Oregon. Eugene. 1970. ERIC ED 075 345.

Teachers' perceptions of the value of material is related to the degree of student achievement when using the material.

1311. Bognar, Carl J. "Dissonant feedback about achievement and teachers' expectations," Alberta Journal of Educational Research 28 No. 3 (1982); 277-87.

Describes future changes in teachers' expectations for individual students resulting from a review of test results.

1312. Bolton, Harold & Mosow, David K. "Microcomputers in the classroom: a foot in the door," Educational Computer 1 No. 3 (1991): 34-36.

Describes changes among teachers and students to more positive attitudes toward computer use for instructional purposes after participation in a simulation.

1313. Boschee, Floyd & Hein, Dennis D. "How effective is inservice education?" Phi Delta Kappan 61 (1980): 427.

Reports that teachers report few changes in attitude and behavior and decreasing opinions about the value of an inservice workshop over time after the workshop.

1314. Boston, Margaret E. & Mitroff, Donna D. Continuing effects: a study of knowledge utilization. 1980. ERIC ED 190 611.

Reports that teachers trained in use of an instructional program continued to use the program in the years after they received training; factors related to continued use include compatibility with usual practices, ease of modification.

1315. Box, Tiara Arlina. Predicting teachers' attitudes toward physically impaired students. Ph.D. dissertation. East Texas State University. 1981.

Describes a limited relationship between teachers' attitudes toward physically impaired students and teachers' characteristics, e.g., teaching level, age, physical health.

1316. Bradbury, Marilee Jean. Experience in curriculum development: some effects of communication, conflict, attitude change, and leadership. Ph.D. dissertation. University of Colorado at Boulder. 1979.

Conflict within groups developing a writing curriculum were associated with lack of change in attitude toward writing instruction.

1317. Braden, Beverly D. "A positive inservice experience in negative behavior change," Educational Leadership 40 No. 1 (1982): 54.

Reports that teachers and administrators became aware of and some changed their negative behavior after participation in a program of positive statements.

1318. Bradford, Juanita S.B. An investigation of job dissatisfaction among elementary teachers within the East Baton Rouge Parish school system. Ed.D. dissertation. George Peabody College for Teachers of Vanderbilt University. 1980.

Describes reasons teachers report for job dissatisfaction among teachers requesting a transfer; no difference by background variables such as sex, race and age.

1319. Brennan, Leonard. Teacher acceptance and rejection of innovation in classroom practice. Ed.D. dissertation. Columbia University. 1971.

Teachers' acceptance of a particular innovation is related to characteristics of teachers as acceptors or rejectors of innovations in general.

1320. Brinkmeier, O.A. & others. Inside the organizational teacher - the relationship between selected characteristics of teachers and their membership in teacher organizations. 1967. ERIC ED 015 542.

Teachers agreed with the position of their professional organization on controversial issues; membership in one of two groups was related to personality characteristics but not to school climate.

1321. Brosnan, William J., Jr. Teacher attitude toward curricular innovation as a function of age and experience within the framework of Rotter's social learning theory. Ed.D. dissertation. Columbia University Teachers College. 1982.

Reports a strong relationship between attitude toward an innovation and the belief that the innovation would result in more student success, with elementary teachers having a more positive attitude than secondary teachers.

1322. Brubaker, Constance K. Reactions of public school teachers to simple and complex technological innovations endorsed by different sources varying in educator role and previous public school teaching experience. Ed.D. dissertation. Indiana University. 1978.

Describes teachers' attitudes toward and willingness to try educational innovations by degree of perceived complexity of the innovation; no greater willingness to try if the innovation is endorsed.

1323. Bruce, Larry R. "A study of the relationship between the SCIS teachers' attitude toward the teacher-student relationship and question type," Journal of Research in Science Teaching 8 (1971): 157-164.

Describes attitudes of teachers, question types used and changes in question type after training; teachers increased the number of fact questions that they asked.

1324. Bryant, Dorothy Taylor. A study of the relationship of inservice education to teachers' attitudes and pupil achievement. Ed.D. dissertation. George Peabody College for Teachers of Vanderbilt University. 1981.

Reports that teachers who participated in a mathematics inservice education program changed their attitudes toward mathematics instruction but not toward inservice education programs.

1325. Bunting, Carolyn. "Leadership style and the instructional role of the principal," Psychology in the Schools 19 No. 4 (1982): 570-72.

Reports a relationship between the principal's leadership style and teachers' attitudes toward classroom roles.

1326. Burgess, Marilyne Powell. A study of the relationships between organizational climate and pupil control ideology. Ph.D. dissertation. George Peabody College for Teachers of Vanderbilt University. 1983.

Reports a relationship between teachers' pupil control ideology and the organizational climate of the school as perceived by the teachers.

1327. Butler, Jesse Joe. Teacher attitude, classroom climate, and the level of implementation of recommended middle school practices in Oklahoma. Ed.D. dissertation. Oklahoma State University. 1983.

Describes a relationship between teachers' attitudes and perceptions of school climate, with a low level of implementation of the concept of the middle school among the schools studied.

1328. Caliguri, Joseph & Levine, Daniel A. "Relationships between teachers' views on education and their socio-economic attitudes," Journal of Experimental Education 35 No. 4 (1967): 42-44.

Reports a relationship between teachers' attitudes toward education, economics and social attitudes (liberal and conservative).

1329. Calloway, Rolland. Teachers' beliefs concerning values and the functions and purposes of schooling. 1979. ERIC ED 177 110.

Describes beliefs teachers have about schooling and the relationship between those attitudes and age, sex, professional level (teacher or student teacher).

1330. Camerota, Elaine C. The effect of dramatic improvisation on the attitudes of high school teachers toward their students. Ed.D. dissertation. Rutgers University. 1980.

Describes teachers' attitudes toward students, limited changes resulting from participation in the experimental improvisation program, and changes toward more negative attitudes toward students during the course of the school year.

1331. Capillupo, Jean Nady. Colorado school finance: teachers' knowledge and attitudes. Ed.D. dissertation. University of Denver. 1980.

Describes teachers' recognition of the importance of school finance issues; greater knowledge of school finance among teachers who own property, have a master's degree, have taken a course or workshop on school finance.

1332. Carter, J.A. & Frankel, Eric A. "The effects of a teacher training program in family life and human sexuality on the knowledge and attitudes of public school teachers," Journal of School Health 53 No. 8 (1983): 459-62.

Reports a change in knowledge but not attitude resulting from participation in a course on human sexuality.

1333. Castiglione, Lawrence V. Potential mobility among career teachers in New York City's middle schools: the relationship between selected occupational characteristics, expectations and attitudes. Center for Urban Education. New York. 1978. ERIC ED 087 732.

Study investigated a relationship between teachers' attitudes, school characteristics and mobility of teachers; reports existence of relationship but small response rate.

1334. Catalino, Salvatore W. Leadership belief systems, attitude toward teacher participation and decisional participation: a study of the relationship of principal belief system, attitude toward teacher participation and teacher decisional deviation. Ed.D. dissertation. State University of New York at Buffalo. 1979.

Reports a relationship between administrators' belief systems and teachers' perceptions of their involvement in decision making, with teachers' decisional deviation associated with the attitude of the principal toward teachers' participation in decision making.

1335. Cathey, Fannie MacW. Teacher perceptions of multicultural education in comparison with their previous multicultural education preparation. Ph.D. dissertation. George Peabody College for Teachers of Vanderbilt University. 1980.

Teachers' race but not previous training in multicultural education is related to attitudes toward multicultural education.

1336. Chai, Heny Keonaona. The effect of knowledge of students beliefs and attitudes on the teacher's attitude and behavior toward that student. Ed.D. dissertation. Arizona State University. 1979.

Describes no change in teachers' attitudes and behavior toward students resulting from knowledge of students' beliefs.

1337. Chanow, Karen Jean. "Teacher effectiveness training": an assessment of the changes in self-reported attitudes and student observed attitudes of junior high school teachers. Ph.D. dissertation. St. John's University. 1980.

Describes changes in teachers' attitudes toward those deemed more desirable as a result of participation in an inservice training program.

1338. Cheser, D. Wayne & others. "The effect of a classroom management course on teachers' disciplinary styles," High School Journal 66 No. 1 (1982): 1-6.

Reports changes in teachers' attitudes toward classroom management and discipline associated with participation in an inservice program.

1339. Chilton, Shirley Ray. Changes of knowledge and attitudes among teachers concerning economic principles and concepts after a course in economics. Ed.D. dissertation. Pepperdine University. 1979.

Describes teachers' attitudes toward and knowledge of economics and changes in knowledge and attitudes resulting from participation in an economics course.

1340. Ciaglia, Anthony Federico. Parents' social background and pupil control attitudes and pupil control attitudes of students and teachers. Ph.D. dissertation. Fordham University. 1980.

Describes pupil control ideologies of students, teachers and parents; reports no differences between students and teachers but differences between parents and the other two groups.

1341. Clapp, Gayle Mary. A comparative study of the attitudes, knowledge, and experience of teachers regarding handicapping conditions and mainstreaming in early childhood programs. Ph.D. dissertation. Michigan State University. 1977.

Describes a relationship between experience, knowledge and attitudes of preschool teachers toward integration of handicapped children but no difference by teacher background variables, e.g., age, race, sex.

1342. Clark, Janet May. A study of the effects of a management-initiated innovation on teacher attitude and student achievement. Ed.D. dissertation. Northern Illinois University. 1979.

Reports no loss of teacher morale or student achievement when teachers were assigned to participate in an innovative program selected and implemented by the school management.

1343. Clark, Larry R. Comparisons of teacher control ideology and student attitudes in elementary Christian schools. Ph.D. dissertation. Oregon State University. 1984.

Reports wide variations in teachers' attitudes toward pupil control ideology, variations in attitudes of students by subject of the attitude measure and limited relationships between teachers' pupil control ideology and students' attitudes toward school.

1344. Claye, C.M. "Barriers to effective teaching," Journal of Negro Education 37 No. 2 (1968): 146-152.

Teacher identification of barriers to effective teaching does not differ by grade taught, sex, experience; experienced teachers were more apt to include among barriers "too many non-teaching duties".

1345. Clifford, Richard M. The relationship between structure-technology, consonance and teacher satisfaction. Ph.D. dissertation. University of North Carolina at Chapel Hill. 1978.

Describes teachers' job satisfaction as related to the degree of fit between school structure and techniques of teaching.

1346. Cochran, Robert B. The effect of white teacher-black student interaction on changing social distance attitude of white teachers. Ed.D. dissertation. Mississippi State University. 1972.

Study found no change in white teachers' social distance toward Negroes after one year of teaching in desegregated schools.

1347. Cohen, Elizabeth G. & others. Organization and instruction in elementary schools: first results, 1973. technical report No. 50. Stanford Center for Research and Development in Teaching. Stanford University, California. 1973. ERIC ED 132 656.

Describes organization in a sample of schools and the effects of organization patterns on teachers' satisfaction.

1348. Coker, Theodore James. The effect of the teachers' attitude on the infusion of career education in South Carolina. Ed.D. dissertation. 1979.

Presents several teacher characteristics that are related to teachers' attitudes toward incorporating career education into elementary school curriculum.

1349. Coladarci, Theodore. Empirical research as inservice teacher education. ERIC ED 222 460.

Describes changes in teachers' attitudes resulting from participation in an inservice program studying causes of school dropping out among native American students.

1350. Cole, Henry P. & Lacefield, Warren E. MACOS: its empirical effects versus its critics. 1980. ERIC ED 194 397.

Relates teachers' attitudes toward use of MACOS, an innovative social studies curriculum, to teachers' characteristics; teachers using MACOS changed their behaviors and their attitudes toward instruction.

1351. Cole, Stephen. "The unionization of teachers: determinants of rank-and-file support," Sociology of Education 41 (1968): 66-87.

Teacher characteristics, i.e., socioeconomic level and religion, related to attitude toward unions in general and teachers' unions in particular and therefore toward militancy.

1352. Coley, Thomas Gregory. The implementation of planned educational change: a multivariate analysis of the decision source for change, organizational commitment, and job satisfaction among elementary school teachers. Ph.D. dissertation. Wisconsin University. 1980. ERIC ED 194 469.

Reports that the source of the decision to implement an innovative program of individualized instruction did not affect teachers' satisfaction with the conditions of their work or their commitment to the success of the educational program.

1353. Colosimo, Mary-Lynn S. The effect of practice or beginning teaching on the self concepts and attitudes of teachers: a quantitative synthesis. Ph.D. dissertation. University of Chicago. 1981.

Identifies factors which are associated with changes in teachers' attitudes during the initial teaching years, as analyzed from selected studies reported in the literature.

1354. Conwell, Catherine L.R. An investigation of changes in elementary teachers' achievement in science and attitude toward teaching science due to matching and mismatching science activities with the Myers-Briggs type indicator. Ph.D. dissertation. Ohio State University. 1983.

Reports a relationship between teachers' personality characteristics and ratings of specific student science activities.

1355. Cooper, Donald Lamar. A study of the effects of an activity based inservice science program on teaching attitudes, science process skills, and teaching style of elementary school teachers. Ed.D. dissertation. University of Southern Mississippi. 1982.

Reports differences in attitudes toward science teaching processes and teachers' personal characteristics, e.g., grade level taught and years of teaching experience, with more positive attitudes resulting from participation in an inservice program.

1356. Cooper, Gary Robert. Collegial supervision: the feasibility of implementation and particular effectiveness on teacher attitudes and job satisfaction. Ed.D. dissertation. University of Pennsylvania. 1983.

Describes teachers' attitudes toward and perceptions of the effectiveness of a pilot program of collegial teacher evaluation, with attitudes generally positive to the program and the teachers' participation in the program.

1357. Corprew, Mary Crumble. The influence of age, experience, and participation in planning and implementing staff development activities on teachers' attitudes, as measured by the Minnesota Teacher Attitude Inventory. Ed.D. dissertation. George Washington University. 1981.

Describes no differences in attitudes toward students, teachers and teaching between teachers who have and have not participated in planning staff development programs.

1358. Covert, Douglas C. Attitudes, actions and communication behavior of teachers before and after experiencing an environmental education workshop. Ph.D. dissertation. Michigan State University. 1982.

Describes teachers' attitudes toward environmental education and the use of various resources available to assist teachers in teaching about the environment, no change in attitude resulting from participation in the inservice program.

1359. Craig, Larry Vernon. The effects of organizational climate and leadership behavior on teacher job satisfaction in selected schools. Ph.D. dissertation. North Texas State University. 1979.

Teacher job satisfaction was related to the organizational climate of the school.

1360. Dandridge, Joyce Annette. The attitudes, knowledge of subject matter and classroom behaviors of teachers using multicultural/multi-ethnic programs.

Ed.D. dissertation. University of Southern California. 1980.

Greater teacher knowledge is associated with more professional preparation and more positive attitudes toward multicultural/multi-ethnic education.

1361. D'Angelo, Sydney John. An investigation of factors influencing the attitudes of educators regarding mainstreaming handicapped children. Ed.D. dissertation. Rutgers University. 1981.

Describes positive attitudes among educators toward mainstreaming, no association between attitudes and personal characteristics but an association between attitudes and perceived need for facilities and support services to facilitate mainstreaming.

1362. Dangharn, Normari. An investigation of teacher innovation and attitude toward participation in curriculum planning and use. Ph.D. dissertation. University of Oklahoma. 1979.

Describes teachers' attitudes toward innovation and involvement in curriculum planning and use; positive relationship between innovation and total teaching experience and exerience in present school; no relationship to formal education and grade level.

1363. Defazio, Richard Joseph. A study of the relationships among teacher job satisfaction, teacher militancy, and school district conflict. Ed.D. dissertation. Syracuse University. 1978.

Teacher militancy is related to job satisfaction - teachers agree that conflict and other district characteristics are not related.

1364. Deluzain, Edward. An analysis of factors which affect teachers' attitudes toward English usage. Florida State University. 1976. ERIC ED 141 813.

Considerable disagreement among teachers' acceptability of disputed items of English usage; related to demographic characteristics of teachers.

1365. Dennis, Stephen. The relationship of principals' and teachers' attitudes toward education, perceptions of the school climate, and perceptions of the principals' leadership behavior. Ph.D. dissertation. New York University. 1978.

Study found no relationship between teachers' attitudes and perceptions of principal leadership behavior and no relationship between attitudes of principals and teachers.

1366. Dettmer, Peggy Ann. The effect of short-term training in personality type on teacher attitudes toward characteristics that define the creatively gifted child. Ph.D. dissertation. Kansas State University. 1979.

Describes changes in teachers' perceptions of gifted children resulting from a training program in personality characteristics.

1367. Diemart, Norman E. & Holdaway, Edward A. "Teacher satisfaction in team and conventional teaching situations," _Alberta Journal of Educational Research 16 No. 2_ (1970): 111-24.

Reports slightly more satisfaction with work among team teachers than teachers in traditional situations.

1368. Dix, Gwen Ellyn. The relationship between teacher's knowledge of alternative programming, teachers' attitudes toward handicapped children, and organizational climate. Ph.D. dissertation. Kent State University. 1979.

Describes differences in variables which teachers and special education experts considered in making placement decisions for handicapped students and greater classroom placement by regular than special education teachers.

1369. Donlan, Dan. Contrastive techniques of training English teachers to become writing consultants. 1980. _ERIC ED_ 240 602.

Describes changes in teachers' attitudes and behaviors resulting from participating in an inservice education program in writing instruction; teachers' characteristics were associated with more and less change in attitudes.

1370. Donlan, Dan. "The effects of two models of staff development on self-awareness and attitudes of teachers with internal vs. external locus of control," _Journal of Experimental Education 51 No. 3_ (1983): 109-13.

Describes no change in teachers' attitudes toward open education after participation in an inservice program.

1371. Donnelly, Mona Mary. A study of elementary teachers' personality traits and attitudes toward teaching selected content areas in the elementary school. Ph.D. dissertation. University of Illinois at Urbana-Champaign. 1971.

Describes differences in attitudes among elementary teachers by background characteristics and between teachers and student teachers.

1372. Doubrava-Harris, Mary J. The relationship of inservice training to the attitudes toward, and knowledge of, mainstreaming of three groups of educators: Elementary teachers, with and without mainstreaming experience, and principals. Ph.D. dissertation. Bowling Green State University. 1982.

Reports that teachers without mainstreaming experience have more positive attitudes toward mainstreaming than teachers with such experience, but no relationship between attitudes and other teacher characteristics.

1373. Driscoll, Amy. The socialization of teachers: career rewards and levels of professional concern. ERIC ED 241 474.

Describes changes in teachers' attitudes toward teaching as a career and their non-work situations associated with years of teaching experience.

1374. Drugan, Elizabeth Ann. Role conflict and the teacher: an empirical study of role conflict and its relationship to classroom organizational patterns and selected teacher characteristics. Ph.D. dissertation. Loyola University of Chicago. 1979.

Describes teachers' perceptions of role conflict - the diverse and specific aspects of teacher roles.

1375. Dunlop, David L. & Fazio, Frank. The effects of a one-day energy workshop on science teachers' attitudes toward energy related topics. ERIC ED 201 490.

Describes positive changes in teachers' attitudes toward energy education resulting from participation in an inservice education program.

1376. D'Zamko, Mary Elizabeth R. Relationship of a program of diagnostic-prescriptive inservice education and regular classroom teacher attitudes toward handicapped pupils. Ed.D. dissertation. University of Florida. 1979.

Describes a teacher inservice program and reports teachers' use of the diagnostic-prescriptive method but no change in teachers' attitudes resulting from the inservice program.

1377. Earl, William Moulton. Competencies and attitudes towards the metric system: a study of the secondary teachers in Utah. Ed.D. dissertation. Brigham Young University. 1979.

Describes teachers' knowledge of and attitude toward the metric system and increases in attitude and knowledge after instruction.

1378. Eberts, Randall W. The effects of district personnel policies and teacher attitudes on teacher mobility. ERIC ED 239 409.

Reports a relationship between teachers' attitudes toward unions and attitudes toward aspects of their teaching situation.

1379. Edgar, Donald E. & Brod, Rodney L. Professional socialization and teacher autonomy. Stanford University. Stanford Center for Research and Development in Teaching. 1970. ERIC ED 046 885.

Describes how new teachers' attitudes toward autonomy differ by the nature of the task involved.

1380. Elkins, Dorothy Mary. An assessment of the relationships between selected teacher characteristics and attitudes of regular classroom teachers toward mainstreaming. Ed.D. dissertation. Western Michigan University. 1983.

Reports a relationship between teachers' attitudes toward mainstreaming and teachers' demographic characteristics, e.g., age, years of teaching experience and teacher perception of the support available to teachers.

1381. Elliott, Stephen N. & Argulewicz, Ed N. "The influence of student ethnicity on teachers' behavior ratings of normal and learning disabled children," Hispanic Journal of Behavioral Science 5 (1983): 337-45.

Reports the effects of student ethnicity group membership on teachers' attitudes toward mainstreamed students, in terms of achievement and motivation.

1382. Emmerich, Walter. Disadvantaged children and their first school experiences. ETS Head Start longitudinal study: preschool teacher's beliefs on effective teaching techniques and their relationships to pupil characteristics. Educational Testing Service. Princeton, New Jersey. 1973. ERIC ED 079 415.

Discribes a relationship between teachers' beliefs and behavior; student characteristics influence teachers' beliefs.

1383. Enoch, Mary Morel. Relationship of teacher attitudes toward mainstreaming with respect to previous special education training, teaching level, and experience with exceptional children. Ph.D. dissertation. George Peabody College for Teachers. 1979.

Describes more positive attitudes toward mainstreaming among elementary than secondary teachers, among teachers with than without training, but no difference by the presence of a mainstreamed student in the teachers' classroom.

1384. Evans, Peter & others. British Columbia reading assessment 1977: report 2: instructional practices. British Columbia Department of Education. Victoria. 1977. ERIC ED 163 414.

Describes teachers' attitudes toward secondary reading instruction and assessment along with demographic characteristics of teachers.

1385. Everson Howard & Tobias, Sigmund. Fear of automation in teachers' attitudes toward instructional media. AERA presentation. 1978. ERIC ED 151 314.

Describes attitudes of teachers toward technology and the role of fear of automation in the negative attitudes.

1386. Faas, Larry A. Characteristics and stress producing factors in a population of RIFfed educators. ERIC ED 232 243.

Describes teachers' attitudes toward aspects of their work situation that cause stress and changes in those attitudes associated with the possiblility of being laid off.

1387. Farris, Charlotte J. Sex fair knowledge, attitudes and behaviors of vocational educators: a research report. ERIC ED 224 996.

Describes the attitudes of vocational teachers toward sex roles and sex equity and the effects of participation in an inservice program on those attitudes.

1388. Faust, Frank Lawrence. An analysis of teacher and student acceptance of program innovations through evaluation of attitudes toward curriculum change and schedule change. Ed.D. dissertation. University of New Orleans. 1980.

Describes positive attitudes of teachers toward the value for students of science in the curriculum and the students' positive attitudes and the teachers' wish that more science had been offered in elementary school.

1389. Feinberg, Ronald Allen. A descriptive study of the relationship between the belief systems, selected personal characteristics and school environmental characteristics of teachers and their attitudes toward teaching. Ph.D. dissertation. New York University. 1981.

Describes attitudes of teachers toward teaching, based on Rokeach's theory of belief systems.

1390. Felton, Randall Garrett. A study of black and white urban social studies teacher perceptions in light of equality of educational opportunity commitments. Ph.D. dissertation. Florida State University. 1979.

Describes attitudes of black and white teachers toward black and white students; attitudes affected by racial composition of the school; low perceptions throughout district of students; low job satisfaction in black schools.

1391. Feng, Dan-Pai. The relationship between characteristics of teachers and their attitudes toward mainstreaming in Pennsylvania AVTSs. Ph.D. dissertation. Pennsylvania State University. 1981.

Reports a relationship between teaching assignment and personal characteristics and attitude toward mainstreaming in vocational programs.

1392. Ferrante, Ruth Ann. Survey of attitudes of regular teachers, teachers of the gifted and talented and administrators toward gifted education. Ed.D. dissertation. University of South Carolina. 1983.

Reports more positive attitudes toward gifted education among teachers of the gifted than among regular teachers; less positive attitudes among teachers in schools with than without programs for the gifted; no relation of attitude and prior course work.

1393. Feshbach, Norma Dutch & Campbell, Michael. Teacher stress and disiplinary practices in schools: a preliminary report. 1978. ERIC ED 162 228.

Survey of teachers about the factors which cause stress and on their attitudes toward corporal punishment.

1394. Fink, Judith. An investigation into the effects of an inservice program in learning disabilities. Ed.D. dissertation. George Peabody College for Teachers of Vanderbilt University. 1980.

Describes teachers' attitudes and behaviors toward students with learning disabilities, an inservice program designed to change attitudes and behaviors, and changes in teacher behaviors resulting from program participation.

1395. Finkelstein, Judith M. A comparison of full day alternate day and half day every day kindergarten in Iowa focusing on instructional time, congruence between goals and outcomes and principal, teacher and pupil attitudes. Ph.D. dissertation. University of Minnesota. 1983.

Describes differences in attitudes of teachers toward the two alternative scheduling plans for kindergarten and differences in the uses of the available instructional time between the two alternate schedules.

1396. Flannery, David Michael. Teacher decision involvement and job satisfaction in Wisconsin high schools. Ph.D. dissertation. University of Wisconsin-Madison. 1980.

Teacher job satisfaction is related to involvement in decisons, with more satisfaction associated with greater involvement in school decisions.

1397. Fletcher, Douglas Kent. The effectiveness of a master teacher inservice program at the middle school level in changing teachers' attitudes and behaviors toward students. Ed.D. dissertation. University of San Francisco. 1979.

Reports some changes in teachers' attitudes toward teacher-student interactions resulting from participation in a master teacher inservice education program.

1398. Fontaine, Ronald. The impact of the California School Improvement Program on teaching attitude and styles. Ed.D. dissertation. University of Southern California. 1981.

Reports positive teacher attitudes toward individualized instruction and no significant change related to participation in a School Improvement Program.

1399. Francis, Marie Sockwell. The effect of a teacher training program on teacher attitude and student attitude, self-esteem, and achievement. Ed.D. dissertation. Johns Hopkins University. 1980.

Describes teachers' attitudes and changes resulting from an inservice program; students' attitudes also changed after teachers participated in the inservice program.

1400. Franklin, Joan. "The high school social studies teacher: his political preferences related to contentment with course content," _Indiana Social Studies Quarterly 27_ (1974): 25-32.

Describes the relationship between teachers' political orientation and attitudes toward the secondary social studies curriculum.

1401. Freck, Joan M. Attitudes of teachers of the gifted toward underachieving gifted students. Ed.D. dissertation. George Peabody College for Teachers. 1979.

Teachers with positive attitudes have four to six years of teaching experience and gifted adults in their family but other teacher demographic variables were not related to attitudes.

1402. Freedman, Sara. The effects of the institutional structure of schools on teachers. _ERIC ED_ 234 047.

Describes teachers' attitudes toward their work situations and the effects on those attitudes of teachers' perceptions of schools and educational goals.

1403. Fritts, Chantrey A. The professional self concept of teachers. 1979. _ERIC ED_ 177 152.

Teachers' concepts of teachers as professionals are related to years of experience; teachers have varying perceptions of the characteristics of the profession.

1404. Fruth, Marvin J. & others. Commitment to teaching: teachers' responses to organizational incentives. ERIC ED 223 557.

Describes the effects on teachers' attitudes toward teaching of school climate and organization.

1405. Fuller, Frances F. "Concerns of teachers: a developmental conceptualization," American Educational Research Journal 6 No. 2 (1969): 207-226.

Reports variations in nature of concerns among persons at each level: pre-teaching amorphous, not related to teaching; early teaching needs self-protection; experienced teaching focused on pupils and outcomes.

1406. Fuller, Frances F. & others. Concerns of teachers: research and reconceptualization. Research and Development Center for Teaching. University of Texas. Austin. 1974. ERIC ED 091 439.

Reports different teachers' concerns pre- and inservice; two dimensions: self adequacy vs. pupil-benefit; teaching performance.

1407. Garrison, William D. The relationship between school organization and teachers' authoritarian attitudes. Final report. University of Washington. Seattle. 1972. ERIC ED 062 294.

Reports on a study of the relationship between the organizational climate of the school and teachers' attitudes toward pupil control and the teacher's role in enforcing discipline.

1408. George, A.A. & Rutherford, W.L. Affective and behavioral change in individuals involved in innovation implementation. Research and Development Center for Teacher Education. University of Texas. Austin. 1978. AERA presentation.

Describes dimensions of teachers' concerns about and levels of use of innovations.

1409. George, Philip Carlyle. An exploratory study of the effects of the Hilda Taba inservice education program on teacher attitudes and thinking skills. Ph.D. dissertation. George Peabody College for Teachers of Vanderbilt University. 1981.

Describes positive teachers' attitudes but no significant differences in those attitudes associated with participation in an inservice education program.

1410. Gier, Frederick John & Leonard, B. Charles. "The relationship between teacher perception of organizational climate and values concerning disadvantaged pupils," Negro Educational Review 22 (1971): 152-159.

Teachers' perceptions of the value of education for disadvantaged students differ slightly according to perceptions of their school climate as "open" or "closed".

1411. Gies, Frederick John & Leonard, B. Charles. "Value consensus concerning disadvantaged pupils in inner city elementary schools," Educational Leadership 30 No. 3 (1972): 254-256.

Teacher values differ by open-closed school climate in inner-city schools; more positive values in an open climate.

1412. Glaser, Mark Leonard. Attitudes of elementary school students and teachers toward hearing impaired children in integrated and nonintegrated settings. Ph.D. dissertation. American University. 1979.

Attitudes of teachers and students in classrooms with mainstreamed hearing impaired students are more positive toward such students than attitudes of other teachers and students.

1413. Glass, Lynn W. "An inservice energy education program for elementary school teachers," Journal of Research in Science Teaching 19 No. 6 (1982): 469-74.

Describes changes in teachers' attitudes toward and knowledge of energy education resulting from participation in an inservice education program.

1414. Goebes, Diane D. & Shore, Milton F. "Behavioral expectations of students as related to the sex of the teacher," Psychology in the Schools 12 No. 2 (1975): 222-224.

Presents teachers' perceptions of students' behavior in relation to the ideal student by teacher sex and student sex; female teachers perceive girls' behavior as closer to ideal than boys' behavior; not so of male teachers.

1415. Gonick, Alan Martin. A study of the influence of selected factors on corporal punishment attitudes and practices of educators in the state of Michigan.

Reports a relationship between educators' attitudes toward use of corporal punishment and educators' personal characteristics, e.g., age, sex, with more positive attitudes among educators who experienced corporal punishment as children.

1416. Grace, Gerald. Teachers, ideology and control: a study in urban education. Routledge & Kegan Paul Ltd. 1978.

Describes the attitudes of teachers who are part of the urban working class and the influence of class membership on their opinions about "good" teachers.

1417. Grayson, Dolores A. & Martin, Mary D. Gender expectations and student achievement: a teachers training program addressing gender disparity in the classroom. ERIC ED 243 829.

Describes a program to change attitudes of teachers and students toward sex stereotypes and changes in behaviors and effects of the inservice program on teachers' attitudes and behaviors.

1418. Greene, George Marion. An investigation of the attitudes fourth- and fifth-grade pupils and teachers exhibit toward selected concepts. Ed.D. dissertation. Northern Arizona University. 1979.

Describes teachers' and students' attitudes and relates them to ethnicity and school climate.

1419. Gubser, M.M. "Authoritarianism among teachers and school principals and its possible relationship to faculty morale," Journal of Educational Research 63 No. 1 (1969): 36-39.

Presents differences in teachers' satisfaction with the principal, with earnings and with community support for education by differences in personality factors.

1420. Guilliams, John D., Jr. Educators' attitudes concerning rights of students and their relationship to teachers' assessment of students' classroom behavior. Ed.D. dissertation. University of Oklahoma. 1972.

Study found differences in teachers' attitudes toward student rights by sex, race, years of experience and subject taught; also found a relationship between attitudes and assessment of classroom behavior of students.

1421. Guskey, Thomas R. "Differences in teachers' perceptions of personal control of positive versus negative student learning outcomes," Contemporary Educational Psychology 7 No. 1 (1982): 70-80.

Reports relationships between teachers' characteristics and teachers' attributions of causation for student positive and negative learning outcomes.

1422. Guskey, Thomas R. "The effects of change in instructional effectiveness on the relationship of teacher expectations and student achievement," Journal of Educational Research 75 No. 6 (1982): 345-49.

Describes a lower relationship between teachers' expectations and student grades for teachers who did not participate in a mastery learning program.

1423. Guskey, Thomas R. The effects of mastery learning on the reasons teachers give for their effectiveness in the classroom. ERIC ED 242 692.

Describes differences in teachers' perceptions of the importance of teaching methods resulting from participation in specific inservice program on mastery learning.

1424. Hagton, Elizabeth Virginia. The effect of an inservice program upon a secondary school faculty's attitude toward and knowledge about handicapped students. Ed.D. dissertation. University of Cincinnati. 1980.

Describes an inservice program, differences in attitudes of teachers who participated in the experimental and control programs, but those differences were related to prior differences in educational experience, not to the experimental program.

1425. Hall, Gene E. & Rutherford, William L. Concerns of teachers about implementing the innovation of team teaching. Procedures for Adopting Educational Innovations Projects. Research and Development Center for Teacher Education. University of Texas. Austin. 1975. ERIC ED 128 930.

Teachers' concerns vary as they progress through the several stages of implementing an innovation.

1426. Hall, Joye Kaye. The relationship between teacher perceived job tension and district commitment to negotiate. Ph.D. dissertation. Illinois State University. 1980.

Describes greater levels of job-related tension for teachers in districts without a written commitment to negotiate with the teacher organization, for teachers of grades 9-12 rather than k-8 and for single than for married teachers.

1427. Hansen, Lee H., Borgatts, Edgart & Lambert Philip. "Teacher perceptions of intra-occupational status relationships among elementary, junior high, and senior high school teaching positions," Journal of Experimental Education 40 (1971): 51-56.

Reports the status perceptions which exist among some, not all, teachers with senior high, junior high and elementary in descending order.

1428. Harasymiw, Stefan J. & Horne, Marcia D. "Integration of handicapped children: its effects on teacher attitudes," Education 96 (1975): 153-158.

Teachers' attitudes toward integration of handicapped children in regular classrooms were related to age but not sex or number of special education courses; there were more favorable attitudes among teachers with handicapped students.

1429. Harris, Annie Rene. The relationship between elementary teachers' attitudes toward and understanding of the application of psychological theory to classroom practice. Ed.D. dissertation. Indiana University. 1983.

Reports no relationship between teachers' attitudes and knowledge but relationships between teachers' attitudes and psychological characteristics.

1430. Hashimoto, Harry Yasushi. A comparative study of the effects of intensive and mandated race/human relations programs on staff attitudes within a school community. Ph.D. dissertation. United States International University. 1979.

Describes attitudes of school staff and students toward the need for a human relations program in a school district involved in voluntary integration.

1431. Hawkes, Richard R. & Dedrick, Charles V. "Teacher characteristics," NASSP Bulletin 67 No. 461 (1983): 78-83.

Reports that teachers' stress is associated with concerns about finances and a need for professional support.

1432. Heck, Shirley Frances. Teacher -- peer interactions. Ph.D. dissertation. University of Wisconsin. 1972.

Describes teachers' perceptions of teacher to teacher interaction which, when active positive, are seen as reinforcing and when negative passive are seen as thwarting career development.

1433. Hendlin, Rochelle Joy. The attitudes of educators toward handicapped children. Ed.D. dissertation. Yeshiva University. 1981.

Reports more positive attitudes toward mainstreaming by teachers with than without handicapped students but no differences by personal characteristics, e.g., years of experience.

1434. Hendricks, Irene & Sloan, Charles A. A study of the impact of an inservice program on the concerns and needs of secondary teachers toward mainstreaming. _ERIC_ _ED_ 243 265.

Reports that participation in an inservice education program had little effect on the negative attitudes of secondary teachers toward mainstreaming.

1435. Herriott, Robert E. & St. John, Nancy Hoyt. _Social class and the urban school: the impact of pupil background on teachers and principals_. John Wiley & Sons, Inc. New York. 1966.

Presents a study of schools and interactions of students' and teachers' socioeconomic status, race; includes a report of differences in teachers' perceptions of students' needs by socioeconomic level and race of students served by the school.

1436. Hight, Donald. The influence of school building age upon teachers' attitudes toward the school building in which they teach. Ed.D. dissertation. University of Georgia. 1983.

Reports higher attitudes of teachers toward their school buildings for new and newly renovated old buildings than old buildings.

1437. Hobbs, Gardner James. Perceived teacher satisfaction with leadership of selected black and white principals in Georgia high schools. Ed.D. dissertation. University of Georgia. 1978.

Study found that the size of school and the race of the principal are not related to teachers' satisfaction with leadership.

1438. Hoferek, Mary J. "Sex role prescriptions and attitudes of physical educators," Sex Roles: A Journal of Research 8 No. 1 (1982): 83-98.

Describes relationships between teachers' sex and sex role definition and expectations for students' physical performance.

1439. Hoffman, Frank Albert. The occupational prestige of teaching as perceived by public school teachers in the state of Louisiana. Ed.D. dissertation. Northeastern Louisiana University. 1979.

Generally no differences in perceptions of occupational status of teaching by teachers' characteristics but school principals and college teachers perceived to be of higher status than elementary, junior high and senior high teachers.

1440. Hogben, Donald & Lawson, Michael J. "Trainee and beginning teacher attitude stability and change: four case studies," Journal of Education for Teaching 10 No. 2 (1984): 135-153.

Describes the influence on teachers' attitudes of the teaching situation and the school's acceptance of the teachers, based on case studies.

1441. Holland, Richard Paul. Teachers' perceived needs in implementing the individualized educational program in accordance with Public Law 94-142 and teachers' attitudes and characteristics. Ed.D. dissertation. Temple University. 1979.

Describes teachers' perceptions of needs for training and relates them to teachers' characteristics.

1442. Horak, Willis James. An analysis of science teachers' beliefs about teacher classroom behaviors. Ph.D. dissertation. University of Iowa. 1975. ERIC ED 104 424.

Defines three types of science teachers by their beliefs in science teaching and found teacher type not related to background characteristics.

1443. Horak, Willis & Lunetts, Vincent N. "Science teacher types: a study of beliefs about the importance of specific teaching behaviors," Journal of Research in Science Teaching 16 (1979): 269-274. ERIC ED 224 302.

Reports a survey which found secondary science teachers grouped into three types by beliefs about science teaching (indirect-student centered-individualized, concern for order and discipline, flexibility most important teaching behavior).

1444. Horn, Ethel. Teachers who remain in the classroom - an interview study of persisting teachers. Division of Teacher Education. City University of New York. 1966. ERIC ED 011 872.

Sex, marital status, age of children, early experiences are all related to persistence in teaching; women intended to remain in classroom; men intended to become principals.

1445. Hornstein, Harvey A., Callahan, D.M., Fisch E. & Benedict, B.A. "Influence and satisfaction in organizations: a replication," Sociology of Education 41 (1968): 380-389.

Reports that teachers' job satisfaction and perceptions of student satisfaction are greater when teachers see themselves and the principal as mutually influential and perceive the principal as an expert.

1446. Hoy, Wayne K. & Blankenship, Jacob W. "A comparison of the ideological orientations and personality characteristics of teacher "acceptors" and "rejectors" of BSCS biology," Science Education 56 No. 1 (1972): 71-77.

Reports that different teacher personality characteristics are related to acceptance or rejection of the rationale for the BSCS approach.

1447. Hudgins, William Baird, Jr. An assessment of effects of a long-term inservice political education program on teacher knowlege and attitudes. Ed.D. dissertation. University of Georgia. 1980.

Describes no changes in teachers' knowledge of political science or instructional strategies but changes in teachers' attitudes toward use of instructional strategies in teaching about politics.

1448. Hulton, Lucreda A. "Calculators: teachers' attitudes and children's ability," Mathematics Teaching 90 (1980): 20-21.

Describes a study in which elementary school students used calculators and teachers became more positive in their attitudes toward the use of calculators.

1449. Hurtado-Portillo, J.L. II. Effects of an inservice education program on the attitudes of regular classroom teachers toward mainstreaming mildly handicapped students. Ph.D. dissertation. University of North Carolina at Chapel Hill. 1980.

Describes attitudes of elementary and secondary teachers toward mainstreamed students and positive changes in those attitudes resulting from participation in an inservice training program.

1450. Hynson, Lawrence M., Jr. "Teachers preferences of children's qualities," Urban Education 11 No. 1 (1976): 49-54.

Qualities in children that teachers preferred are related to grade taught and place of residence; reports different responses from general public.

1451. Itzko, Mitchell Sidney. A study of selected beliefs and attitudes of secondary social studies teachers concerning teaching and curriculum practices. Ed.D. dissertation. Temple University. 1981.

Describes teachers' attitudes as positive toward components of the curriculum and flexible in terms of inclusion of content; personal characteristics, e.g., age, were associated with differences in attitude.

1452. James, James Lee. The effects of inservice sensitivity training on self concepts and attitudes of first-year teachers. Ph.D. dissertation. Georgia State University. 1980.

Describes teachers' attitudes but no changes in attitude resulting from participation in an inservice program designed to increase teacher sensitivity toward student characteristics.

1453. Jenkins, Charles Kevin. A study of selected religious opinions and attitudes as held by two groups of Indiana public secondary school social studies teachers. Ph.D. dissertation. Indiana State University. 1981.

Describes attitudes of secondary social studies teachers who did and did not participate in an inservice program toward use of religious materials in the classroom.

1454. Johanningmeier, L.L. LaR. The attitudes of Iowa teachers toward women in educational administration positions. Ph.D. dissertation. University of Iowa. 1979.

Describes attitudes of teachers as differing by sex of teachers but not by other characteristics such as years of experience.

1455. Johnson, Alex B. & Cartwright, Carol A. "The roles of information and experience in improving teachers' knowledge and attitudes about mainstreaming," Journal of Special Education 13 No. 4 (1979): 453-462.

Describes teachers' attitudes toward mainstreaming and handicapped children as related to level of information and experience of regular classroom teachers.

1456. Joki, Russell Alex. A study of the relationship between eupsychian behavior and satisfaction with teacher negotiation results. Ed.D. dissertation. University of Idaho. 1980.

Study found no relationship between teacher humanistic skills and satisfaction with results of teacher contract negotiations.

1457. Jones, David, Jr. The relationship among professional educators' attitudes, students' attitudes, and organizational climate. Ed.D. dissertation. George Peabody College for Teachers of Vanderbilt University. 1983.

Reports no differences in attitudes toward students and toward teaching among teachers in open and traditional school settings.

1458. Jones, Melanie Matthews. Motivation of male and female teachers for seeking upward mobility via administrative positions: a study based on expectancy theory. Ph.D. dissertation. Kent State University. 1979.

Describes teachers' motivational pressures for upward mobility in terms of perceived ability to perform administrative tasks, perceived support, perceived expectancy of others and perceived career advantage.

1459. Jones, Ruth S. "Teachers, change, and political socialization," Urban Education 7 (1972): 119-130.

Describes attitudes of teachers toward social change and related background characteristics; found greater and lesser positive attitudes toward change.

1460. Jordan, John E. & Proctor, Doris J. "Relationships between knowledge of exceptional children, kind and amount of experience with them, and teacher attitudes toward their classroom integration," Journal of Special Education 3 No. 4 (1969): 433-439.

Teachers' attitudes toward integration of handicapped children are not related to experience with programs for such children.

1461. Jovick, Thomas & Milich, Robyn. Impact of unitization on the behavior and attitudes of teachers: a cross-sectional replication of the Meyer and Cohen study. Center for Educational Policy and Management. University of Oregon. Eugene. 1976. ERIC ED 124 519.

Extensive work collaborating in team teaching curtailed teachers' sense of control of their own work; the effect of work collaboration was not unidimensional.

1462. Jury, L.E. & others. "Teacher self-actualization and pupil control ideology," Alberta Journal of Educational Research 21 No. 4 (1975): 295-301.

Relates teachers' level of self-actualization to pupil control ideology.

1463. Justice, Betheda Fries. The impact of selected structural characteristics of schools upon teacher response to innovative social studies curricula. Ph.D. dissertation. University of North Carolina at Chapel Hill. 1978.

Teachers' responses toward innovative curricula are related to characteristics of the school social structure.

1464. Kanell, Karen L. A comparison of principals' preferences for "change via credibility" and its relation to organzational climate, principals' leader behavior, and teachers' attitudes toward change. Ph.D. University of Pittsburgh. 1980.

Describes no relationship between principals' attitudes and behaviors and teachers' attitudes toward innovations and change.

1465. Katz, Alexander I.J. The relationahip of individual needs and perceived organizational stress to job satisfaction in a comparative study of elementary school principals and teachers. Ph.D. dissertation. New York University. 1980.

Role conflict is related to lack of job satisfaction, varies by level in school hierarchy and role ambiguity has a negative effect for those higher in the school hierarchy.

1466. Katz, Harry C. Labor relations and public school desegregation in Los Angeles, Dade County and Boston. ERIC ED 209 410.

Describes the effects of desegregation of the schools in teachers' attitudes toward unions and labor relations.

1467. Keel, James L. "Teacher 'restlessness' and decision making," Clearing House 52 No. 9 (1979): 410-412.

Teacher restlessness is related to lack of involvement in school site decisions.

1468. Keith, Pat M. "Correlates of role strain in the classroom," Urban Education 14 No. 1 (1979): 19-30.

Reports factors related to role strain in self-contained and team teaching classrooms.

1469. Keith, Pat. Sources and correlates of role strain among teachers in varied settings. AERA presentation. 1970. ERIC ED 050 024.

More teacher strain in less formalized settings - teacher teams with no training in teaming, teacher teams with less agreement on teacher role, teacher teams with new teaming program; no difference self-contained and team teaching.

1470. Keller, Aubrey Munford. A typology of administrator and teacher perceptions toward curriculum and instruction within a large urban school system. Ed.D. dissertation. Memphis State University. 1978.

Describes perceptions of teachers toward curriculum and instruction and relates differences in attitudes to teachers' characteristics.

1471. Keller, Paul F.G. & Johnson, Kerry A. How are ITV users different? ERIC ED 223 224.

Describes teachers' attitudes toward the use of instructional television and the effects of teacher's characteristics on teachers' attitudes.

1472. Kelley, Edgar A. & others. Teacher perceptions of school climate and the implementation of Individually Guided Education (IGE). Teachers College. University of Nebraska. Lincoln. 1973. ERIC ED 083 229.

Teachers' perceptions of the environment lead to different degrees of implementing IGE.

1473. Kelley, James M. The relationship between teacher anxiety levels and teacher perceptions and expectations of the disciplinary process. Ph.D. dissertation. George Peabody College for Teachers. 1979.

Teachers' anxiety was influenced more by teachers' perceptions of than expectations for the disciplinary process within schools.

1474. Kendall, Robbie M.G. The correlative attitudes of a selected group of regular education teachers in the Detroit public schools regarding mainstreaming. Ph.D. dissertation. University of Michigan. 1979.

Teachers have limited knowledge about handicapped students but a willingness to learn and their attitude is not related to factors such as age or number of courses.

1475. Kennedy, Cecilia R. The relationship of teacher training in nutrition education to subsequent nutrition knowledge and attitudes of teachers and students. Ed.D. dissertation. University of South Dakota. 1983.

Describes no differences in teachers' knowledge about and attitudes toward nutrition education resulting from participation in a workshop about nutrition education.

1476. Khan, Sar B. & Traub, Ross E. "Teachers' attitudes in open and traditional schools," _Canadian Journal of Education 5_ (1980): 5-14.

Teachers in open programs or physically more open schools had more positive attitudes toward education, teaching, pupils and innovations than teachers in less open programs or environments.

1477. Knivetan, Bromley. "Teacher attitudes and self perceptions: an age/sex comparison," _Educational Studies 2 No. 3_ (1976): 185-191.

Points out differences in teachers by sex and age in attitudes toward self and achievement of students.

1478. Knopp, Robert & O'Reilly, Robert A. Job satisfaction of teachers and organizational effectiveness of elementary schools. 1978. _ERIC ED_ 177 719.

Teachers' perceptions of effectiveness of schools is related to satisfaction, other teachers and leadership of principals.

1479. Kornacker, Mildrid. "The ethnic teacher in the urban classroom: differential orientations to the teaching role," Education and Urban Society 1 No. 3 (1969): 247-264.

Reports differences in teachers' attitudes toward teaching role, by sex, level of education and urban/rural; no difference in socioeconomic background or subject matter taught.

1480. Kozey, Louisa Mina. A study of secondary teachers' perceptions of importance, qualifications, and implementation of content area reading instruction. Ph.D. dissertation. University of Oregon. 1980.

Describes teachers' perceptions of responsibility and training for secondary reading instruction related to content area taught and training but not years of teaching experience.

1481. Krakow, Jere L. Which history is most important? views from secondary history teachers. 1974. ERIC ED 159 128.

Presents history teachers' rankings of areas of study - rankings differ by teachers' demographics (years of experience, geographic area in which teaching).

1482. Kremer, Lya & Lifmann, Margot. "Locus of control and its reflection in teachers' professional attributions," College Student Journal 16 No. 3 (1982): 209-15.

Reports that teachers' locus of control is related to teachers' attribution of responsibility to teachers and students in classroom settings.

1483. Kreutzkampf, June E. Teachers' conceptual systems as a predictor of beliefs about the teaching process. AERA presentation. 1979. ERIC ED 171 666.

Teachers' level of conceptualization is related to what teachers believe about the long-range effects of teaching.

1484. Kulpa, Carol Mary. A structural model of teacher alienation. Ph.D. dissertation. University of Wisconsin-Madison. 1980.

Describes differences in teachers' perceptions of their roles and relationships to the school system and resulting alienation from work.

1485. Kulwin, Maury Harold. The effect of teacher advice on the attitudes of neophyte teachers. Ph.D. dissertation. Northwestern University. 1978.

Describes beginning teachers' attitudes and responses to suggestions from experienced teachers and the school socialization process.

1486. Lagana, Joseph F. What happens to the attitudes of beginning teachers? Interstate Printers & Publishers Inc. Danville, Illinois. 1970. Reviewed in Grade Teacher 88 (1970): 8.

Describes a study of first year teachers' attitudes toward the profession, changes in attitude in the first year of teaching, and related teacher background characteristics.

1487. Lam, Y.L. Jack. "Determinants of teacher professionalism," Alberta Journal of Educational Research 29 No. 3 (1983): 168-79.

Describes the effects of personal, school and district characteristics on teachers' attitudes toward aspects of their own teaching and teaching as a profession.

1488. Larrivee, Barbara & Cook, Linda. "Mainstreaming: a study of the variables affecting teacher attitude," Journal of Special Education 13 (1979): 315-324.

The teacher's perception of success in dealing with handicapped students had the greatest influence on the regular classroom teacher's attitude toward mainstreaming.

1489. Laurento, Louis Michael. A study designed to investigate the relationship between the strength of the professional employee' contract and the degree of teachers' job satisfaction. Ed.D. dissertation. Temple University. 1980.

Study found no relationship between strength of the employment contract, in terms of certain types of contract language, and teachers' job satisfaction.

1490. Lawrenz, Frances P. "An evaluation of the effect of two different lengths of inservice training on teacher attitudes," Journal of Research in Science Teaching 21 No. 5 (1984): 497-506.

Reports changes in teachers' attitudes toward science education but not toward energy issues resulting from participation in an inservice program.

1491. Layton, James R. & Chappell, Harold. "An analysis of teacher opinion regarding student academic achievement and teacher ability to cope with underachievement," Colorado Journal of Educational Research 15 No. 2 (1976): 17-27. 1975. ERIC ED 113 682.

Describes attitudes of teachers toward student achievement and relates those attitudes to teachers' characteristics.

1492. Lazarowitz, Rueven. "Does use of curriculum change teachers' attitudes toward inquiry?" Journal of Research in Science Teaching 13 No. 6 (1976): 547-552.

Years of teachers' experience with new curricula are related to positive attitudes toward inquiry strategies.

1493. Lazarowitz, Reuven. The development and use of a technique for determining the inquiry teaching attitude of secondary school science teachers. 1973. ERIC ED 094 973.

Reports that different personal characteristics of teachers lead to different attitudes toward inquiry.

1494. Leake, John Benjamin. A study of attitudes of elementary teachers toward science. Ed.D. dissertation. Oklahoma State University. 1966.

Describes attitudes of elementary teachers toward science; no changes resulting from an inservice course in science.

1495. Leary, Jim. The effectiveness of concerns-based staff development in facilitating curriculum implementation. ERIC ED 231 788.

Describes teachers' attitudes toward their own teaching, their effects on student learning and the effects of aspects of the teaching situation that influence their sense of efficacy.

1496. Lebowitz, Ruth. The relationship of the views women elementary teachers have of their work and their attitudes toward the feminist movement. Ed.D. dissertation. Columbia University Teachers College. 1979.

Describes the attitudes of teachers toward feminism (strong support) and relates those attitudes to teachers' characteristics and other attitudes.

1497. Lenz, O. Victor, Jr. The effects of reduction in force on the morale of elementary classroom teachers. Ph.D. dissertation. Saint Louis University. 1978.

Describes morale of teachers as lower in schools experiencing staff reductions than in schools with no lay-offs.

1498. Levin, James & Jones, Craig. Elementary teachers attitudes toward science in four areas related to gender differences in students science performance. <u>ERIC</u> <u>ED</u> 229 230.

Reports differences in teachers' attitudes toward science instruction associated with sex, grade level taught, prior science courses completed.

1499. Linden, Kayhryn W. & Linden, James D. "A longitudinal study of teachers' attitudes and personality characteristics," <u>Journal of Teacher Education</u> <u>20</u> (1969): 351-360.

Describes teachers' attitudes toward children and control of pupils with MTAI given prior to and after student teaching and after teaching experience; reports some changes in attitude after teaching experience.

1500. Lipka, Richard P. & Gaulet, L.R. "Aging- and experience-related changes in teacher attitudes toward the profession," <u>Educational Research Quarterly</u> <u>4</u> (1979): 19-28.

Indicates that there are few changes in teachers' attitudes toward the profession after the first few years of teaching, based on teachers' recollections.

1501. Lloyd, James Leroy. A study of the relationship between psychological stress and public school tenured teachers. Ed.D. dissertation. George Peabody College for Teachers. 1980.

Study found no difference in stress by teachers' characteristics such as age, sex and whether tenured.

1502. Loble, Naomi Kaufman. The impact of P.L. 94-142 on elementary teacher attitudes and needs for personnel, resources, and staff preparation in an atypical New Jersey school district. Ed.D. dissertation. Rutgers University. 1980.

Describes attitudes of parents and teachers toward mainstreaming and changes in those attitudes during a school year.

1503. McArthur, John. The first five years of teaching. ERIC ED 240 087.

Describes changes in teachers' attitudes toward discipline resulting from experiences during the first year and subsequent years of teaching.

1504. McAulay, J.D. "Social-political attitudes of elementary teachers," Journal of Teacher Education 19 (1968): 405-409.

Describes attitudes of teachers on social and political issues, reporting differences by geographic location and some characteristics of the teachers.

1505. McCallon, Earl L. "Interpersonal perception characteristics of teachers," Journal of Experimental Education 34 No. 3 (1966): 97-100.

Relates teachers' years of experience and perceptions of self to perceptions of the students who are most desirable to teach.

1506. McCaskill, Edwin O. & others. A research study about teachers' perceptions of job satisfaction. 1979. ERIC ED 184 205.

Describes teachers' job satisfaction related to the nature of the teaching contract becoming more negative as class size and total student load increase; low salary is related to low job satisfaction; the principal is perceived as knowledgeable but not often enough available.

1507. McClain, Anita Joyce Bell. A study of the modification of teachers' attitudes toward the hearing-impaired using two different types of treatment workshops. Ed.D. dissertation. Portland State University. 1983.

Describes no differences in the attitudes of teachers who participated in different workshops in their attitudes toward mainstreaming of hearing-impaired students.

1508. McDowell, Everett E. A study of three teacher variables and their relationships to individualized instruction. Ph.D. dissertation. Northwestern University. 1979.

Describes a relationship between teachers' individualization of instruction and knowledge of individual differences, belief in importance of individual differences and attitude toward students and grade taught.

1509. McFarlane, Peter J., Jr. A study of the effect of teaching-learning units and consultant services on the attitude of second and third grade teachers toward science and the teaching of science. Ed.D. dissertation. Southern Illinois University at Edwardsville. 1983.

Describes teachers' attitudes toward the teaching of science associated with teachers' characteristics, e.g., grade taught and years of experience.

1510. McFaul, Shirley A. & Cooper, James M. "Peer clinical supervision in an urban elementary school," Journal of Teacher Education 34 No. 5 (Sept.-Oct. 1983): 34-38.

Describes attitudes of teachers toward clinical supervision and changes in those attitudes after participation in a clinical supervison program.

1511. McGowan, James Robert. An investigation of the relationship between certain situational variables, personality variables and job satisfaction within the path-goal model of management among public school teachers. Ph.D. dissertation. University of Maryland. 1980.

Describes a relationship between teachers' satisfaction with work and perceived involvement with decision making.

1512. McRainey, Gay. Teacher-pupil contact as a factor in the development of positive teacher attitudes toward handicapped students. Ph.D. dissertation. George Peabody College for Teachers of Vanderbilt University. 1981.

Reports that teachers' attitudes toward handicapped students improved with more knowledge but did not change with contact with handicapped students.

1513. Madsen-Nuemann, Kay Lynne. The effects on teachers of public school enrollment decline: a case study of an urban school district. Ph.D. dissertation. Michigan State University. 1983.

Describes a decline in teachers' morale over the period of years during which a school district experienced an enrollment decline, with teachers concerned about the quality of instruction when facing conditions of job insecurity due to reduction in the number of teachers.

1514. Mahar, Carolyn Fae. The professionalized self-concept of teachers. Ph.D. dissertation. University of Michigan. 1979.

Describes teachers' professional self-concept in relation to years of teaching experience.

1515. Major, Cherie R. The effects of the organizational structure of middle school and junior high school on teacher attitudes, student attitudes and student self-concept. Ed.D. dissertation. Utah State University. 1983.

Describes few variations in teachers' attitudes associated with school organizational structure, although teachers differed in their preference for smaller or larger school size.

1516. Mallett, Claudia G. Relationship between perceived need deficiencies of teachers and inservice education perceived to be important. Ed.D. dissertation. Wayne State University. 1979.

Study found no relationship between teachers' needs, based on Maslow's need hierarchy, and teachers' perceptions of the importance of inservice topics.

1517. Mandell, Colleen J. & Strain, Phillip S. "An analysis of factors related to the attitudes of regular classroom teacher toward mainstreaming mildly handicapped children," Contemporary Educational Psychology 3 No. 2 (1978): 154-162.

Describes a relationship among teachers' personal characteristics and their attitudes toward mainstreaming.

1518. Mark, Frank Dieter. The attitudes of elementary teachers toward the mainstreaming of educable mentally retarded students in northwestern Ohio school districts. Ph.D. dissertation. Bowling Green State University. 1980.

Reports more positive attitudes toward educable mentally retarded students among teachers with mainstreaming experience but no differences by teacher age, degree level, years of teaching or teaching level.

1519. Martin, Betty J.C. Teacher attitudes as a function of an inservice program on the phenomenon of professional growth. Ph.D. dissertation. George Peabody College for Teachers of Vanderbilt University. 1980.

Reports no change after an inservice program in teachers' attitudes toward the four concepts, professionalism, individualism, rigidity and controlling.

1520. Meador, Linda Margaret. A descriptive study of teacher self-concept and mental health status in a large metropolitan public school system. Ph.D. dissertation. George Peabody College for Teachers of Vanderbilt University. 1978.

Describes teachers' self-concept and finds no relationship to years of teaching or between the two.

1521. Meehan, Merrill L. "Inservice teachers' predispositions and attitudes towards arts education impacted by unique workshop," College Student Journal 17 No. 1 (1983): 83-88.

Describes changes in teachers' attitudes toward art education as a result of participation in an inservice program.

1522. Melvin, Opal Williams. The perceptions of teachers on competency-based education. Ph.D. dissertation. Claremont Graduate School. 1978.

Describes attitudes of teachers toward CBE and finds no relationship with characteristics and teaching assignment except with the attitudes of teachers working with different classrooms and resource teachers.

1523. Meyer, John & others. The impact of the open-space school upon teacher influence and autonomy: the effects of an organizational innovation. Technical Report No. 21. Stanford Center for Research and Development in Teaching. Stanford University. 1971. ERIC ED 062 291.

Study found a different attitude toward the job among open-space and traditional teachers; organizational innovation led to a change in teachers' attitudes.

1524. Meyers, Barbara & others. Formative evaluation and teacher decision making: a follow-up investigation. 1980. ERIC ED 203 586.

Reports that teachers who participated in an inservice program did not consistently use the methods taught in the program and did not report positive perceptions of the effectiveness of the inservice program.

1525. Mickelson, Grace Erdahl. Evaluation of attitudinal changes in teachers in South Dakota with regard to unionism, professionalism, and political activity since the advent of Uniserv. Ph.D. dissertation. University of Wyoming. 1979.

School board members and superintendents viewed teachers as less professional and more involved in the union since the advent of a specialized NEA program, while legislators viewed teachers as more legislatively active but no less professional.

1526. Miller, Peter J. "Responding to children's needs: unconscious reactions and professional judgements," Elements: Translating Theory into Practice 6 No. 8 (1975): 4-6.

Teachers' responses to students (self report) are related to teachers' personality characteristics.

1527. Miskel, Cecil. Demographic characteristics, faculty attitudes and school structure. AERA presentation. 1979. ERIC ED 170 855.

Describes attitudes of teachers toward and teachers' perceptions of more effective schools having more participative organizational processes, less centralized decision-making structures, more formalized general rules and more complex professional activities.

1528. Miskel, Cecil & others. Expectancy work motivation, central life interests, voluntarism, organizational situation, job satisfaction, and perceived teaching performance. AERA presentation. 1979. ERIC ED 170 279.

Teachers' attitudes and expectancy motivation beliefs about work are related to their job satisfaction.

1529. Miskel, Cecil & others. Structural and expectancy linkages within schools and organizational effectiveness. Educational Administration Quarterly 19 No. 1 (1983): 49-82.

Describes the effects of characteristics of schools on the attitudes of teachers toward their schools and their jobs.

1530. Mitchell, Janet L.W. Teacher attitudes toward handicapped children and selected components of Public Law 94-142. Ed.D. dissertation. University of Alabama. 1980.

Describes attitudes of teachers, with positive attitudes toward some handicaps and negative attitudes toward others; amount of in-service training in the education of the handicapped related to attitudes.

1531. Moeller, Gerald H. & Charters, W.W. Relation of bureaucratization to sense of power among teachers. In Carver, Fred D. & Sergiovanni, Thomas J. (eds), Organization and Human Behavior: Focus on Schools. McGraw-Hill Book Company. New York. 1969. 235-248. & Administrative Science Quarterly 10 (1966): 444-465.

Describes teachers' sense of power as stronger in schools with greater bureaucratization but declining after first year of teaching.

1532. Mokey, Anoush-Irawan. Job satisfaction in the education industry: a case study of teachers' interaction with work conditions in high school. DBA dissertation. United States International University. 1980.

Describes job satisfaction of teachers by sex and age and aspects of work with which teachers were and were not satisfied.

1533. Molnar, Sheila R.F. Decision-making interaction in teaching teams and the teacher's sense of influence and autonomy. Ph.D. dissertation. Stanford University. 1971.

Teachers' feelings of autonomy are related to degree of participation in team planning; in some teams all participate equally, in other teams one teacher dominates.

1534. Monroe, Donald Stuart. An investigation of the effects on job satisfaction of the interaction of teachers' orientation to locus of control and the degree of bureaucratization of selected secondary schools. Ed.D. dissertation. University of Illinois. 1969.

Internal locus of control teachers were more job satisfied than external; degree of school bureaucratization was related to job satisfaction, which may be general satisfaction and not job-related.

1535. Moore, Helen A. & Johnson, David R. A reexamination of elementary school teacher expectations: evidence of sex and ethnic segmentation. Social Science Quarterly 64 (1983): 460-75.

Describes teachers' attitudes toward students' career options as influenced by students' sex and ethnic group membership.

1536. Moore, Mary Louise Eddy. A discriptive survey of secondary English teachers attitudes toward language norms and variation. Ph.D. dissertation. Ohio State University. 1978.

Describes instructional development and attitudes of teachers toward English teaching; finds no relation to background characteristics.

1537. Morawa, Edward Charles. Teachers' perceptions of need fulfillment and self-esteem and their attitudes toward change. Ph.D. dissertation. University of Connecticut. 1983.

Reports a relationship between some aspects of teachers' need and change in teachers' attitudes resulting from participation in an innovative program.

1538. Morrison, Jane A.C. Perceptions of administrators and teachers concerning Public Law 94-142 in Wichita Falls, Texas. Ed.D. dissertation. Baylor University. 1980.

Describes differences by type of job but not levels of education, experience or sex in attitudes toward P.L. 94-142, with special education teachers and central office personnel having greater concern than administators and regular classroom teachers.

1539. Muller, Gene Edward. The effects on teacher knowledge, attitude and classroom behavior of simulated practice versus application of behavior management techniques during in-service instruction. Ph.D. dissertation. University of Texas at Austin. 1978.

Reports more positive changes in teachers' attitudes from inservice programs in which teachers learn both concepts and their application to the classroom concurrently rather than programs in which teachers learn concepts first and then their application to the class.

1540. Murstein, Alberta Sue. Reaction of Saint Louis County public school teachers to the "least restrictive environment" as outlined in Public Law

94-142. Ph.D. dissertation. Saint Louis University. 1979.

Describes attitudes of teachers toward mainstreaming; finds no relationship by teachers' sex, experience or level of teaching.

1541. Muth, Rodney. "Teacher perceptions of power, conflict, and consensus," Administrator's Notebook 21 No. 4 (1972): 1-4.

Describes teachers' views on the power of the principal and teachers' perceptions of coercive behaviors of principals as related to conflicts.

1542. Natyke, John H. & Bennett, William S., Jr. "Teacher aide use and role satisfaction of inner-city teachers," Education and Urban Society 2 No. 3 (1970): 295-314.

Use of teacher aides is related to greater teacher job satisfaction and lower intensity in teachers' sense of problems.

1543. Nicely, Robert F., Jr. & others. "Teachers attitudes toward gifted children and programs - implications for instructional leadership," Education 101 (1980): 12-15.

Results of a survey indicate that the more teachers know about gifted children and pull-out programs for them, the more willing they are to have children pulled from their classrooms for such programs.

1544. Nicholson, Everett W. & Tracy, Saundra J. Principal's influence on teacher's attitude and implementation of curricular change. ERIC EJ 273 141.

Reports that principals' attitudes toward and knowledge of an innovation and their participation influence teachers' attitudes toward an innovative program.

1545. Nickell, Ted A. A study of the relationship between white teacher atttitudes toward minorities and their opinions about the effects of integration. Ph.D. dissertation. University of Missouri, Columbia. 1979.

Describes teachers' attitudes' toward minorities and integration and demonstrates a slight relationship.

1546. North, George E. & Buchanan, O. Lee. "Teacher views of poverty area children," _Journal of Educational Research 61_ (1967): 53-55.

Study found that teachers' characteristics are not related to views of children of poverty; teachers with a greater number of such children had greater frustration; teachers rated effective had less frustration and more favorable disposition toward such children.

1547. Null, Eldon J. "Relationships between personal variables of teachers and their perception of the behavior of school personnel," _Journal of Educational Research 64_ (1971): 351-354.

Teachers' personality variables are related to perceptions of behavior of teachers and principals and attitudes toward children.

1548. Nunmer, Donald Nicklos. Teacher morale, student morale and selected teacher characteristics. Ed.D. dissertation. University of South Dakota. 1977.

Describes a relationship between teachers' characteristics and morale and finds no relationship between teacher morale and student morale.

1549. Nussel, Edward J. & Wiersma, William. Inservice education in multicultural education and its effect on teacher attitudes. _ERIC ED_ 227 200.

Describes changes in teachers' attitudes toward multicultural education resulting from participation in an inservice program.

1550. Oborny, William Joseph. The relationship of teachers' perceptions of their professionalism, the organizational structure of schools, and the leadership behavior of their principals. Ed.D. dissertation. Oklahoma State University. 1970.

Study reports some unclear relationships between teachers' views of their school environment and their own attitudes toward teaching.

1551. O'Quinn, Betty Brumbelow. Perceived teacher satisfaction with selected leadership behaviors of female as compared with male principals in selected Georgia elementary schools. Ed.D. dissertation. University of Georgia. 1978.

Reports that teachers' perceptions of principals' leadership are related to teachers', not principals', sex.

1552. Orlando, Vincent P. Effects of a content area reading class of attitudes and practices of secondary teachers. ERIC ED 240 575.

Reports that the subject matter taught influences secondary teachers' attitudes toward reading instruction.

1553. Orsini-Romano, Clara. "Progressive-traditional beliefs and personal orientations of preservice, inservice, and reentry teachers," Delta Kappa Gamma Bulletin 46 (1980): 53-55.

Describes teachers as mixed rather than favoring one or the other end of a belief continuum and reports that beliefs are related to other personal characteristics.

1554. O'Sullivan, P.S. "A model for the effect of an inservice program on junior high school student science achievement," Journal of Research in Science Teaching 18 No. 3 (1981): 199-207.

Describes positive effects of an inservice education program on teachers' attitudes toward science education.

1555. Pace, Cynthia Omara. A comparison of three types of teacher education workshops on sexually transmissible diseases: their effects on knowledge and attitudes of educators. Ph.D. dissertation. Ohio State University. 1979.

Describes attitudes of educators and changes in those attitudes and in knowledge resulting from inservice programs, reporting educators' preference for inservice programs accompanied by graduate credit rather than money.

1556. Palmer, Douglas J. "The effect of educable mental retardation descriptive information on regular classroom teachers' attributions and instructional prescriptions," Mental Retardation 18 (1980): 171-175.

Reports that information about students and labels attached to mentally retarded students influence teachers' expectations for and instructional plans for mentally retarded pupils.

1557. Parsons, Margaret A. Teachers racial and educational attitudes coincident with metropolitan school desegregation. ERIC ED 228 364.

Reports differences in attitudes toward quality education, race and school desegregation associated with personal characteristics, e.g., sex, and changes in attitudes over time.

1558. Partain, James Douglas. An assessment of energy cognizance, attitude toward energy conservation, and perceived energy conservation behavior of selected public school educators. Ed.D. dissertation. Texas A & M University. 1979.

Reports changes in teachers' knowledge of and attitudes toward energy conservation as a result of an inservice education program.

1559. Partridge, Robyn Hayes. Teacher beliefs about the educative process: test of the interaction-congruity hypothesis. Ph.D. dissertation. University of Oregon. 1979.

Describes changes in teachers' beliefs about education from involvement in team teaching.

1560. Paskal, Dolores. "Innovative orientations of secondary teachers: as functions of system-environment exchanges," Education 91 (1970): 53-60.

Teachers' orientation to innovation is related to organization complexity of the school and status orientation of the faculty; teachers' expectations for professional and organizational lives may change with orientation.

1561. Passarella, Lawrence A. The relationship of class size to teacher morale and to teachers' perceptions of their own educational effectiveness. Ed.D. dissertation. Rutgers University. 1977.

Teachers' morale and class size are related and both are related to teachers' perceptions of effectiveness.

1562. Pastor, Margaret C.B. Higher order need strength and job satisfaction in secondary public school teachers. Ph.D. dissertation. Texas A & M University. 1980.

Describes teachers' reports of their needs and presents a strong relationship between needs and job satisfaction, which is also related to school district and personal characteristics.

1563. Pederson, Jerry Allen. A study of teacher morale in selected Minnesota elementary schools. Ph.D. dissertation. University of Minnesota. 1980.

Aspects of teachers' morale are related to patterns of school enrollment (increasing, stable, declining).

1564. Pedhazur, Elazar, J. "Pseudoprogressivism and assessment of teacher behavior," Educational and Psychological Measurement 29 No. 2 (1969): 377-386.

Ratings of teachers' behavior varied in accordance with classification of their educational beliefs as pseudoprogressive or progressive.

1565. Perry, Howard Louis. The effect of special education supportive services on teacher attitudes toward regular class integration of mildly handicapped children. Ed.D. dissertation. George Washington University. 1979.

The types of support services available influence the attitudes of teachers toward mainstreamed students and the importance which those teachers attach to those services in supporting student success in the classroom.

1566. Peterson, John Duncan. Patterns of teacher alienation. Ed.D. dissertation. Wayne State University. 1979.

Describes levels of alienation of teachers, reporting the highest in middle school teachers, then high school and elementary; related to effects of school administration, relations with hostile students and effects of federally controlled programs.

1567. Peterson, Richard B. Teacher attitudes toward professionalism, job satisfaction and collective negotiations: a cross cultural study. Final report. 1972. ERIC ED 063 279.

Teachers' attitudes are related to personal characteristics; there are differences between teachers' attitudes and principals' perceptions of teachers' attitudes.

1568. Phillips, Barbara K. The relationships of race, sex, length of service and tenure status to the organizational climate perceptions of principals and teachers in thirty-seven elementary schools. Ed.D. dissertation. University of North Carolina. 1979.

Demonstrates a congruence of teachers' and principals' perceptions of school climate.

1569. Piegari, Pasquale. The relationship between elementary school climate and attitudes toward teacher evaluation. Ed.D. dissertation. Rutgers University. 1979.

Teachers' attitudes toward evaluation were related to the extent that the educational environment of the school was categorized as "open."

1570. Pietras, Thomas & Lamb, Pose. "Attitudes of selected elementary teachers toward non-standard black dialects," _Journal of Educational Research_ _71_ (1978): 292-297.

Describes teachers' attitudes toward non-standard black dialects as not related to teachers' characteristics such as age and academic background before training but as related after teachers received training in black dialects.

1571. Pietroski, Michalene S. An analysis of background variables associated with classroom teachers' attitudes toward mainstreaming. Ed.D. dissertation. Boston University. 1979.

Teachers' attitudes toward mainstreaming are related to the level of support services available to the teacher and student and the teachers' prior training, but not to age, sex, level of training.

1572. Piou, Edouardo Louis. An investigation of the relationship between teachers' work motivation and management processes. Ed.D. dissertation. Virginia Polytechnic Institute and State University. 1980.

Describes teachers' work motivaton as multidimensional and related to the level of teachers' involvement in making decisions they are interested in making and to principals' use of constructive and negative feedback.

1573. Placke, Jean Elizabeth. A study of the relationship of teacher attitude toward computers and leadership style. Ed.D. dissertation. University of Tulsa. 1983.

Reports that teachers with positive past experiences with computers have more positive attitudes toward them, but no relationship between teachers' demographic characteristics and attitudes toward computers and leadership style.

1574. Poll, Dwayne Carroll. The relationship between selected aspects of teacher verbal behavior and characteristics of intermediate grade teachers in

Lutheran elementary schools. Ed.D. dissertation. St. John's University. 1972.

Study found no relationship between teachers' attitudes toward teaching, teachers' years of experience and teachers' behaviors.

1575. Powell, Norman Dean. The relationship existing between clinical supervision and certain teacher attitudes. Ed.D. dissertation. University of Southern California. 1982.

Reports more positive attitudes toward supervision among teachers participating in a program of clinical supervision when the program is well implemented and well monitored.

1576. Pratt, John. "Percieved stress among teachers: the effects of age and background of children taught," Educational Review 30 No. 1 (1978): 3-14.

Describes five areas which cause stress to elementary teachers; inability to cope with teaching problems, aggressive students, non-cooperative students, concern for student learning and staff relations.

1577. Price, Antoinette T. An investigation of competencies of regular secondary teachers for meeting the needs of handicapped children in least restrictive environments. Ed.D. dissertation. Northwestern State University of Louisiana. 1979.

Teachers differed in the competencies they considered important for working with handicapped students in regular secondary classrooms by courses taken but not by age, degree, sex, subjects taught and years of teaching experience.

1578. Primeaux, Angelita F. The relationship between pupil control ideology, pupil control behavior and the political attitudes of elementary school teachers. Ed.D. dissertation. Pennsylvania State University. 1979.

Study found a relationship between teachers' political attitudes and pupil control ideology, but not between pupil control ideology and behavior.

1579. Pringle, Celestine Ann. The effects of teachers' attitudes toward dialects on their expectations for students' academic competence. Ph.D. dissertation. Kent State University. 1980.

Describes differences in teachers' attitudes toward speakers of dialects by groups of teachers, such as urban and suburban, elementary and secondary teachers, and lower academic expectations among teachers for students who speak non-standard English dialects.

1580. Proctor, Doris Ione. An investigaton of the relationships between knowledge of exceptional children, kind and amount of experience, and attitudes toward their classroom integration. Ph.D. dissertation. Michigan State University. 1967.

Teachers had a positive attitude and an increase in knowledge with more contact and coursework.

1581. Quade, Barbara Ann. The effects of consultation time scheduling by elementary LD resource teachers on regular teachers' attitude and use of model. Ed.D. dissertation. Southern Illinois University at Edwardsville. 1983.

Reports that teachers acknowledge a need for consultation with resource teachers and will continue to use such consultation services when the services are provided during a consistent block of time throughout the school year.

1582. Rafford, Ray L. The impact of an inservice program on school personnel: their awareness and attitudes toward special education. Ed.D. dissertation. Wayne State University. 1980.

Describes an inservice education program and changes in teachers' attitudes toward special education and paraprofessional attitudes toward a school service department resulting from the program.

1583. Rake, Kenneth Melvin. An attitude study toward children of elementary and secondary educated teachers in selected middle schools. Ph.D. dissertation. United States International University. 1976.

Some characteristics, not type of training, are related to attitude of teachers toward students in middle schools.

1584. Reed, Donald B. & Paznokas, Mary A. Teacher transfer and job satisfaction: an exploratory field study. <u>ERIC</u> <u>ED</u> 233 438.

Decribes teachers' attitudes toward their teaching situation and transfers and affect of a transfer on teachers' job satisfaction.

1585. Reese, Clara Cook. North Carolina public school teacher morale during 1978-1979. Ed.D. dissertation. North Carolina University at Raleigh. 1980.

Describes teachers' morale, with no difference by age but female and non-white teachers had higher morale; other characteristics were not found to be related to morale.

1586. Reid, Edward John. A study of the relationship between job security, feelings of security, job satisfaction and role involvement of teachers in selected public secondary schools in New York state. Ed.D. dissertation. State University of New York at Albany. 1979.

Teacher job satisfaction is related to role involvement; job security to feelings of job security; but no relationship between job satisfaction and objective job security; job security alone did not lead to job satisfaction.

1587. Rempel, Averno M. & Bentley, Ralph R. "Teacher morale: relationship with selected factors," _Journal of Teacher Education 21 No. 4_ (1970): 478-483.

Teachers' morale is related to teachers' characteristics, sex, degree status, etc.

1588. Renninger, K. Ann & Snyder, Samuel S. "Effects of cognitive style on perceived satisfaction and performance among students and teachers," _Journal of Educational Psychology 75 No. 5_ (1983): 668-76.

Describes teachers and students reporting greater satisfaction with the educational process when teachers and students are matched in cognitive style.

1589. Richards, William Howard. The effect of a professional growth and evaluation cycle upon experienced teacher attitudes. Ed.D. dissertation. Boston University. 1983.

Describes attitudes of experienced teachers toward evaluation as relatively stable and unchangeable and reports no changes in attitudes as a result of participation in an educational program.

1590. Richardson, W.D. & Johnson, Linda. Measuring teachers' attitudes about energy and related subjects. 1980. _ERIC ED_ 194 367.

Reports that teachers who participated in a workshop changed their attitudes toward energy use and the inclusion of instruction about energy within the curriculum.

1591. Riggott, Stephen T. The relationship between selected parochial school teacher characteristics and attitudes toward gifted elementary school children. Ed.D. dissertation. Catholic University of America. 1980.

Describes more positive attitudes toward gifted than average children and a relationship between teachers' attitudes and teachers' characteristics, e.g., educational level and years of teaching.

1592. Robinson, Linwood. Selected correlates of teachers' attitudes toward minority-group students in urban classrooms. Ph.D. dissertation. University of Connecticut. 1979.

Teachers' attitudes toward students were related to teachers' demographic characteristics, assignment choices and transfer plans; teachers had more positive attitudes toward middle than low socioeconomic status students.

1593. Rodriquez, Felicita. A study of the relationship between dogmatism and personal variables with perceived obstacles to curriculum change by secondary school teachers of Puerto Rico. Ph.D. dissertation. University of Connecticut. 1980.

Teachers' characteristics such as sex and age are related to perceptions of obstacles to curriculum change in two categories of factors internal and external to teacher.

1594. Ross-Reynolds, Gary G. The effect of gender and sex role on teacher referral bias and perception of student pathology. Ph.D. dissertation. Fordham University. 1980.

Teachers rated androgynous behavior as most healthy, followed by stereotypically masculine and then feminine behavior.

1595. Ruck, Jane E. Weber. Teachers' attitudes toward teacher evaluation in selected Connecticut school districts in relation to level of compliance of teacher evaluation programs with P.A. 74-278 (an act concerning teacher evaluation). Ph.D. dissertation. University of Connecticut. 1979.

Describes attitudes teachers have toward teacher evaluation as not related to the type of evaluation or legal compliance with the evaluation requirement.

1596. Rumstein, Regina. "Teachers' evaluation of research findings in educational psychology," California Journal of Educational Research 23 (1972): 71-82.

Teachers' background factors have some relationship to their views about the validity of research findings; the greater the validity the greater the significance of the findings.

1597. Russell, Earl B. & Warmbrod, J. Robert. "Change orientation of educators: a potential tool for change advocates in state-level educational agencies," Journal of Research and Development in Education 10 (1977): 50-62.

Teachers' attitudes toward change differ and are related to personality factors and observable behaviors.

1598. Russell, Jack Paul. Modifying attitudes of public school teachers toward computers and their use in the classroom through computer literacy workshops. Ph.D. dissertation. North Texas State University. 1983.

Reports changes in both teachers' attitudes toward and knowledge of computers resulting from participation in a workshop on computer literacy.

1599. Ryans, David G. Characteristics of teachers in relation to financial and cultural conditions in their childhood homes. 1972. ERIC ED 086 700.

Reports differences in teachers' attitudes and beliefs by socioeconomic level and financial conditions of the childhood home.

1600. Sacks, Melvin I. Teacher absenteeism, organizational behavior, and other variables. Ph.D. dissertation. Yeshiva University. 1983.

Reports no relationship between days absent and teachers' personal characteristics, e.g., sex, or teachers' attitudes, e.g., toward work, sense of job involvement, and perceptions of organizational behavior.

1601. Salend, Spencer J. & Johns, Janet. "A tale of two teachers, changing teacher commitment to mainstreaming," Teaching Exceptional Children 15 No. 2 (1983): 82-85.

Describes the changes in attitudes of teachers resulting from one positive experience with a mainstreamed student.

1602. Sanders, John & Merritt, Daniel L. Relationship between perceived supervisor style and teacher attitudes. AERA presentation. 1974. ERIC ED 090 663.

Reports attitude changes over time and that teachers' perceptions of supervisor style are related to attitudes.

1603. Sawayer, Audrey Evelyn. Teachers' sense-of-control in the school organization and its relationship to their attitude toward open education. Ed.D. dissertation. University of Massachusetts. 1979.

Reports no relationship between teachers' sense of control and teachers' characteristics and attitudes toward open education.

1604. Scherr, Barbara Joan. An investigation of the relationship between teacher level of development and school receptivity to change. Ed.D. dissertation. Columbia University. 1980.

Describes a complex relationship between level of response of individual teachers to innovations and readiness of the school for change.

1605. Schlageter, J. Noel. Student cognition, attitudes, and action orientation and teacher attitudes toward environmental education concepts at the seventh grade level. Ed.D. dissertation. University of Rochester. 1980.

Describes positive teachers' and students' attitudes toward environmental management concepts and the study of environmental issues.

1606. Schober, Howard M. "An analysis of the impact of teachers training in economics," Theory and Research in Social Education 12 No. 1 (1984): 1-12.

Describes changes in teachers' attitudes toward economics education resulting from participation in an inservice program.

1607. Schoeneberger, Mary M. & Russell, Thomas L. Add a little frill: science in the elementary school. ERIC ED 229 227.

Reports that teachers' characteristics, e.g., science courses, and support, e.g., available materials, are related to teachers' attitudes toward science instruction.

1608. Schulz, Michael Joseph. A study of elementary teachers' perceptions of their daily operational problems and the relationship to the racial composition of the schools in Flint, Michigan. Ed.D. dissertation. Wayne State University. 1978.

Describes teachers' perceptions of daily problems in relation to teachers' characteristics.

1609. Schwirian, Patricia M. "Characteristics of elementary teachers related to attitudes toward science," _Journal of Research in Science Teaching 6 No. 3_ 203-213.

Describes the relationship between elementary teachers' characteristics and their attitudes toward science.

1610. Scott, Judith & Brantley, John C. "Development of an inventory of teachers' attitudes towards sex-role stereotyping and knowledge of differences," _Sex Roles: A Journal of Research 9 No. 3_ (1983): 341-53.

Reports a limited relationship between teachers' knowledge of sex differences and attitudes toward sex stereotyping and describes the development of a measurement instrument.

1611. Seffens, Alda Louise. A field study of clothing behavior as it relates to teacher-student first impression situations in secondary education. Ed.D. dissertation. Wayne State University. 1972.

Study reports that teachers perceive dress differences among students and relates teachers' attitudes toward students according to dress; teachers are more sensitive to female dress type.

1612. Sergiovanni, Thomas J. "Factors which affect satisfaction and dissatisfaction of teachers," in Carver, Fred P. and Sergiovanni, Thomas J. (eds.): _Focus on Schools_. McGraw-Hill Book Company. New York. (1969): 249-260. reprinted in _Journal of Educational Administration 5_ (1967): 66-82.

Factors associated with high teacher attitudes are related to work while factors associated with low attitudes are related to conditions of the work.

1613. Shapson, Stan M. & others. "An experimental study of the effects of class size," American Educational Research Journal 17 (1980): 141-152.

Reports that changes in class size were associated with changes in teachers' expectations and student mathematics achievement but not to other teacher attitudes or student achievement in other subject areas.

1614. Shaw, Marvin E., Stratil, Michael & Reynolds, Gerald. "Team teaching: a source of support for teacher attitudes toward teaching," Education 93 (1973): 295-300.

Teachers' attitude maintenance depends on social support and attitude toward teaching; instructional practice tends to become more negative over the school year, there was less change among team teachers than among self-contained classroom teachers.

1615. Shaw, Rex Frederick. Teachers' professional preparation, experience, and work setting as determinants of their knowledge and attitude toward mental retardation and mainstreaming. Ed.D. dissertation. Columbia University Teachers College. 1980.

Special education teachers had more knowledge of but not more positive attitudes toward handicapped students; attitudes toward handicapped students were related to attitudes toward mainstreaming.

1616. Short, Byrl G. & Szabo, Michael. Secondary school teachers' knowledge of and attitudes toward educational research. AERA presentation. 1972. ERIC ED 061 177. Journal of Experimental Education 43 (1974): 75-78.

Coursework and research participation result in changes in attitude and knowledge; the changes do not remain after five years.

1617. Shotel, Jay R., Iano, Richard P. & McGettigan, James F. "Teacher attitudes associated with the integration of handicapped children," Exceptional Children 38 (1972): 677-683.

Reports that teachers were slightly to moderately more positive in attitude toward handicapped children in schools with an integrative resource room program than in schools with a self-contained special class program.

1618. Showers, Beverly Kay. Self-efficacy as a predictor of teacher participation in school decision making. Ph.D. dissertation. Stanford University. 1980.

Describes greater feelings of efficacy among teachers associated with greater participation in decision making within the school.

1619. Shrigley, Robert L. & Johnson, Theodore M. "The attitude of in-service elementary teachers toward science," _School Science and Mathematics_ _74_ _No. 5_ (1974): 437-447.

Elementary teachers' attitudes toward science are related to characteristics such as sex.

1621. Signoretti, Lorraine F. & Oratio, Albert R. "A multivariate analysis of teachers attitudes toward public school speech pathology services," _Language, Speech, and Hearing Services in the Schools_ _12_ _No. 3_ (1981): 178-87.

Describes teachers' attitudes toward speech impaired students and factors that influenced those attitudes.

1622. Simpson, Gloria R. An exploratory study of the influence of special education coursework on the attitudes and knowledge of regular classroom teachers. Ed.D. dissertation. University of Alabama. 1982.

Reports a high initial attitude toward special education coursework among regular classroom teachers and no change in attitude or knowledge as a result of participation in an introductory course.

1623. Simpson, Richard L. "Sex stereotypes of secondary school teaching subjects: male and female status gains and losses," _Sociology of Education_ _47_ (1974): 388-398.

Some subjects are perceived best taught by men or women, persons teaching subjects opposite to those perceived best taught by their sex had lesser sex-stereotyped perceptions; among teachers, men's prestige is more strongly related to conformity to sex stereotypes than is women's prestige.

1624. Slaven, Thomas M. "Evaluating professional education in drug use and abuse," _Journal of Drug Education_ _10_ (1980): 313-318.

Reports that teachers changed their attitudes toward and knowledge about drug abuse after participation in a training program but notes the tentativeness of the data about attitude changes.

1625. Smith, Gloria Jean. Teacher-judged giftedness: the effects of inservice, attitude, and teaching experience on identification accuracy. Ed.D. dissertation. Arizona State University. 1980.

Describes attitudes of teachers toward characteristics of gifted children and more positive attitudes resulting from participation in an inservice education program.

1626. Smith, Gloria Jean. Analysis of the impact of a staff development program on teacher attitudes toward mainstreamed handicapped students. Ph.D. dissertation. Michigan State University. 1983.

Reports no differences in attitudes associated with participation in the inservice program, with no differences in attitude change associated with differences in personal characteristics.

1627. Smith, Kenneth Eugene. Male teachers in early childhood education: a personal construct investigation of sex-role perceptions. Ed.D. dissertation. Loyola University of Chicago. 1979.

Study found a slight relationship between teachers' sex and sexism which was not related to preschool or second teachers' positions.

1628. Smith, Mary Lynne. Experience in open-space and traditionally constructed elementary schools and teacher attitudes toward open education. Ed.D. dissertation. North Texas State University. 1981.

Reports a relationship between teaching experience and attitude toward open education, with teachers with more years of experience in teaching in traditional programs having more positive attitudes.

1629. Smith, Sara Dawn & Smith, William D. Relationships between community demographic variables and teacher perceptions of organizational climate. 1980. ERIC ED 197 025.

Reports that teachers' perceptions of school climate are not affected by community variables and factors external to the school.

1630. Sobania, LeRoy Eric. A study of individual change proneness in relationship to observed attitude of K-12 teachers toward instructional development.

Ph.D. dissertation. University of Wisconsin-Madison. 1980.

Describes a change in teachers' attitudes toward instructional development but no relationship between degree of change and initial proneness to attitudinal change.

1631. Sokol, Marian G. Herbert. Attitudinal change and concerns of classroom teachers toward the integration of handicapped children. Ph.D. dissertation. University of Texas at Austin. 1979.

Study found no change in teachers' attitudes toward integration of handicapped children after five months of experience with the integration of handicapped children.

1632. Sontag, Marvin. Attitudes toward education and perception of desirable teacher behaviors - a Q study. AERA presentation. 1967. _ERIC ED_ 011 881.

Progressive/traditional differences in educational philosophy are related to teachers' selection (Q sort) of desirable teacher behaviors - progressive teachers select concern for pupils, traditionalist teachers select structure (discipline) and subject matter.

1633. Sontag, Marvin. Attitudes toward education and perception of teacher behaviors. Ph.D. dissertation. New York University. 1967.

Teaching level and educational attitudes interact to influence teachers' perceptions of teaching behaviors.

1634. Spanjer, R. Allan & Layne, B.H. "Teacher attitudes toward language: effects of training in a process approach to writing," _Journal of Educational Research_ _77_ (1983): 60.

Describes changes in teachers' attitudes toward writing and writing instruction as a result of participation in an inservice program.

1635. Sparks, Georgea Mohlman. Inservice education: training activities, teacher attitudes, and behavior change. Ph.D. dissertation. Stanford University. 1983.

Describes differences in teachers' use of specific instructional behaviors resulting from participation in inservice plus peer support, with teachers' attitudes associated with use of the recommended teaching behaviors.

1636. Spearly, David Joseph. Teacher inbreeding and pupil control ideology. Ph.D. dissertation. Pennsylvania State University. 1979.

Study found no differences in the pupil control ideology or extra-school behaviors between teachers teaching in the high schools they attended or in the community in which they grew up and teachers hired from outside the community.

1637. Speers, Mary Louise L. Teachers' attitudes toward a consumer economic education in-service program based on involvement in planning. Ph.D. dissertation. University of Michigan. 1981.

Describes no relationship between teachers' participation in planning an inservice program and attitudes toward the concepts presented in the program; no relationship between other characteristics, e.g., age, and attitude.

1638. Spooner, William E. & others. "The influence of a five-day teacher workshop on attitudes of elementary school teachers toward science and science teaching part II," School Science and Mathematics 82 No. 8 (1982): 629-36.

Reports changes in teachers' attitudes toward science education resulting from participation in an inservice program.

1639. Stahl, Richard Layne. Teacher participation and attitudes, innovation characteristics and the adoption of behavioral objectives. Ph.D. dissertation. Florida State University. 1972.

Describes teachers' attitudes and participation as related to adoption of behavioral objectives.

1640. Stainback, Susan & others. "Preparing regular classroom teachers for the integration of severely handicapped students: an experimental study," Education and Training of the Mentally Retarded 18 No. 3 (1983): 204-09.

Describes changes in teachers' attitudes toward mainstreaming resulting from participation in an inservice program.

1641. Steeg, Jeannie Lenore. Behavioral and attitudinal changes of teachers toward low achieving students as a result of the TESA program. Ed.D. dissertation. United States International University. 1982.

Describes changes in teachers' behaviors resulting from participation in a training program and concludes that attitudinal changes accompany the behavior changes.

1642. Steen, Marcia Ruth. Simulation activities as a means of modifying teacher attitudes toward handicapped individuals. Ed.D. dissertation. Texas Tech University. 1980.

Describes teachers' attitudes toward handicapped children, a simulation program designed to change those attitudes and reports no differences in attitudes between teachers who did and did not participate in the simulation.

1643. Stenzel, Leroy George, Jr. Teacher attitudes toward computer literacy. Ed.D. dissertation. Louisiana State University and Agricultural and Mechanical College. 1982.

Describes attitudes of teachers toward computers, with more positive attitudes associated with more education, but no relationship between attitudes and other personal characteristics; the majority of teachers expressed an interest in learning about computers.

1644. Stiegliz, Ezra L. "Effects of a content area reading course on teacher attitude and practices: a four-year study," _Journal of Reading_ _26_ _No. 8_ (1983): 690-96.

Describes positive changes in teachers' attitudes toward reading instruction at the secondary school resulting from participation in a course.

1645. Stoen, Linda Leone. The effect of a teacher inservice course on the writing skills and attitudes of fourth grade writers and their teachers. Ed.D. dissertation. University of South Dakota. 1983.

Reports no relationship between participation in an inservice program and teachers' attitudes toward writing, and no effect on students' attitudes and writing skills.

1646. Stoops, Charles Emerson. The relationship between militancy and pupil control ideology among public secondary school teachers. Ed.D. dissertation. Pennsylvania State University. 1980.

Study found no relationship between a militant posture toward collective bargaining and custodial ideology of pupil control.

1647. Strawitz, Barbara M. Dogmatism and the beliefs of preservice and inservice elementary science teachers. 1975. ERIC ED 123 032.

Reports that teachers' beliefs are related to teachers' level of dogmatism.

1648. Strebeck, Walter Ray. Relationships of teacher role conflicts to teaching situations and Myers-Briggs personality preference types of secondary teachers. Ed.D. dissertation. Florida State University. 1980.

Teachers report greater role conflicts for role behaviors not directly related to classroom instruction; the level of role conflict was related to personality factors.

1648A. Swartz, David Leroy. An analysis of the attitudes of Nebraska teachers toward three early retirement incentive programs. Ed.D. dissertation. University of Nebraska-Lincoln. 1981.

Reports a relationship between teachers' characteristics and attitudes toward each of three early retirement options available in Nebraska.

1649. Symington, David J. & Fensham, Peter J. "Elementary school teachers' closed-mindedness, attitudes toward science, and congruence with a new curriculum," Journal of Research in Science Teaching 13 No. 5 (1976): 441-447.

Teachers' attitudes toward a new science curriculum are correlated negatively with teachers' dogmatism.

1650. Tabachnick, B. Robert. The development of teacher perspectives. ERIC ED 240 112.

Describes changes in the attitudes of teachers from student teaching through the first year of teaching.

1651. Tisdale, Pamela C. & Fowler, Robert E. "The effects of labels on teachers' perceptions of the prevalence of emotionally disturbed children and youth," Education 103 No. 3 (1983): 278-80.

Reports that labels do effect teachers' attitudes toward emotionally disturbed children in the classroom.

1652. Tobias, S. "Dimensions of teachers' attitudes toward instructional media," American Educational Research Journal 5 No. 1 (1968): 91-98.

Describes differences in teachers' experiences with different media and fear of automation as it influences attitudes.

1653. Tobias, Sigmund. Special education referrals: failure to replicate student-teacher ethnicity interaction. ERIC ED 224 221.

Describes teachers' attitudes toward students and referrals to special education programs as related to teachers' characteristics.

1654. Tolman, Richard R. & Barufaldi, James P. "The effects of teaching the Biological Sciences Curriculum Study Elementary School Science Program on attitudes toward science among elementary school teachers," Journal of Research in Science Teaching 16 No. 5 (1979): 401-406.

Describes effects of teaching using the Elementary School Science Program curriculum on teachers' attitudes toward science.

1655. Tracy, Saundra Johnston. The elementary school principal's influence on teacher attitude toward and implementation of curricular change. Ph.D. dissertation. Purdue University. 1981.

Reports that teachers' sense of involvement in a change was the major factor determining teachers' attitudes toward the innovation and that principals' knowlege of the innovation influenced teachers' attitudes.

1656. Turbett, J. Patrick & O'Toole, Richard. "Teachers' recognition and reporting of child abuse," Journal of School Health 53 (1982): 605-9.

Describes the influences on teachers' attitudes toward child abuse of information about parents' characteristics and child's type of injury.

1657. Turley, James David. Attitudes of Rhode Island secondary school English teachers toward certain objectives in the teaching of English. 1969. ERIC ED 048 264.

Professional characteristics influence teachers' acceptance of goals to some extent; goals related to English are more accepted than goals related to social and humanistic implications.

1658. Twitty, Gaila Marie. An analysis of factors that relate to the attitudes of regular classroom teachers toward the integration of handicapped children in regular public elementary classes. Ph.D. dissertation. University of Maryland. 1979.

Teachers' knowledge of and experience with handicapped students is related to positive attitudes toward those students.

1659. Uskiewicz, Vincent D. & Willower, Donald J. "Perceived pupil control ideology consensus and teacher job satisfaction," Urban Education 8 No. 3 (1973): 231-238.

Relationship found between pupil control ideology consensus among teachers and principals within schools and teachers' job satisfaction.

1660. Vacca, Richard T. & Gove, Mary K. Teacher reflections on the use and adaptation of instructional innovation presented during staff development. ERIC ED 217 389.

Describes factors, including participation in an inservice program, associated with changes in teachers' attitudes toward the teaching of reading in content area classrooms.

1661. Vavrus, Michael Joseph. The relationship of teacher alienation to school workplace characteristics and career stages of teachers. Ph.D. dissertation. Michigan State University. 1978.

Describes teachers' attitudes toward work, opportunity for teachers' self-actualization and years of teaching experience.

1662. Vedral, N.M. "Educational viewpoints and teaching patterns of junior high school teachers," Illinois School Research 7 No. 2 (1971): 24-28.

Teachers' attitudes toward education varied by whether they taught separate subjects or combined subjects, and students' perceptions of teachers varied by teaching organization.

1663. Villeme, Melvin G. "The relation of teacher attitude to major, employment status, teaching level, and satisfaction with teaching for first-year teachers," Humanist Educator 19 (1980): 85-90.

Reports no relationship between new teachers' attitudes and sex, employment status, satisfaction with teaching and long-range teaching plans.

1664. Vitale, Michael R. & others. Using multidimensional scaling and unfolding to explore teacher perceptual biases for selected special education referral categories," Journal of Experimental Education 51 No. 3 (1983): 134-41.

Describes attitudes of teachers toward handicapped students and effects on their attitudes of labels and students' ethnic group membership.

1665. Wachs, Brian Jay. The mathematics anxieties and attitudes of urban public school teachers. Ed.D. dissertation. Yeshiva University. 1983.

Reports relationships between mathematics attitudes and several personal characteristics of teachers, e.g., sex, number of mathematics courses, achievement in mathematics courses.

1666. Wagoner, Roderic L. & O'Hanlon, James P. "Teacher attitudes toward evaluation," Journal of Teacher Education 19 (1968): 471-475.

A survey of teachers' attitudes toward evaluation found that "better" and tenured teachers had more positive attitudes; other differences, e.g., sex, level of teaching, showed a small, non-significant difference.

1667. Wallace, Mildred Glover. Attitudes toward mainstreaming, impact of an inservice training program on participants. Ph.D. dissertation. George Peabody College for Teachers of Vanderbilt University. 1980.

Describes teachers' attitudes toward mainstreaming, reporting that more experience with mainstreamed students was associated with less positive attitudes toward mainstreaming.

1668. Wangen, Nancy Register. Receptivity to change in small schools: a study of teachers willingness to accept the risks of innovation. ERIC ED 242 082.

Describes personal characterisitcs of teachers associated with teachers' support for a resistance to educational innovations.

1669. Watson, Judith Binish. Effects of modes of instruction in metrics on the attitudes and knowledge of elementary school inservice teachers. Ph.D. dissertation. Fordham University. 1981.

Describes a relationship between teachers' personal characteristics, e.g., age, and attitudes toward metric education after participation in an inservice program.

1670. Weissenburger, Jacalyn W. "The relationship of selected consultant/teacher characteristics to consultation outcomes," Journal of School Psychology 20 No. 4 (1983): 263-70.

Describes the relationship between teachers' perceptions of the effectiveness of consultants and several teachers' characteristics, e.g., dogmatism, years of teaching.

1671. Welch, Kenneth Verne. The effects of university special education inservice taken by regular classroom teachers upon their attitude toward and knowledge of appropriate program placements for handicapped children. Ph.D. dissertation. University of Wyoming. 1983.

Reports differences in teachers' knowledge about handicapped students and their placement but not attitude differences resulting from participation in an inservice program.

1672. Westerhouse, Mary Ann. The effects of tenure, role conflict and role conflict resolution on the work orientation and burn-out of teachers. Ph.D. dissertation. University of California. Berkeley. 1979.

Little self-reported burn-out among a sample of secondary private school teachers; they use compromise to resolve conflicts.

1673. Wilcox, Kay Ellen. Motivation, central life interests, voluntarism, and demographic variables as predicators of job satisfaction and perceived performance of teachers. Ed.D. dissertation. University of Kansas. 1979.

Teachers' life interests, motivation and voluntarism are related to teachers' job satisfaction.

1674. Wiley, Mary Glenn & Eskilson, Arlene. "Why did you learn in school today? teachers' perceptions of causality," Sociology of Education 51 No. 4 (1978): 261-269.

Teachers' attributions of causality are related to students' race, not sex or past performance.

1675. Wilke, Richard John. An analysis of three strategies designed to influence teacher use of, knowledge of, and attitudes toward educational resource use in environmental education. Ph.D. dissertation. Southern Illinois University at Carbondale. 1980.

Describes teachers' use of knowledge of and attitudes toward resources available for environmental education, and changes in knowledge and attitudes resulting from inservice education programs.

1676. Wilkite, James Wesley. The congruence of pupil control ideology between principals and teachers as related to teacher job satisfaction. Ed.D. dissertation. Oklahoma State University. 1978.

No relationship found between congruence of teachers' and principals' pupil control ideology and teachers' job satisfaction.

1677. Willard, David Thomas. An assessment of the effects of a staff evaluation model developed from Douglas McGregor's theory "Y" upon the attitudes of teachers and supervisors toward evaluation. Ph.D. dissertation. Saint Louis University. 1979.

Describes teachers' attitudes toward evaluation; they perceive that evaluation is more likely to be done to comply with tenure laws and less likely to help teachers identify strengths and weaknesses but should help teachers identify inservice needs.

1678. Williams, Frederick. Explorations of the linguistic attitudes of teachers. Newbury House Publishers. Inc. Rowley, Massachusetts. 1976. ERIC ED 146 797.

Describes two research projects on teachers' attitudes toward students' differences (ethnic and linguistic) and reports a relationship between attitudes and behavior.

1679. Willower, Donald J. & Heckert, J. Wayne. Teacher pupil control ideology - behavior congruence and job satisfaction. AERA presentation. 1977. ERIC ED 138 569.

Congruence of teachers' pupil control ideology and behavior related to teachers' job satisfaction.

1680. Willower, Donald J. & Landis, Charles A. III. "Pupil control ideology and professional orientation of school faculty," Journal of Secondary Education 45 No. 3 (1970): 118-123.

Reports a slight relationship between teachers' professional orientation and pupil control ideology.

1681. Willower, Donald J. & Lawrence, James D. "Teachers' perceptions of student threat to teacher status and teacher pupil control ideology," _Psychology in the Schools_ _16_ _No. 4_ (1979): 586-590.

Reports relationship between teachers' perceptions of threats from students toward the status of teachers and teachers' pupil control ideology.

1682. Winchester, Elwood O. Differences on an interactive combination of degree of democratic orientation and positive self-evaluation among teachers with varying levels of teaching. Ed.D. dissertation. University of Oklahoma. 1975.

Study found a relationship between teachers' attitudes and number of years teaching.

1683. Wlodarczyk, Steven Albert. The impact of an inservice program on the attitudes of teachers toward mainstreaming handicapped students. Ph.D. dissertation. University of Illinois at Urbana-Champaign. 1981.

Describes the attitudes of teachers who did and did not participate in an inservice program toward the mainstreaming of handicapped children.

1684. Wood, Judith Gay Walker. A comparison of the effects of experimental special education inservice programs on the classroom teacher's attitude toward handicapped children in the public schools. Ph.D. dissertation. University of Southern Mississippi. 1979.

Describes teachers' attitudes toward handicapped students and changes in those attitudes resulting from inservice education programs; teachers' perceptions of support from a resource teacher were more strongly related to a positive attitude than to experience.

1685. Yager, Phyllis M. Crable. A study of secondary teacher attitudes toward nonsexist education and factors related to teaching. Ph.D. dissertation. University of Iowa. 1983.

Reports that teachers have a positive attitude toward nonsexist education, with differences in attitude associated with teachers' sex, teaching assignment, proportion of female students in classes.

1686. Yap, Kim Onn. "Teachers' education and teachers' attitudes toward children and learning," _Elementary School Journal_ _78_ _No. 1_ (1977): 38-43.

Found few relationships between teachers' background characteristics and attitudes.

1687. Young, I. Phillip & Kasten, Katherine. The relationship between school climate and implementation of an innovation in elementary schools. 1980. ERIC ED 199 925.

Reports that teachers changed their attitudes toward their school and toward individualized education as they participated in a staff development program designed to assist them to implement individualized instruction.

1688. Ysseldyke, James E. & others. Judgment under uncertainty: how many children are handicapped?" Exceptional Children 48 No. 6 (1982): 531-34.

Describes teachers' estimates of whether students were handicapped and influence of student characteristics, e.g., sex, on those estimates.

1689. Yuskiewicz, Vincent D. & Donaldson, William S. Job satisfaction of the public school teacher, a function of subculture consensus with respect to pupil control ideology. AERA presentation. 1972. ERIC ED 061 178.

Teachers' job satisfaction is related to teachers' attitude, pupil control ideology, experience and teaching level.

1690. Zahorik, John A. "Teacher verbal behavior: perceived value, source of acquisition, and method of justification," Journal of Teacher Education 28 No. 4 (1977): 50-55.

Describes how teachers value different verbal behaviors and how they justify their own verbal behavior.

1691. Zaremba, John Philip. Relationship of teacher motivation to innovativeness and job satisfaction. Ph.D. dissertation. University of Wisconsin - Madison. 1978.

Describes teachers' motivation in relation to job satisfaction and reported degree of innovation.

1692. Zeichner, Kenneth M. & Tabachnick, B. Robert. Teacher perspectives in the face of institutional press. ERIC ED 240 113.

Describes changes in attitudes of four teachers toward teaching, curriculum, classroom management, during their first years of teaching.

1693. Zelanak, Mel J. & Snider, Bill C. "Teacher perceptions of the teacher evaluation process," _California Journal of Educational Research_ _25_ (1974): 116-120.

Teachers who view evaluation as serving administrative purposes have a negative attitude toward evaluation while those who view it as serving an instructional purpose have a positive attitude toward evaluation.

VI. EFFECTS OF ATTITUDES

1694. Alexander, Alice Crayton. Regular-classroom teachers' attitudes toward mainstreaming handicapped students: a study of the stated attitude and its relation to selected variables and acceptance behaviors. Ed.D. dissertation. West Virginia University. 1983.

Describes relationships between teachers' attitudes toward mainstreaming and their sense of district support for mainstreaming, but attitudes do not vary by characteristics such as numbers of handicapped students taught.

1695. Alexander, William. Pupil achievement, attendance rate, and teacher attitudes toward pupils in differing organizational climates. Ed.D. dissertation. Northeastern University. 1978.

Reports that student achievement in reading and mathematics is related to teachers' attitudes and school climate.

1696. Algozzine, Bob & others. The influence of teachers' tolerances for specific kinds of behaviors on their ratings of a third grade student. ERIC ED 224 190.

Reports that teachers' responses to described student behaviors were related to teachers' attitudes and characteristics.

1697. Archer, Peter & Edwards, John R. "Predicting school achievement from data on pupils obtained from teachers: toward a screening device for disadvantage," *Journal of Educational Psychology* 74 No. 5 (1982): 761-70.

Reports that teachers' attitudes toward students and perceptions of personal characteristics are related to later student achievement.

1698. Auttonen, Ralph G. & Deighan, William. An exploration into teacher and student arithmetic attitude at grades 3, 5 and 6. AERA presentation. 1971. ERIC ED 047 983.

Reports no relationship between teachers' and students' attitudes toward arithmetic; significant decline in students' attitudes from grades 3 to 6.

1699. Babad, Elisha Y. & others. "Pygmalion, Galatea, and the Golem: investigations of biased and unbiased teachers," Journal of Educational Psychology 74 No. 4 (1982): 459-74.

Describes differences in positive and negative teacher expectations and their effects on teaching behavior and student achievement.

1700. Bauch, Patricia A. Predicting elementary classroom teaching practices from teachers' educational beliefs. ERIC ED 226 437.

Reports teachers' attitudes and the effects of those attitudes on their teaching practices as identified by four types of teachers.

1701. Bean, James Stevens & Hoy, Wayne K. "Pupil control ideology of teachers and instructional climate in the classroom," High School Journal 58 No. 2 (1974): 61-39.

Describes a relation between classroom climate variables and teachers' pupil control ideology.

1702. Beecher, Clarence. "Curriculum practices: their effect and/or relationship to selected biographical and professional variables," Journal of Experimental Education 46 No. 2 (1978): 31-41.

Describes a relationship between teachers' characteristics and attitudes toward involvement in curriculum planning, use and study.

1703. Benninga, Jacques S. & others. Selected attitudes of teachers and student perceptions of instruction at the primary level. International Congress on Early Childhood Education. Tel Aviv. 1980. ERIC ED 186 115.

Describes teachers' self confidence and perceptions of causes of pupil learning as related to attitude toward teaching, toward student freedom and toward teacher democratic values.

1704. Bhest, Ross S. & Willower, Donald J. "Organizational pressure, personal ideology and teacher pupil control behavior," Journal of Educational Administration 17 No. 1 (1979): 68-74.

Teachers' views of pupil control, not pressure of perceived colleagues' views of pupil control, are related to teachers' actual pupil control behavior.

1705. Blanton, Mary Ellen & Uffelmann, Gerald Watter. High school teacher perceptions of innovative concepts. Ed.D. dissertation. University of Southern California. 1978.

Describes teachers' attitudes toward different innovations and relates teachers' uses of those innovations to reported attitudes.

1706. Blevins, Sandra Lee C. The interrelationships of parent, teacher, and student attitudes toward mathematics and student achievement in mathematics. Ed.D. dissertation. East Tennessee State University. 1979.

Study found no relationship between students' attitudes toward math and prior teachers' attitudes toward math; did find a relationship between students' and parents' attitudes toward math.

1707. Boger, David. High school chemistry teachers and teacher-student attitudes and perceptions of chemistry. Ph.D. dissertation. University of New Mexico. 1973.

Teachers' attitudes are related to students' attitudes; reports a relationship between student enrollment and students' characteristics; students' perceptions are related to teachers' characteristics.

1708. Breen, Michael J. "Teacher interest and student attitude toward four areas of elementary school curriculum," Education 100 No. 1 (1979): 63-66.

Reports a slight relationship between teachers' and students' attitudes toward and interest in specific subject areas.

1709. Browning, Maurice E., Jr. The relationships among secondary school teachers role orientation, pupil control ideology, and pupil control behavior. Ed.D. dissertation. Northeastern Illinois University. 1979.

Describes a relationship between teachers' pupil control ideology and professional orientation toward pupil control behavior.

1710. Brummett, David Carl. The effects of teacher understanding of and attitude toward ITV science lesson content on student understanding of and attitude toward ITV science lesson content. Ed.D. dissertation. University of Virginia. 1978.

Teachers' attitudes toward and understanding of instructional TV science lessons are related to students' attitudes and understanding.

1711. Buckley, Michael Francis. The relationship of philosophical orientation, participation in decision making and degree of fulfillment of expectations about participation in decision making to elementary school teacher attitudes toward leaders, leader-teacher interaction and membership in the organization. Ph.D. dissertation. University of Connecticut. 1981.

Describes teachers' attitudes as more positive when they do than when they do not participate in decision making; attitudes toward human nature are associated with attitudes toward teaching.

1712. Carey, R.S.M. Judith A. The interrelationship between teacher skill knowledge, attitude toward, knowledge of and behavioral interactions with handicapped children in the regular classroom. Ph.D. dissertation. University of Connecticut. 1978.

Study found a relationship between teachers' knowledge and attitudes; between attitudes and behavior toward children; different teacher interactions with handicapped and non-handicapped students; and no relationship between knowledge and behavior toward students.

1713. Carter, Larry George. The relationship between teacher attitudes toward education and teacher ratings of selected behavioral objectives for elementary social studies. Ph.D. dissertation. University of Michigan. 1974. ERIC ED 097 242.

Describes teachers' attitudes toward education and philosophy of education as related to teachers' selection of affective, not cognitive, behavioral objectives for elementary social studies.

1714. Childress, Bill & Dobson, Russell. "Elementary teachers' philosophies of human nature and students' perceptions of the elementary school," Journal of the Student Personnel Association for Teacher Education 11 No. 4 (1973): 153-161.

Study found no relationship between teachers' beliefs about human nature and students' perceptions.

1715. Clark, Christopher M. Understanding writing in school: a descriptive study of writing and its instruction in two classrooms. ERIC ED 239 257.

Describes teachers' attitudes toward writing and writing instruction and the effects of those attitudes on teachers' classroom writing activities.

1716. Clements, Barbara S. The relationship of teacher perceptions to classroom processes and student outcomes. 1980. ERIC ED 195 545.

Describes teachers' beliefs about education, instruction, relationships between teachers and students, and allocation of decision making between teachers and students as related in a complex manner to teachers' behaviors in the classroom.

1717. Coleman, Dolores Shirley. The relationship of teacher disciplinary attitudes and teacher disciplinary behavior. Ed.D. dissertation. University of Pennsylvania. 1983.

Reports no relationship between teachers' pupil control ideology and sense of authority and numbers of referrals of students to school administrators for discipline problems.

1718. Coley, J.W. The Biological Sciences Curriculum Study: its present status as perceived by certain biology teachers in Florida high schools. Florida State University. Tallahassee. 1966. ERIC ED 028 073.

Reports a relationship between teachers' perceptions of the Biological Sciences Curriculum Study (BSCS) and their own teaching of biology.

1719. Cooper, Harris & others. "Relations between student achievement and various indexes of teacher expectations," Journal of Educational Psychology 74 No. 4 (1982): 577-79.

Reports that teachers' expectations and the discrepancy between teachers' perceptions and students' abilities were associated with changes in students' achievement.

1720. Cox, H.R. Effects of maternal attitudes, teacher attitudes, and the types of nursery school training on the abilities of preschool children. Final report. Catholic University of America. Washington, D.C. 1968. ERIC ED 028 844.

Teachers' democratic attitudes and maternal attitudes are not related to academic achievement of preschool children in Montessori and traditional nursery schools.

1721. Decker, Alexander H. A correlational study of elementary school teacher perception of school climate dimensions and preference for participation in decision-making in the Durham County school system. Ed.D. dissertation. University of North Carolina at Chapel Hill. 1980.

Teachers' preference for participation in most types of educational decison-making is not related to most measures of school climate.

1722. Demps, Henry Wilie. A study of the relationship between teachers' perceptions of job satisfaction and their perceptions of the level of implementation of eighteen basic middle school characteristics. Ph.D. dissertation. Michigan State University. 1978.

Middle school teachers' job satisfaction is related to their perceptions of characteristics of their school.

1723. Dilendik, John R., Jr. Teacher-student attitude similarities and information retention. Ph.D. dissertation. State University of New York at Buffalo. 1973. American Educational Research Journal 12 (1973): 405-414.

Describes a relationship between teachers' and students' attitudes and students' learning; experiment presented teachers on film.

1724. Dillingham, McKinley & Johnson, T. Bradford. "The effect of teacher attitudes and self-concept of students on academic success," Education of the Disadvantaged Child 1 No. 4 (1973): 15-21.

Relationship between teachers' attitudes and students' self-concept to students' achievement.

1725. Divers, Arthur Jesse. An analysis of the relationship of teacher job satisfaction and teacher union activism in the Detroit public school system. Ph.D. dissertation. University of Michigan. 1980.

Reports that teachers who were most satisfied with their work environment were least active in the union.

1726. Driver, Paul Joseph. A study of public school biology teachers theory of science as related to student achievement. Florida University. 1969. ERIC ED 049 041.

Teachers with a strong belief in experimentalism have students with higher scores on biology achievement tests than teachers with strong opposition toward experimentation in science classes.

1727. Duke, Daniel L., Showers, Beverly K. & Imber, Michael. "Teachers and shared decision making: the costs and benefits of involvement," Educational Administration Quarterly 16 (1980): 93-106.

Describes teachers' views on the low cost and high benefit of teachers' involvement in decisions at the school level; identifies teachers' hesitation to get involved because of an expectation that involvement would have a limited effect on decisions actually made.

1728. Echols, Patricia S. A study of the relationships among students' attitudes toward mathematics and the variables of teacher attitude, parental attitude, achievement, ability, sex of the student and grade level of the student. Ed.D. dissertation. University of Houston. 1981.

Reports a limited relationship between teachers' and students' attitudes toward mathematics; parental attitudes had a stronger relationship to students attitudes.

1729. Elias, Susan F. & Elias, Jeffrey W. "Open education and teacher attitudes toward openness: the impact on students," Education 99 No. 2 (1978): 208-214.

Describes teachers' attitudes in traditional classrooms toward open education and the relationship of attitudes to students' self-esteem and curiosity.

1730. Emans, Robert. "Teacher attitudes as a function of values," Journal of Educational Research 62 (1969): 459-463.

Reports that teachers' values are related to teachers' approval of the school curriculum.

1731. Erez, Miriam & Israeli, Rachael. "Work-value orientations and their relationships to teachers' activities," Journal of Educational Administration 18 (1980): 88-97.

Describes a study which found that teachers' attitudes are related to their orientations toward the value of work, local orientation and bureaucratic orientation.

1732. Evertson, Carolyn M. & Brophy, Jere E. The Texas Teacher Effectiveness Project: quesionnaire and interview data. Research and Development Center for Teacher Education. University of Texas. Austin. 1974. report 4005. ERIC ED 099 346.

Reports that teachers' attitudes, beliefs and classroom instructional practices are related to students' achievement.

1733. Felsenthal, Helen. Sex differences in teacher-pupil interaction in first grade reading instruction. AERA presentation. 1970. ERIC ED 039 106.

Female teachers behave differently toward boys and girls; the behavior differences are related to teachers' attitudes.

1734. Fielding, Marianne A. & Gall, Meredith D. Personality and situational correlates of teacher stress and burnout. ERIC ED 219 353.

Describes a relationship between teachers' characteristics and attitudes and teachers' perceptions of factors associated with stress.

1735. Foley, Walter J. & Brooks, Robert. "Pupil control ideology in predicting teacher discipline referrals," Educational Administration Quarterly 14 No. 3 (1978): 104-112.

Teachers' pupil control ideology is related to the number of referrals of students for discipline problems.

1736. Ford, Carolyn Brown. A study of the relationships among pupil perception of teacher social power base, teacher pupil control ideology and teacher concern level in teachers of secondary mathematics. Ed.D. dissertation. University of Houston. 1976.

Describes teachers' level of concern related to pupil control ideology and students' perceptions of teachers' power.

1737. Funderburk, Charles & Shaw, Paul C. "Teachers' political attitudes: implications for political socialization," _Indiana Social Studies Quarterly 29 No. 3_ (1976-77): 29-37.

Describes teachers' political beliefs as supportive of the established political order.

1738. Gansneder, Bruce M. The relationship between teachers' attitudes toward pupils and pupils' attitudes and achievement. AERA presentation. 1970. _ERIC ED_ 137 788.

Teachers' attitudes as measured by a fourteen-item questionnaire are not related to students' achievement at the school level; reports a correlation between teachers' attitudes and community support for schools.

1739. Garza, Gonzalo. A study of teacher-student interaction in sixth grades of ethnically imbalanced schools. Ph.D. dissertation. University of Texas at Austin. 1976.

Teachers' attitudes and experiences are related to teachers' perceptions of student behavior and both are related to actual student behavior.

1740. Gilbert, Charles D. & Cooper, Dwight. "The relationship between teacher/student attitudes and the competency levels of sixth grade students," _School Science and Mathematics 79_ (1976): 469-176.

No relationship found between teachers' reports of feeling of competency to teach math and attitudes toward teaching math and attitudes of students toward math; reports a negative relationship between teachers' and students' attitudes toward math.

1741. Gitlin, Ellen Claire. Teachers' attitudes towards students and teachers' attitudes towards the teaching of mathematics as it relates to students' performances in sixth grade mathematics. Ed.D. dissertation. Wayne State University. 1979.

Reports that teachers' attitudes toward math are not related to student achievement in math.

1742. Glass, Lynn William. An analysis of the influence of selected teacher behaviors upon development of corresponding student behaviors. Ph.D. dissertation. University of Iowa. 1970. _ERIC ED_ 113 128.

Students adopt an attitude toward biology similar to teachers' attitudes; attitudes are not related to achievement.

1743. Golas, Anthony. Interaction analysis as a means of studying the effects of an attitudinal group experience on the classroom behavior of teachers. Ph.D. dissertation. Kent State University. 1966.

Study found a relationship between attitude and behavior; teachers with strong attitudes and training demonstrate changes in verbal behaviors.

1744. Good, Thomas L. & Brophy, Jere E. "Behavioral expresson of teacher attitudes," Journal of Educational Psychology 63 No. 6 (1972): 617-624.

Reports that different behaviors of teachers toward students (attachment, concern, indifference, rejection) are related to teachers' attitudes toward those students.

1745. Gove, Mary K. Conceptual frameworks of reading held by teachers. ERIC ED 119 641.

Describes differences in teachers' beliefs about the ways that children learn to read and reports that beliefs are associated with differences in teaching methods.

1746. Greene, Carol Malk. Relationship of teacher attitude to individualization of instruction practices in early childhood education. Ph.D. dissertation. Northwestern University. 1981.

Reports relationships between teachers' attitudes toward some instructional approaches and concepts concerning education and use of those approaches in early childhood classrooms.

1747. Greenwood, Gordon E. & Soar, Robert S. "Some relationships between teacher morale and teacher behavior," Journal of Educational Psychology 64 No. 1 (1973): 105-108.

Describes the relationship between teachers' morale and their verbal behavior.

1748. Griffith, Albert T. & London, Clement B.G. "Student relations among inner city teachers: a comparative study by teacher race," Education 101 (1980): 139-147.

Reports that differences in black and white teachers' attitudes toward students and teaching are related to behaviors of those teachers with their students in urban schools.

1749. Halpern, Marcia S. "First-grade teachers' goals and children's developing perceptions of school," Journal of Educational Psychology 68 No. 5 (1976): 633-648.

Teachers' beliefs influence students' behavior and perceptions of school.

1750. Harding, Robert Charles. The relationship of teacher attitudes toward homework and the academic achievement of primary grade students. Ed.D. dissertation. Lehigh University. 1979.

Describes differences in teachers' attitudes toward homework and the lack of a relationship between amount of homework and students' grades.

1751. Hargrove, Martha Lois. The relationship of teachers' attitudes and perceptions of ESEA Title 1 programs to the academic achievement of their students. Ed.D. dissertation. University of San Francisco. 1981.

Describes differences in student achievement as related to differences in teachers' characteristics, e.g., race, and teachers' attitudes toward their students.

1752. Harvey, O.J. "Beliefs and behavior: some implications for education," Science Teacher 37 No. 9 (1970): 10-14.

Reports that a relationship between teachers' and students' belief systems influences changes in students' attitudes; describes four major belief systems based on studies of teachers and students.

1753. Haviland, Jeannette M. "Teachers' and students' beliefs about punishment," Journal of Educational Psychology 71 No. 4 (1979): 563-570.

Students' beliefs about punishment are somewhat related to teachers' beliefs about punishment.

1754. Hawk, Thomas Dale. A comparison of teachers' preference for specific inservice activity approaches and their measured learning styles. Ph.D. dissertation. Kansas State University. 1983.

Reports a relationship between teachers' learning style and preferences for types of inservice education activities but that teachers have a limited experience with a range of possible inservice activities.

1755. Hess, Robert D. & Kirst, Michael W. "Political orientations and behavior patterns: linkages between teachers and children," Education and Urban Society 3 No. 4 (1971): 453-477.

Describes the relationship between teachers' and students' political orientations during the 1960s.

1756. Hinojasa, David. A study of the relationships between the organizational climate, the pupil control ideology and the self-esteem and power dimensions of the students' self-concept in selected elementary schools in the Corpus Christi Independent School District. Ph.D. dissertation. University of Houston. 1977.

Reports that when teachers' pupil control ideology is more open, students have greater self-esteem scores.

1757. Hirsch, Vicki E. A study of instructional approaches to spelling: student achievement and teacher attitudes. Ed.D. dissertation. University of Cincinnati. 1980.

Reported no differences between groups of teachers in attitude toward spelling instructional methods.

1758. Houston, Jacqueline G. A survey of teachers' attitudes related to behavior contracts in suburban and urban area school settings. Ph.D. dissertation. George Peabody College for Teachers of Vanderbilt University. 1979.

Describes teachers as believing that behavioral contracting will result in changes in students' behavior; differences in attitudes are not associated with personal characteristics.

1759. Hoy, Wayne K. & Jalovick, Judith M. "Open education and pupil control ideologies of teachers," Journal of Educational Research 73 No. 1 (1979): 45-49.

Reports a relationship between the openness of teachers' attitudes toward pupil control and teachers' use of open education practices.

1760. Hummelke, Helen Louise. The relationship between teachers' belief systems and perceptions of organizational climate in high and low change-oriented elementary schools. Ed.D dissertation. Oklahoma State University. 1980.

Study found no relationship between teachers' belief systems and perceptions of the organizational climate of schools.

1761. Israelson, J. "Toward a realistic image of parents: a teacher's point of view," Exceptional Parent 10 (1980): 53-54.

Describes reactions of teachers toward parents of handicapped children as those reactions are related to teachers' ideal of a model parent.

1762. Jalali, Ahmad. An exploration of the relationship between teachers' attitudes and their perception of classroom problems as a possible means for screening and selecting teacher-counselors. Ph.D. dissertation. George Peabody College for Teachers of Vanderbilt University. 1978.

Teachers' attitudes are not related to perceptions of problem behaviors among students in the classroom.

1763. Jett, Virginia Margaret. Relationships among teachers' attitudes, teachers' ratings of leadership characteristics, and children's perceptions of leadership opportunities. Ed.D. dissertation. University of Tennessee. 1982.

Reports no differences in students' perceptions of leadership opportunities with autocratic and democratic teachers, or between male and female students.

1764. Johnson, Lesley. "Teacher professional role orientation and its relationship to teacher attitudes and reported classroom practices," Australian Journal of Education 18 No. 1 (1974): 86-93.

Describes a relationship between teachers' attitudes toward the profession and their teaching practices.

1765. Johnston, Allen Curtis. A study of the statistical interaction of student belief systems, teacher belief systems and student perception of teacher performance. Ph.D. dissertation. University of Pittsburgh. 1973.

Reports no relationship between teachers' and students' belief systems and students' perceptions of teachers.

1766. Jones, Lynn. The relationship of pupil control ideology to students' rights attitudes. M.Ed. thesis. Wilkes College. 1979. ERIC ED 177 133.

Teachers' acceptance of student rights is related to the degree of teachers' humanistic attitudes toward pupil control.

1767. Jones, Paul Linus. An analysis of the relationship between biology teachers' control ideology and their classroom practices. 1970. ERIC ED 069 487.

Teachers' humanistic control ideology is related to greater acceptance of a range of behaviors in classrooms using a BSCS science curriculum.

1768. Jones, Paul L. & Blankenship, Jacob W. "A correlation of biology teachers' pupil control ideology and their classroom teaching practices," Science Education 54 (1970): 263-265. ERIC ED 025 365.

Teachers with strong pupil custodial control beliefs demonstrated a negative correlation with students' reports of inquiry teaching behavior; a weaker relation was found in a biology laboratory setting.

1769. Karagan, Nicholas James. The relationship between similarity of teacher pupil interests and school grades. Ph.D. dissertation. University of Iowa. 1972.

Reports a slight relationship between teachers' and students' interests and students' grade point averages for female but not male students.

1770. Keane, Daniel Ford. Relatonships among teacher attitude, student attitude, and student achievement in elementary school arithmetic. 1968. ERIC ED 055 774.

Study found no relationship between students' and teachers' attitudes or attitudes and achievement; socioeconomic level is related to students' attitudes but not achievement.

1771. Kedar-Vaivodas, Gita. Teachers' attitudes toward young deviant children. Ph.D. dissertation. Columbia University. 1977.

Reports that student behavior is a major factor in teachers' expectations and predictions, more important than teachers' assessment of students' current status; its effect varies by type of student behavior.

1772. Kendall, Frances E. The relationship of teachers' racial attitudes and their use of a multicultural approach to the education of young children. Ph.D. dissertation. University of North Carolina at Chapel Hill. 1980.

Study found no relationship between teachers' racial attitudes and use of a unit on multicultural education with primary grade children.

1773. Kerlinger, Fred & Pedhazur, Elazar. Educational attitudes and perceptions of desirable traits of teachers. AERA presentation. 1967.

Describes how teachers' and raters' philosophies of education relate to characteristics of teachers that are valued by teachers and raters.

1774. Klumb, Roger William. The effects of monitoring pupil performance and two incentive treatments for teachers on pupils' reading skill development and teachers' attitudes. Research and Development Center for Cognitive Learning. University of Wisconsin. Madison. 1973. ERIC ED 092 933.

Study found no change in teachers' behaviors or perceptions between treatment groups; also found no differences in student achievement associated with differences in the teaching skills in which teachers received training.

1775. Kourilsky, Marilyn & Keislor, Evan. "The effect of the success-oriented teacher on pupils' perceived personal control and attitude toward learning," Contemporary Educational Psychology 8 No. 2 (1983): 158-67.

Reports a relationship between teachers' attitudes toward teaching students and student achievement.

1776. Larkin, Ralph W. "Social exchange in the elementary school classroom: the problem of teacher legitimation of social power," Sociology of Education 48 No. 4 (1975): 400-410.

Reports that teachers' task and talk orientations are related to classroom climate.

1777. Larson, Martha Lelia. Selected parent-teacher factors that influence reading in the kindergarten. Ph.D. dissertation. University of Arizona. 1978.

Describes attitudes of teachers and parents toward behavior of teachers in reading-related instruction.

1778. Lathrop, Robert F. A study of the relationship between teacher absence behavior and morale. Ed.D. dissertation. Northern Illinois University. 1979.

Study found no relationship between teachers' morale and absences; morale was related to teachers' characteristics, e.g., sex, age, grade level, rapport with principal.

1779. Lawrence, Gordon. Use of systematic classroom observation to validate a measurement of teacher beliefs about teaching. AERA presentation. 1972. ERIC ED 064 390.

Describes a correlation between observations and reports of teachers' attitudes.

1780. Lawton, Joseph T. & Brown, Deborah L. Teacher and child verbalizations during small group and related learning activities. Research and Development Center for Individualized Schooling. University of Wisconsin. Madison, Wisconsin. 1978. ERIC ED 164 090.

Teachers' philosophy was found not highly related to teachers' behaviors in interaction with students, based on an analysis of the behaviors and philosophies of Piagetian and Ausubelian preschool teachers.

1781. LeMaster, Fredrick A. The relationships between teacher stress, attitudes toward the profession and organizational climate. Ed.D. dissertation. Oklahoma State University. 1981.

Reports a relationship between teachers' self-perceptions of stress and both attitudes toward teaching as a profession and the organizational climate of the teachers' school.

1782. Lewis, Angel Lucille F. Job satisfaction, decisional discrepancy, academic social climate, and academic achievement in selected Title I elementary schools. Ph.D. dissertation. Fordham University. 1981.

Describes a relationship between teachers' job satisfaction and aspects of the teaching situation, e.g., school climate and achievement level of students.

1783. Lewis, William Hiram. The effect of mutual precise goal-setting on teacher- and student-attitudes and on student achievement in elementary science curriculum. 1972. ERIC ED 077 643.

Describes the results of an eight week experiment where goal setting had a greater effect than did the relationship between teacher and principal.

1784. Lindholm, Mary E.N. The relationship of student and teacher attitudinal perception to student reading achievement, student spelling achievement, student IQ and teaching patterns. Ed.D. dissertation. George Washington University. 1981.

Reports that teachers do not accurately predict student achievement on standardized tests; teachers provide more positive feedback to students with more positive self-images and teachers are aware of students' self-images.

1785. Liston, John McTyeire. The relationship of attitudes of superintendents, principals, and social studies teachers to the utilization of closed circuit television in the senior public high schools of South Carolina. Ed.D. dissertation. University of South Carolina. 1981.

Reports consistent attitudes toward and use of instructional television among superintendents, principals and social studies teachers.

1786. Littrell, Dennis Martin. Teachers' pupil control ideology, pupil control behavior, and student discipline. Ed.D. dissertation. University of Missouri - Columbia. 1980.

Reports that teachers' pupil control ideology is more strict than students perceive the teachers' behavior to be, but no differences in the types of disipline problems that occur in classrooms by whether the teacher has a custodial or humanistic pupil control ideology.

1787. Loughran, Paul Andrew. Administrator and teacher attitude, work environment, and mathematics achievement in system and non-system approaches. Ph.D. dissertation. Fordham University. 1979.

Study compares two methods of mathematics system approaches, finding variations in student achievement and teacher satisfaction with the work environment; results were also related to teachers' age and training.

1788. Lynam, Robert John. An exploratory investigation of the relationship between teacher morale, attendance pressure, and absenteeism. Ph.D. dissertation. George Peabody College for Teachers of Vanderbilt University. 1979.

Low teacher morale was associated with more absence, more pressure not to be absent; the greater the frequency of teacher absences, the more pressure to be present.

1789. McAdams, Martha L.W. The effects of regular education inservice training on teacher anxiety, knowledge about individualization, and attitudes toward mainstreaming. Ph.D. dissertation. University of Florida. 1981.

Reports limited relationships between teachers' knowledge about mainstreaming and attitudes toward and anxiety about mainstreaming, with no changes resulting from participation in an inservice program.

1790. McCann, S.J.H. & Fisher, R.J. "The interactive relationships of teacher directiveness and student authoritarianism and dogmatism to grades and satisfaction," _Alberta Journal of Educational Research 23 No. 1_ (1977): 71-84.

Describes a relationship between students' and teachers' dogmatism, authoritarianism and students' grades and satisfaction.

1791. McKiney. James Allen. A correlational comparison of the relationship between interpersonal values of teachers and the measured self-esteem and social behavior of early adolescent students in selected middle schools and junior high schools. Ph.D. dissertation. Michigan State University. 1971.

Study found a relationship between interpersonal values of teachers and self-concept and social behavior of students.

1792. McMahon, Albert J., Jr. The relationship between the pupil control ideology of mathematics teachers and student attitudes toward mathematics. Ph.D. dissertation. Saint Louis University. 1979.

Describes a relationship between teachers' pupil control ideology and grade 9 students' attitudes toward mathematics.

1793. McNeil, Terry Scott. A study of the relationship between the biology teachers' attitude toward the BSCS biology program and the students' perception of the type of laboratory and classroom activity. 1971. _ERIC ED_ 068 305.

Reports that teachers' attitudes bore no relationship to students' perceptions of laboratory activities.

1794. Maestas, Leo C. "Academic performance across cultures: an examination of the effects of value similarity," Educational Research Quarterly 7 No. 4 (1983): 24-34.

Reports that discrepancies in teachers' and students' attitudes and values are associated with greater student achievement.

1795. Mager, Gerald M. "The conditions which influence a teacher in initiating contact with parents," Journal of Educational Research 73 (1980): 276-282.

Reports that teachers who more frequently make contact with parents believe that they have a responsibility to initiate and continue such contact but those teachers thought that they received less support from parents than did teachers who made less frequent contact.

1796. Mallula, Sandra Ann. Teacher competency, teacher attitude and student attitude toward reading. Ph.D. dissertation. University of Georgia. 1978.

Reports that teachers' attitudes are related to teachers' competence and student achievement in junior high school reading content areas.

1797. Manganiello, Louis P. A study to determine the relationship of teacher self-acceptance and other selected variables to teacher absence behavior. Ed.D. dissertation. University of Miami. 1972.

Reports no relationship between teachers' self-acceptance and absence behavior, teachers' sex, number of children or years of teaching experience.

1798. Mascagna, Dominic Rocco. Successful and unsuccessful teacher behaviors in selected flexible modular scheduled public high schools in Connecticut. Ed.D. dissertaiton. Fordham University. 1975.

Teachers' belief systems, pupil control ideology and sex are rated differently by teachers and supervisors in rating as successful and unsuccessful those behaviors used by teachers in flexible modular scheduling.

1799. Matthews, G. P. "An example of the teacher expectation effect in mixed ability teaching," Journal of Research in Science Teaching 1 No. 6 (1982): 497-502.

Describes teachers' expectations for various classes and different patterns of student science achievement than predicted by teachers' expectations.

1800. Mattioli, Michael J. The effect ot genuine progressive and pseudoprogressive educational attitudes and susceptibility to an authoritative source on the marking behavior of 4th, 5th, and 6th grade teachers and students of education preparing to teach. Ph.D. dissertation. New York University. 1972.

Study found a relationship between teachers' genuine progressive attitude and grades given to low and average achieving students; a relationship between experience and grades - inexperienced teachers gave higher grades.

1801. Mitchell, Marlene. Teacher "attitude" vs. teacher behavior. Ph.D. dissertation. Nova University. 1972. ERIC ED 063 280.

Study found that teachers' attitudes and expressed goals predicted teachers' activities.

1802. Mitchell, Patricia T. Organizational climates of elementary schools and teachers' perceptions of principals' effectiveness. Ph.D. dissertation. Catholic University of America. 1978.

Study found a relationship between teachers' characteristics and teachers' perceptions of the effectiveness of the principal.

1803. Modisette, Barbara Jane. A study of the attitudes of teachers and intermediate and middle school students toward the handicapped in their classrooms. Ed.D. dissertation. East Texas State University. 1983.

Reports positive attitudes among teachers toward handicapped students and a relationship between teachers' attitudes and attitudes of students toward handicapped students.

1804. Moore, Robert Lee. Elementary teachers' attitudes toward student-centered science as related to teacher concerns. Ph.D. dissertation. University of Southern Mississippi. 1982.

Reports relationships between teachers' concerns for tasks and themselves and their attitudes toward student-centered science instruction.

1805. Morawa, Edward C. & Sheathelm, Herbert H. Teachers perceptions of need fulfillment and self-esteem and their attitudes toward change. ERIC ED 243 843.

Describes teachers' attitudes toward change as related to but not fully explained by, teachers' levels of self-esteem and need fulfillment.

1806. Morrison, Gale M. & others. "Influences on the sociometric ratings of mildly handicapped children: a path analysis," Journal of Educational Psychology 75 No. 1 (1983): 63-74.

Describes teachers' attitudes toward handicapped students as influencing the social status of those students.

1807. Mullarney, Patrick B. A study of the relationship between the verbal interaction of teachers and their philosophical and educational beliefs in experimentalism. Ph.D. dissertation. University of Michigan. 1972.

Three observations of twenty teachers using Flanders Interaction Analysis demonstrated a relationship between teachers' belief in Dewey's experimentalism and teacher behavior; those with a higher belief were more indirect.

1808. O'Connell, Dennis Lee. A comparison of three middle schools involving a study of relationships among school climate, perceived teacher needs and student attitudes. Ed.D. dissertation. University of Toledo. 1979.

Describes teachers' self-reported needs and the relationship of those needs to school morale and students' attitudes.

1809. Oliver, Bernard & Taylor, John L. "Teacher characteristics and classroom behavior," Journal of Classroom Interaction 16 (1980): 11-18.

Reports that teachers' attitudes and characteristics are related to teachers' behavior in elementary physical education instruction.

1810. O'Rourke, Anne Patrice. A comparison of principal and teacher attitudes toward handicapped students and the relationship between those attitudes and school morale of handicapped students. Ed.D. dissertation. University of Nebraska - Lincoln. 1979.

Study found a relationship between teachers' and principals' attitudes toward handicapped students and some relationship between those attitudes and the morale of handicapped students in those schools.

1811. Patton, Virginia Ann. The relationship of educators' attitudes toward handicapped children and the handicapped children's attitude toward the quality of school life. Ph.D. dissertation. Kent State University. 1981.

Reports few relationships between attitudes of teachers and attitudes of handicapped and non-handicapped students.

1812. Pecheone, Raymond Lee. Investigating the meaning of needs assessment data: the relationship between the in-service training needs of classroom teachers and the teachers' demographic characteristics, attitude toward, and knowledge of mainstreamed children. Ph.D. dissertation. University of Connecticut. 1979.

Reports that teachers who rated themselves high in attitude toward mainstreaming also rated themselves high in competence to deal with mainstreamed children and that teacher demographic variables did not relate to attitudes.

1813. Peretti, Peter O. "Effects of teachers' attitudes on discipline problems in schools recently desegregated," _Education_ _97_ _No._ _2_ (1976): 136-140.

Reports that teachers' attitudes toward bussing for integration are related to the presence of classroom discipline problems.

1814. Perkins, Karen L. & others. "Influence of teachers' attitudes toward the school lunch program on student participation," _Journal of Nutrition Education_ _12_ _No._ _2_ (1980): 55-60.

Reports that teachers' attitudes toward the school lunch program and toward eating with students influence students' attitudes toward and participation in the school lunch program.

1815. Peters, William H. "Research and selected aspects of a statement on the preparation of teachers of English," _English Education_ _11_ (1980): 202-219.

Describes a study of the relationship between teachers' belief systems and classroom environments and their influence on students, related to statement of teacher competencies.

1816. Phillips, Douglas Jay. Teachers' role concepts and the qualities of teacher-student relationships. Ph.D. dissertation. University of Alabama. 1978.

Reports that teachers' ideal behavior is related to student teachers' ratings of teachers' behaviors.

1817. Politzer, Robert L. & Hoover, Mary Rhodes. Teachers' and pupils' attitudes toward black English speech varieties and black pupils' achievement. Research and development memorandum No. 145. Stanford Center for Research and Development in Teaching. Stanford University. California. 1976. ERIC ED 128 527.

Describes attitudes of teachers toward black English and finds some relationships between attitudes and teachers' assigned grades, but not between attitudes and students' achievement gains on reading tests.

1818. Powell, Douglas R. "Correlates of parent-teacher communication frequency and diversity," Journal of Educational Research 71 (1978): 333-341.

Identifies several factors related to the frequency and diversity of communication between preschool students' parents and teachers: teachers' role status, attitudes toward appropriate parent-teacher communication content, professional education and experience.

1819. Radecki, Henry & Evans, Susan. The teacher's strike study. ERIC ED 232 247.

Describes attitudes of teachers toward events leading to a teacher strike and the effects of the strike on teachers' attitudes toward the school system.

1820. Ralston, Elizabeth W. The relationship between teacher and principal attitude and student achievement in the Title I reading program. Ed.D. dissertation. Memphis State University. 1978.

Study found that teachers' and principals' attitudes had a significant relationship to student achievement.

1821. Rasmusen, Mary V.W. Predictors of teacher turnover. Ed.D. dissertation. University of Houston. 1980.

Describes a relationship between several teachers' attitudes, such as toward quitting, and teacher turnover.

1822. Rescigno, Ronald C. A study of the relationship between parent and teacher satisfaction with their involvement in a school's decison-making process and student attitude toward school. Ed.D. dissertation. University of Northern Colorado. 1977.

Describes attitudes of parents and teachers: teachers had a more positive attitude when decisions were made at the school, not district, level.

1823. Rexford, Gene Erwin. The relationship between pupil control ideology and observed verbal behavior of selected secondary teachers. Ed.D. dissertation. Pennsylvania State University. 1970.

Investigated the relationship between pupil control ideology and classroom behavior of teachers; teachers' indirect and direct influence are more closely related to teachers' pupil control ideology than to the percentage of teacher talk in the classroom.

1824. Rexford, Gene E., Willower, Donald J. & Lynch, Patrick D. "Teachers' pupil control ideology and classroom verbal behavior," Journal of Experimental Education 40 No. 4 (1972): 78-82.

Teachers with a custodial pupil control ideology are more direct but exhibit no greater talk than teachers with a humanistic pupil control ideology.

1825. Richardson, Donald E. Teacher work values and decisional states. Ph.D. dissertation. University of Oklahoma. 1978.

Study found a relationship between teachers' work values and their interest in involvement in school decisions.

1826. Rogers, Jimmy Weber. The school-based attitudes of students and their relationships to the school-based attitudes of administrators, teachers, and parents in Colorado Seventh Day Adventist church schools. Ed.D. dissertation. University of Colorado at Boulder. 1980.

Describes differences in attitudes toward the school program among students, teachers and parents, with less positive attitudes among students.

1827. Rookey, Thomas J. & Reardon, Francis, J. Teacher behavior related to pupil creativity and assessment strategem. AERA presentation. 1973. ERIC ED 076 704.

Teachers' attitudes are not correlated with student creativity; teachers' behaviors are correlated with student creative ability but not attitudes.

1828. Rubin, K.H. & Hansen, R. "Teaching attitudes and behaviors of preschool personnel: curriculum variations," Alberta Journal of Educational Research 22 No. 3 (1976): 261-269.

Reports a relationship between teachers' attitudes with respect to instructional strategies and students' and teachers' behaviors.

1829. Schmidt, William H. & Buchmann, Margret. "Six teachers' beliefs and attitudes and their curricular time allocations," Elementary School Journal 84 (1983): 162-71.

Describes teachers' attitudes toward subject areas of instruction and the effects of those attitudes on time allocations.

1830. Seyfarth, John T. & Canady, Robert L. "Assessing causes of teachers' attitudes toward team teaching," Education 98 No. 3 (1978): 297-300.

Reports that teachers' experiences and values are related to teachers' reactions toward team teaching.

1831. Shaw, Stanley F. An assessment and comparison of elementary classroom teachers' attitudes and behaviors in relation to mildly handicapped children. Ed.D. dissertation. University of Oregon. 1971.

Study found differences in teachers' attitudes toward average and mildly handicapped (attitudes favor average students), differences by school, no relationship between attitudes and behaviors, and no difference in teachers' behavior toward average and mildly handicapped.

1832. Shearin, Wiley H., Jr. "The relationship between student alienation and extent of faculty agreement on pupil control ideology," High School Journal 66 No. 1 (1982): 32-35.

Reports less student alienation in schools with greater agreement among teachers about pupil control ideology.

1833. Skinner, Janet E. A study of teacher attitudes as related to voluntary participation in a program designed to promote preventive discipline in desegregated elementary schools. Ed.D. dissertation. East Texas State University. 1980.

Describes teachers' flexibility and child-centeredness and changes in those attitudes resulting from participation in an inservice education program.

1834. Smith, Joanna Brashaber. Teachers' attitudes and peer acceptance of mainstreamed handicapped students. Ph.D. dissertation. Purdue University. 1983.

Reports a relationship between teachers' attitudes toward mainstreaming and the presence in their classroom of mainstreamed students; no relationship between teachers' attitudes and level of students' acceptance of mainstreamed student.

1835. Smith, Kenneth Robert. Teacher preference compared with teacher effectiveness evidenced by product measurement: an indicator for teacher placement in grouped classes. Ed.D. dissertation. University of Oklahoma. 1971.

Teachers' preferences for ability levels within grade are related to teachers' effectiveness as measured by achievement scores of students.

1836. Stedman, James M. & Adams, Russell L. "Teacher perceptions of behavioral adjustment as a function of linguistic ability in Mexican-American Head Start children," Psychology in the Schools 10 No 2 (1973): 221-223.

Study reports a relationship between teachers' ratings and students' proficiency in the English language.

1837. Steiner, Laurie Levine. A study of female kindergarten teachers' sex-role attitudes and their effect on kindergarten girls' sex-typed toy preferences. Ed.D. dissertation. University of Houston. 1980.

Describes differences between "feminist" and "traditional" teachers and the effects of "traditional" teachers on the toy choices of their female students.

1838. Stern, William Alvin. Teacher absenteeism at the secondary school level: an investigation of work-related attitudes and demographic correlates. Ph.D. dissertation. Michigan State University. 1980.

Describes a relationship between teachers' job satisfaction and absenteeism; dissatisfaction with specific aspects of job assignments is associated with greater absenteeism.

1839. Taylor, Janet B. "Influence of speech variety on teachers' evaluation of reading comprehension," Journal of Educational Psychology 75 No. 5 (1983): 662-67.

Describes teachers' attitudes toward non-standard English and the effects of those attitudes in teachers' assessments of students' reading skills.

1840. Taylor, Janet M.B. The influence of speech variety on teachers' evaluation of reading comprehension during an oral reading and recall task. Ph.D. dissertation. Florida State University. 1979.

Teachers' attitudes toward black English are related to teachers' evaluations of students' oral reading and comprehension skills with negative attitudes associated with lower evaluations in a tape simulation.

1841. Tomaras, Sophronia N. Nonstandard dialects in the classroom: a study of elementary and secondary teachers' perceptions, expectations, and coping strategies in a selected school district. Ph.D. dissertation. University of Washington. 1980.

Reported ambivalence among teachers about whether nonstandard dialects are different languages or a deficient language; teachers who believed the latter had lower expectations for speakers of nonstandard dialects.

1842. Van de Walle, John A. Attitudes and perceptions of elementary mathematics possessed by third and sixth grade teachers as related to student attitude and achievement in mathematics. 1973. ERIC ED 076 425.

Study found no relationship between teachers' attitudes and perceptions and student achievement.

1843. Victor, James B. & Otis, James P. "Teacher strength and sensitivity behavior: attitude personality correlates," Journal of Experimental Education 49 (1980): 9-15.

Reports that teachers' attitudes are related more strongly than personality characteristics to teachers' sensitivity to the learner and ratings of strength of the teachers' teaching performances.

1844. Villpiano, Albert J. A study of elementary school teachers' and support personnel's democratic classroom behaviors and their attitudes toward education. Ed.D. dissertation. Boston University School of Education. 1983.

Reports a relationship between teachers' attitudes toward education and teachers' democratic behavior in the classroom, with teachers' attitudes varying by demographic characteristics, e.g., degree level and income.

1845. von Eschenbach, John F. "Effects of a collaborative in-service model on middle school teachers' perceptions of their professional competence," <u>High School Journal 64</u> (1980): 8-12.

Reports increases in teachers' perceptions of their professional competence in twenty-four areas after participation in the planning and implementation of an inservice education program.

1846. Watson, Robert Stone. The effect of teacher knowledge and attitude on teaching about alcohol. Ph.D. dissertation. University of South Carolina. 1981.

Reports that teachers' knowledge about and attitudes toward alcohol was not related to teachers' beliefs in student-centered or teacher-centered teaching.

1847. Weber, Margaret B. & others. The relationship between teachers' sex role attitudes and stereotypic reinforcements of student behaviors. AERA presentation. 1978. <u>ERIC ED</u> 151 333.

Reports that teachers' stereotypic attitudes are not related to stereotypic behavior or grade taught.

1848. Westbrook, Arlen. "Teachers' recognition of problem behaviors and referrals of children to pupil personnel services," <u>Journal of Educational Research 63 No. 9</u> (1970): 391-394.

Teachers' referrals reflect and are related to teachers' concerns for the educational needs of their students.

1849. Wilson, William Lynn. Organizational climate, teachers' attitudes, teachers' demographic data, and perceived effectiveness of teachers. Ed.D. dissertation. University of Kansas. 1980.

Principals' ratings of teacher effectiveness are related to teachers' attitudes toward students, teachers' demographic characteristics, and school organizational climate.

1850. Winkler, Donald R. Project on research in student learning. Final report. 1976. ERIC ED 113 820.

Describes teachers' attitudes toward levels of student achievement and the effects of years of schooling on the range of student achievement, student work effort and achievement.

1851. Wu, Shi-Chang. The foundations of student suspension. 1980. ERIC ED 201 054.

Reports that rates of suspension of students from school are associated with teachers' attitudes toward students, bias toward minority and low achieving students, and degree of formality and rigidity in school procedures for handling discipline problems.

1852. Zulich, Jan Leigh. The relationship between secondary students' attitudes toward women and their teachers' attitudes toward women. Ph.D. dissertation. Indiana University. 1983.

Reports a relationship between teachers' sex and age and attitudes toward women, with female and younger teachers having more feminist attitudes; student attitudes were related to the attitudes of their current, not model, teachers.

VII. REVIEWS OF RESEARCH ON ATTITUDES

1853. Aiken, Lewis R., Jr. & Aiken, Dorothy R. "Recent research on attitudes concerning science," Science Education 53 No. 4 (1969): 295-305.

Describes and reviews research on and development of attitudes toward science among elementary, secondary and college students and relates their attitudes to teachers' attitudes.

1854. Aldana, Ana L. & Ogletree, Earl J. What research says about the attitudes toward and the opinions of bilingual education. ERIC ED 227 993.

Reviews research on teachers' attitudes toward bilingual education, the maintenance of a language other than English, and the relationship of bilingual education to other institutional efforts.

1855. Alexander, Cara & Strain, Phillip S. "A review of educators' attitudes toward handicapped children and the concept of mainstreaming," Psychology in the Schools 15 No. 3 (1978): 390-396.

The review indicates that educators view handicapped students as less able to benefit from schooling and therefore they don't favor mainstreaming.

1856. Arganbright, Jerry L. "Teacher expectations -- a critical factor for student achievement," NASSP Bulletin 67 (Sept. 1983): 93-95,

Review of research describes the influence of teachers' expectations for students on student motivation and achievement.

1857. Ashbaugh, Carl R. "What is job satisfaction?" Planning and Changing 13 No. 4 (1982): 195-203.

Reviews research in teachers' job satisfaction, factors which cause discontent and ways to increase job satisfaction.

1858. Awender, M.A. & Plantus, M. "Discipline and pupil control ideologies," Education Canada 23 No. 1 (1983): 36-39.

Reviews literature on teachers' attitudes toward discipline in schools.

1859. Ayers, George E. "Teacher attitudes and black children," Kappa Delta Pi Record 7 No. 1 (1970): 22-24.

Article reviews literature on teachers' attitudes toward black children.

1860. Blanbergs, Maija S. "Sex-role stereotyping and gifted girls' experience and education," Roeper Review 2 No. 3 (1980): 13-15.

Review of literature reveals sex stereotyped attitudes of teachers, parents and counselors toward abilities of gifted girls.

1861. Bloland, Paul A. & Selby, Thomas J. "Factors associated with career change among secondary school teachers: a review of the literature," Educational Research Quarterly 5 No. 3 (1980): 13-24.

Describes changes in teachers' attitudes toward teaching as a career and the relationship of personality factors and career patterns.

1862. Blosser, Patricia E. & Mayer, Victor J. (eds.). "Investigations in science education" Investigations in Science Education 9 No 2.

Reviews studies of teachers' attitudes toward science education and programs designed to change those attitudes.

1863. Brooks, Benjamin L. & Simms, Rochelle B. "Are handicapped children welcome in Catholic schools?" Momentum 15 No. 1 (1984): 44-46.

Reviews research on attitudes of educators toward handicapped students, describing variables related to positive attitudes, e.g., teaching experience.

1864. Brophy, Jere E. Research on the self-fulfilling prophecy and teacher expectations. ERIC ED 221 530.

Describes research on teachers' expectations for students, the role of individual student differences and the implications of the research for teachers and teacher education.

1865. Brophy, Jere E. Teachers' cognitive activities and overt behavior. 1980. ERIC ED 200 561.

Reviews research on teacher planning and decision making, describing teachers' planning as based on perceived needs of students rather than instructional objectives; teachers' expectations for students are accurate and form a basis for planning.

1866. Buchmann, Margret & Schmidt, William H. The school day and content commitments. ERIC ED 204 282.

Describes the patterns of time commitment to specific areas of the curriculum for six teachers and relates those patterns to the teachers' attitudes and perceptions of their teaching skills.

1867. Clement, Frank J. "Affective considerations in computer-based education," Educational Technology 21 NO. 4 (1981): 28-32.

Reviews research on attitudes of teachers, administrators and students toward instructional uses of computers.

1868. Coates, Thomas J. & Thoresen, Carl E. Teacher anxiety: a review with recommendations. Research and development memorandum no. 123. Stanford Center for Research and Development in Teaching. Stanford University. California. 1974. ERIC ED 092 518.

Reviews studies of teachers' anxiety and stress: incidences of, causes, effects, ways of reducing stress.

1869. Cohen, Elizabeth G. "Status of teachers," Review of Educational Research 37 (1967): 280-295.

Reviews research on the status of teachers and factors affecting status, such as slum schools.

1870. Conver, Michael E. "Minimal competency testing, the professionals, the handicapped, and the law," Illinois School Research and Development 19 No. 1 (1982): 26-31.

Reviews studies of teachers' negative attitudes toward minimum competency testing and other factors, including the widespread use of such testing.

1871. Crohn, Leslie. Toward excellence: student and teacher behaviors as predictors of school success. ERIC ED 242 704.

Reviews research on teachers' expectations and students' self-concept and their effects on student achievement.

1872. Daniels, Harvey A. & others. What teachers believe: an historical investigation of language attitudes and the implications for bidialectalism in the schools. 1975. ERIC ED 125 288.

Historic review of teachers' attitudes toward language use in the classroom.

1873. Duckworth, Kenneth & De Bevoise, Wynn (eds.). The effects of collective bargaining on school administrative leadership. ERIC ED 227 547.

Summarizes effects of collective bargaining on attitudes of teachers and administrators.

1874. Dusek, Jerome B. & Joseph, Gail. "The bases of teacher expectancies: a meta-analysis," Journal of Educational Psychology 75 (1983): 327-46.

Reviews studies of teachers' expectations for students and identifies factors affecting expectations, e.g., student attractiveness.

1877. ERIC Information Analysis Center for Science Education. Science education information report. general bibliography. Series 10. Teacher characteristics. Student characteristics. 1968. ERIC ED 021 773.

General bibliography of teachers' and students' characteristics in science including research reports.

1875. Educational Research Service. Summary of research on open education. Educational Research Service. Washington, D.C. 1974. ERIC ED 087 769.

Review of studies on open education including teachers' attitudes toward behaviors and effects of open education on students' attitudes and achievement (includes bibliography).

1876. Enz, Judith. Review and analysis of reports of science inservice projects: recommendations for the future. ERIC ED 216 883.

Reviews studies of effects of inservice programs on teachers' and students' knowledge and attitudes, concluding that inservice education is effective.

1878. Flaxman, E. A selected bibliography on teacher attitude. ERIC-IRCD Urban Disadvantaged. Columbia University. New York City. 1969. ERIC ED 027 357.

Annotated bibliography of studies of teachers' attitude and its relation to student-teacher interactions; of programs of inservice training to modify teachers' attitudes; and of essays about attitudes and expectations.

1879. Freeman, Evelyn B. "The Ann Arbor decision: the importance of teacher attitudes toward language," Elementary School Journal 83 No. 1 (1982): 41-47.

Reviews studies of teachers' attitudes toward students' use of non-standard English.

1880. Glickman, Carl D. Directions for research on supervisory conference approaches appropriate to developmental levels of teachers. ERIC ED 230 513.

Reviews research on teacher supervision and the effects of teachers' attitudes and personality characteristics on teachers' attitudes toward methods of supervision.

1881. Hannah, Mary Elizabeth & Pliner, Susan. "Teacher attitudes toward handicapped children: a review and synthesis," School Psychology Review 12 NO. 1 (1983): 12-25.

Reviews studies of teachers' attitudes toward handicapped students and the relationship between teachers' characteristics and attitudes.

1882. Helgeson, Stanley E. & Blosser, Patricia E. (eds.). Investigations into science education 4 No. 1. Expanded abstracts and critical analyses of recent research. 1978. ERIC ED 164 327.

Review of students' and teachers' attitudes and characteristics in science classes.

1883. Higdon, D.W. Prospective and experienced elementary teachers: a comparison of mathematical achievement and attitudes. 1972. ERIC ED 107 528.

Describes the attitudes toward and achievement in mathematics of experienced teachers and teachers in training; grade 4-6 teachers have a more positive attitude than those in grades k-3.

1884. Hoge, Robert D. "The definition and measurement of teacher expectations: problems and prospects," Canadian Journal of Education 9 No. 2 (1984): 213-228.

Describes weaknesses in researchers' views of and research on teachers' expectation for student performance.

1885. Horne, Marcia D. How attitudes are measured: a review of investigations of professional, peer, and parent attitudes toward the handicapped. 1980. ERIC ED 198 154.

Reviews various procedures for measurement of attitudes of several groups toward handicapped students, focusing on measurement issues more than on the attitudes measured.

1886. Jayatilleke, Raja. Human relations in the classroom. an annotated bibliography: supplement I. Series No. 28. ERIC-IRDC Urban Disadvantaged. Columbia University. New York City. 1972. ERIC ED 064 417.

Annotated bibliography of citations which appeared in ERIC or were published in 1971 covering many aspects of relations in the classroom, such as attitudes of teachers and students, multicultural curriculum development, student-teacher relationships.

1887. Johnston, John M. & Ryan, Kevin. Research on the beginning teacher: implications for teacher education. 1980. ERIC ED 209 188.

Describes the writings on and research about teachers' induction to teaching, including an overview of historical perspectives on induction, research on initial socialization of teachers and evaluations of programs to assist beginning teachers.

1888. Keavney, Glenese & Sinclair, Kenneth E. "Teacher concerns and teacher anxiety: a neglected topic of classroom research," Review of Educational Research 48 (1978): 273-290.

Reviews teachers' anxiety, sources and consequences for survival or non-survival in teaching; affective impact of students' achievement; coping styles of teachers.

1889. Kedar-Voivodas, Gita. "The impact of elementary children's school roles and sex roles on teacher attitudes: an interaction analysis," Review of Educational Research 53 (1983): 514.

Reviews research on teachers' attitudes toward students and identifies three major roles for students, as pupils, receptive learners and active learners.

1890. Koenke, Karl. "One view of improving the teaching of reading," Reading Teacher 34 (1980): 90-92.

Reviews research on teachers' conceptions of reading and learning to read as well as their behaviors during reading instruction, diagnosis of reading problems and remediation instruction.

1891. Kurtz, Sandra. An annotated bibliography of literature dealing with stress in the teaching profession. Master's thesis. Indiana University. South Bend, Indiana. 1980. ERIC ED 187 707.

A bibliography on causes of teachers' stress and teachers' responses to stress.

1892. Kyriacou, Chris. "Social support and occupational stress among school teachers," Educational Studies 7 No. 1 55-60.

Reviews documents on teachers' stress and the ways that teachers can use social support to lessen stress.

1893. Lasley, Thomas J. & Galloway, Charles M. "Achieving professional status: a problem in what teachers believe," Clearing House 57 (1983): 5-8.

Reviews studies of teachers' perceptions of teaching as a profession and three potential roles of teachers.

1894. Leibowicz, Joseph. "ERIC/RCS report: classrooms, teachers, and nonstandard speakers," Language Arts 61 No. 1 (1984): 88-91.

Reviews studies of teachers' attitudes toward speakers of non-standard English and the effects of those attitudes on students' performance.

1895. Loop, Liza & Christensen, Paul. Exploring the microcomputer learning environment. 1980. ERIC ED 201 307.

Reviews studies of teachers' uses of, attitudes toward, and expressions of training needs related to the use of computers in the classroom and instruction in computer literacy.

1896. Loree, M. Ray. "Shaping teachers' attitudes," Research in Teacher Education: a Symposium (Smith, B.O., ed.). Prentice-Hall, Inc. Englewood Cliffs, New Jersey (1971): 99-118.

Describes programs of teacher education intended to influence teachers' attitudes, methods of measuring teachers' attitudes and briefly reviews studies of effects of teachers' attitudes.

1897. Luftig, Jeffrey T. Review and synthesis of the theory of occupational choice literature with special application to public school teaching. 1974. ERIC ED 095 409.

Review of career choice literature as it relates to teaching, including characteristics of teachers and the job of teaching; develops a model of the process of career choice.

1898. Mancuso, James C. & Eimer, Bruce N. A constructivist view of reprimand in the classroom. ERIC ED 273 591.

Reviews studies of classroom management and student discipline to develop a coherent approach to classroom management.

1899. Meyer, Ruth A. Attitudes of elementary teachers toward mathematics. 1980. ERIC ED 190 388.

Reports the existence of equal numbers of elementary student teachers with positive and negative attitudes toward mathematics and reviews prior research on teachers' attitudes toward mathematics.

1900. Monteith, Mary K. "Black English, teacher attitudes, and reading: ERIC/RICS report," Language Arts 57 (1980): 908-912.

Review of selected studies of teachers' attitudes toward black English and teachers' behavior in response to black English.

1901. National Science Teachers Association. Selected bibliographies: report of the deans' grants. ERIC ED 224 238.

Bibliographies of documents describing teachers' attitudes toward handicapped students and special programs for mainstreaming.

1902. Pedhazur, Elazar, J. "Do teacher attitudes make a difference?" N.Y. University Education Quarterly 4 No. 3 (1973): 14-21.

Reviews some research on teachers' attitudes and problems in defining and measuring them.

1903. Pitkoff, Evan. Teacher participation in school decision making. ERIC ED 204 302.

Reviews studies of teachers' participation in school decision making and the attitudes of teachers and administrators toward that participation.

1904. Proctor, C. Patrick. "Teacher expectations: a model for school improvement," Elementary School Journal 84 No. 4 (1984): 469-81.

Reviews research on teachers' expectations and the implications of the research for school improvement.

1905. Robinson, Sharon P. & others. "Desegregation: a bibliographic review of teacher attitudes and black students," Negro Education Review 31 No. 2 (1980): 48-59.

Describes attitudes of teachers toward black students in desegregated schools, based upon several reviewed studies, and discusses the importance of teacher-student relations to successful desegregation of schools.

1906. Rudner, Lawrence M. (ed.). Testing in our schools. ERIC ED 237 579.

Collection of papers about testing and teachers' attitudes toward the use of information from testing.

1907. Sacay, Valerie H. (ed.). Teachers and teaching: annotated bibliographies on selected topics. Volume 2: analyzing teacher attitudes toward students and behavioral interaction in the classroom. 1976. ERIC ED 111 777.

Describes selected research articles and reports, 1968-1972.

1908. Sacay, Valerie H. (ed.). Teachers and teaching: annotated bibliographies on selected topics. Volume 3: characteristics, attitudes, and values of teachers. 1975. ERIC ED 111 778.

Annotated bibliography of research reports on teachers' characteristics and attitudes.

1909. Sarris, Sharon & others. Professional staff development. ERIC ED 219 382.

Collected papers review research on several aspects of staff development, including studies of teachers' attitudes toward staff development.

1910. Short, Edmund C. Competence: analysis, critique, reassessment. 1980. ERIC ED 229 237.

Contains the papers presented at a conference on teacher competence, the historical development of the conception of competence and teachers' characteristics associated with the desire to develop competencies.

1911. Smith, Mary Lee & Glass, Gene V. "Meta-analysis of research on class size and its relationship to attitudes and instruction," American Educational Research Journal 17 (1980): 419-433.

Reports a relationship between class size and teachers' attitudes toward teaching and the teaching situation, based on an analysis of results of several prior studies of class size.

1912. Stern, Carolyn & Kieslar, Evan R. "Teacher attitudes and attitude change: a research review," Journal of Research and Development in Education 10 No. 2 (1977): 63-76.

Reviews studies of teachers' attitudes toward curriculum, students, innovation and the relationship of teachers' attitudes and student achievement.

1913. Stern, Carolyn & Keislar, Evan R. Teacher attitudes and attitude change. Volume 2: summary and analysis of recent research. 1975. ERIC ED 109 073.

A research review of studies of teachers' attitudes and factors associated with changes in teachers' attitudes.

1914. Stern, Carolyn & Keisler, Evan R. Teacher attitudes and attitude change. Volume 3: comprehensive bibliography for volumes 1 & 2. 1975. ERIC ED 109 074.

Presents a bibliography of research on teachers' attitudes and attitude change.

1915. Stern, Paula & Shavelson, Richard J. "Reading teachers' judgments, plans, and decision making," Reading Teacher 37 No. 3 (1983): 280-86.

Reviews research on teachers' perceptions of students, planning for instruction and decision making and their effects on instruction.

1916. Theis, Al, Jr. Teacher attitudes toward in-service programs. ERIC ED 210 251.

Reviews the literature on teachers' attitudes toward the structure and content of inservice education programs.

1917. VanDeMark, Christy L. Implementation of microcomputers in the classroom: problems and potentials. ERIC ED 234 749.

Reviews studies of uses of computers in educational settings, including studies of teachers' attitudes toward the use of computers.

1918. Webber, R.D. "An overview of language attitude studies with special reference to teachers' language attitudes," Educational Review 31 No. 3 (1979): 217-232.

Reviews studies of students' and teachers' attitudes toward language, especially toward the language of West Indian and black American students.

1919. Willoughby, Stephen S. "Mathematics," Encyclopedia of Educational Research Ebel, Robert L. (ed.). Macmillan Company (1969): 766-777.

Reviews the history of mathematics curriculum developments, studies of student acquisition of math skills, studies of methods of teaching math and of teachers' knowledge of and attitudes toward mathematics.

1920. Yarborough, Thelma B. Teacher attitudes toward participation in decision-making. Master's thesis. University of Maryland. 1976. ERIC ED 142 521.

Reviews studies of teachers who favor participation in decision making.

1921. Yinger, Robert J. & Clark, Christopher M. Self-reports of teacher judgment. ERIC ED 241 495.

Reviews studies of teachers' decision making about curriculum content and instructional activities and interactions with students.

AUTHOR INDEX

TITLE INDEX

SUBJECT INDEX